The Magic Bullet?

The Magic Bullet?

UNDERSTANDING THE 'REVOLUTION IN MILITARY AFFAIRS'

Tim Benbow

BRASSEY'S

First published in Great Britain in 2004 by Brassey's

An imprint of **Chrysalis** Books Group

The Chrysalis Building
Bramley Road
London W10 6SP
www.chrysalisbooks.co.uk

British Library Cataloguing in Publication Data
A record of this title is available on request from the British Library

ISBN 1 85753 314 3

Printed in Great Britain

Contents

Acknowledgements

Many people have made significant contributions to this project and to the development of my ideas and arguments. I would like to offer all of the following my grateful thanks.

Commodore Guy Challands (Royal Navy, retired) and Captain Peter Hore (Royal Navy, retired) took the helm in initiating the original research project and in encouraging me to undertake it. Professor Robert O'Neill, my doctoral supervisor, has continued to be very supportive even after doing so has ceased to be part of his job.

Professor Archie Brown and the Warden and Fellows of St. Antony's College, Oxford, elected me a Senior Associate Member of the College, providing a highly conducive location to conduct research for two years.

Dr Roger Forder, Steve Lea and John Herrington from the Defence Evaluation and Research Agency, now dstl and Qinetiq, contributed many useful comments. Numerous Ministry of Defence officials and officers from across the UK and several foreign armed services have been generous with their time and advice.

Britannia Royal Naval College has provided a stimulating environment in which to think about conflict; I am grateful to my colleagues in the Department of Strategic Studies and International Affairs, in particular Dr Geoff Sloan and my colleague in the international 'Britannia Briefings' series, Dr Simon Murden. The staff of the Royal Naval College library are the most helpful librarians that I have ever encountered.

A number of people who are both friends and colleagues have been endlessly patient over many years, particularly Professor Anand Menon, Dr Nick Redman, Professor Jay Rubenstein, Dr Lawrence Tal, Colonel Mike Walker and Dr Lee Willett. Ali, as ever, provided a 'sauce' of inspiration. Special mention must go, of course, to my parents.

Many students have contributed far more than they realise by forcing me to explain things and by asking tricky questions. I would particularly mention the Oxford PPE students whom I have taught International Relations, the graduate students of the Oxford M.Phil. Strategic Studies course, the Royal Navy and Royal Marine young officers at Britannia Royal Naval College, and the students of the 'War in World History' course of the Oxford Tradition summer programme.

The views expressed in this book are my own and do not necessarily represent those of the Ministry of Defence.

List of Abbreviations

AIFV	Armoured Infantry Fighting Vehicle
APC	Armoured Personnel Carrier
ASM	Air-to-Surface Missile
ASTOR	Airborne Stand-Off Radar (UK)
ATGW	Anti-Tank Guided Weapon
AW	Asymmetric Warfare
AWACS	Airborne Warning and Control System
C2W	Command and Control Warfare
C4ISR	Command, Control, Communications, Computers, Intelligence, Surveillance and Reconnaissance
C4ISTAR	Command, Control, Communications, Computers, Intelligence, Surveillance, Target Acquisition and Reconnaissance
CEC	Co-operative Engagement Capability
CNA	Computer Network Attack
CND	Computer Network Defence
DOD	Department of Defense (US)
EMP	Electro-Magnetic Pulse
ERRF	European Rapid Reaction Force
EW	Electronic Warfare
FIST	Future Integrated Soldier Technology (UK)
GPS	Global Positioning System
HERF	High Energy Radio Frequency
ICBM	Inter-Continental Ballistic Missile
IFOR	(NATO, Bosnia) Implementation Force
IO	Information Operations
ISTAR	Intelligence, Surveillance, Target Acquisition and Reconnaissance
IT	Information Technology
IW	Information Warfare
JDAM	Joint Direct Attack Munition (US)
JSTARS	Joint Surveillance and Target Attack Radar System (US)
MAD	Mutually Assured Destruction
MEM	Micro Electro-mechanical Machine
MIRV	Multiple Independently-targetable Re-entry Vehicle
MLRS	Multiple-Launch Rocket System

MOD	Ministry of Defence (UK)
MOOTW	Military Operations Other Than War (*see also* OOTW)
MOUT	Military Operations in Urban Terrain
MTR	Military-Technical Revolution
NWC	Network-Centric Warfare
OODA	Observe, Orient, Decide, Act
OOTW	Operations Other Than War (*see also* MOOTW)
PGM	Precision-Guided Munitions
RMA	Revolution in Military Affairs
ROE	Rules of Engagement
SAC	Strategic Air Command (US)
SAM	Surface-to-Air Missile
SFOR	(NATO, Bosnia) Stabilisation Force
TLAM	Tomahawk Land Attack Missile
UAV	Unmanned (or Unoccupied) Aerial Vehicle
UCAV	Unmanned (or Unoccupied) Combat Aerial Vehicle
UGV	Unmanned (or Unoccupied) Ground Vehicle
UNPROFOR	United Nations Protection Force (Croatia & Bosnia)
WMD	Weapons of Mass Destruction

Introduction

One of the most prominent and significant debates in strategic studies and defence policy since the end of the Cold War has been whether a 'Revolution in Military Affairs' (RMA) is underway and, if so, what its implications might be for the future of warfare. It is an important issue, since if a genuine RMA truly is afoot, it will have enormous implications across a whole range of vital issues. What is the role of force and military power in the post-Cold War international system? Which states (or even actors other than states) and which sorts of military strategies and systems will have an advantage? What form will future warfare and military operations take? What should be the composition of the future armed forces: is there still a need for heavy armour, manned aircraft or surface warships, either at all or in the same numbers as today? How will the armed forces deploy, operate and fight? What new systems and techniques for military intervention, or even alternatives to it, will be added to the means used in conflict? Will the current paradigm of warfare evolve, be radically changed or even be entirely superseded? All of these questions are raised by the RMA.

Assessing the impact on warfare of technological change is undoubtedly important. There are many historical examples of battles, campaigns and wars being decided by the failure of one belligerent to appreciate developments in technology and either to incorporate or to counter them. On the other hand, of course, there are numerous cases of one side with an enormous advantage in military technology failing to achieve its objectives. Since 1945 alone, the list would include France in Indochina, the US in Vietnam, the USSR in Afghanistan, Israel in Lebanon, the US in Somalia and Russia in Chechnya. Technology is not always the key to victory and is never a panacea. It is only one of the factors that needs to be considered for a full understanding of change in warfare; other critical elements include the organisation, concepts and doctrine that form the immediate framework within which technology is used and, most of all, the political and strategic factors that form the wider background.

It might be felt that the Revolution in Military Affairs has long since transcended the status of buzz word and entered the 'done to death' category. Why, then, inflict yet another work about this subject on a weary world? This book seeks to fill a surprising gap in the existing literature: there is no single volume that examines the broad concept of RMA in both historical and contemporary contexts, as well as the claims and counter-claims surrounding how to interpret recent technological and conceptual developments and their effects.

The aim of this book is to understand the RMA, setting the topic in its proper context of international politics, strategic thought and military history. It therefore does not go into great detail about specific technical programmes or government policies (though both areas are touched upon). Rather, it attempts a wider investigation, drawing on broad historical and political issues and taking account of the strategic and international background – indeed, it will be argued that much writing on military technological change in general and the RMA in particular is flawed precisely because it tends to look at systems and capabilities too much in isolation and abstracted from the context of their use. The book concentrates on the major Western powers, though it does discuss their interaction with other parts of the world. An important part of the argument is that not only do military improvements spread beyond their originators, and do so increasingly quickly, but also that in practice their effect tends to be blunted by other states' and cultures' distinctive approaches to international politics, warfare and strategy.

This book began as a research project on the implications of the Revolution in Military Affairs for British foreign and defence policy, which was sponsored by the Defence Evaluation and Research Agency (DERA, since reincarnated as dstl and Qinetiq), the research arm of the UK Ministry of Defence. The project was unclassified and based on open sources, though it has benefited greatly from discussions with many MOD civil servants and officers from the British and some foreign armed services. It originally took the form of a series of stand-alone papers written between 1999 and 2002. These papers have been revised to create the current book which, like the earlier research project, represents the personal views of the author and not necessarily the official opinion of the Ministry of Defence. The individual papers that constituted the initial study were completed before the 2003 intervention in Iraq. I have resisted the temptation to inflict on what follows a fundamental re-write in the light of recent events, because it is too soon for an accurate understanding; events are still changing rapidly and rushed revisions seldom have lasting value. Nevertheless, I believe that the arguments of the book stand up tolerably well.

Chapter One explores the concept of a 'Revolution in Military Affairs', examining the ways in which various writers have understood it. It explores contrasting approaches to the concept, looking at some of the events and periods that tend to be seen as RMAs. Chapter Two goes into a little more detail, studying a number of cases that are widely acknowledged to be RMAs, specifically the French Revolutionary and Napoleonic Wars, the Industrial Revolution, the period of the two World Wars and the advent of nuclear weapons. It then outlines the developments in conventional warfare that form the origins of the contemporary RMA. The Gulf conflict of 1990-91 was enormously influential in the rise of the idea that an RMA is underway, and is the subject of Chapter Three. A number of schools of thought have interpreted this war as providing evidence for the existence of different RMAs and the claims of each one are examined. Chapter Four sets out the arguments surrounding the current purported Revolution in Military Affairs. It explains the sources and nature of the developments on which RMA proponents base their case and looks at the effects that they expect it to have. It then sets out several reasons for caution in too quickly accepting the more far-reaching predictions as well as some grounds for outright scepticism. This chapter then defines a number of different perspectives from which the RMA can be analysed, which are used in the following chapters to explore the various specific arguments and issues that they cover.

Information is generally placed at the heart of the RMA. Some analysts even envisage it giving rise to an entirely new form of warfare that will not require any physical deployment of forces. Chapter Five discusses 'Information Warfare', distinguishing among the contrasting approaches to the subject according to the level of strategy with which they are principally concerned. Chapter Six looks at the spectrum of conflict, to explore whether the RMA is equally applicable in the lower intensity, intra-state conflicts that seem increasingly prevalent in the contemporary strategic environment. RMA proponents tend to focus on higher intensity, conventional, state-against-state warfare, which risks resulting in a mismatch between what the armed forces can do and what they are required to do. The last two chapters consider slightly broader issues that have important implications for the RMA, not least in drawing attention to the wider political and strategic context. Chapter Seven provides a more detailed account of asymmetric warfare. This issue has demanded a great deal of attention in recent years and potentially has serious implications for post-RMA forces: the more any RMA enhances the existing Western advantage in conventional warfare, the more any future challenger will be pushed towards alternative options. The RMA also presents a number of dilemmas for alliance relationships within the Western world. Chapter Eight investigates the possible implications of the RMA for the US-European alliance and for relations within Europe.

Whether or not one concludes that an RMA is currently underway, and how many previous cases one acknowledges, depend on the precise definition used. A solely terminological debate over the existence of an RMA and how many there have been throughout history risks becoming somewhat sterile. Yet it does matter. Among writers who identify a current RMA are some who proclaim that it is only the second in the whole of history and others who count six or eight in the twentieth century alone. The argument developed in this book is that a Revolution in Military Affairs probably is underway that bears comparison with several previous cases that are generally accepted as RMAs. Contemporary developments may be seen as comparable with some of the changes introduced during the period from the middle of World War I to the middle of World War II, even if they are not quite on a par with the changes unleashed by the French Revolution or Industrialisation. However, there is a need for a little realism about the effects even of the latter two cases: neither produced a new set of military capabilities that applied equally across all forms and intensities of warfare and neither provided military means that could compensate for fundamental flaws in grand strategy. The title of this book is not intended to deny that there is any substance in the RMA debate, nor to dismiss its implications, nor to argue that the possible advantages it offers should be spurned. Rather, it was chosen to urge a little scepticism towards some of the claims made on behalf of the current RMA and also to suggest some caution in assessing the impact of RMAs in general. It does not matter a great deal if the reader comes to a different conclusion about the existence or otherwise of a current RMA; the approach taken in this book is to outline different perspectives on whether one truly exists, including sceptical viewpoints, and to use these multiple points of view to explore the possible ramifications. In any case, what label is attached to the current period is less important than the implications – positive or negative – of the political and military developments that are acknowledged to be underway even by those who deny that they amount to an RMA or who doubt that the concept itself has any validity.

Chapter 1
Revolutions in Military Affairs

The concept of 'Revolution in Military Affairs' is a controversial one that has been responsible for the spilling of a great deal of ink. There is widespread disagreement over how many there have been and even over a basic definition of the term. It is no doubt rather frustrating for policy-makers and practitioners to observe what might appear to be analysts debating how many RMAs can dance on the head of a pin. Yet this dispute is far more than academic pedantry. It is significant because it relates to the consequences that can be expected from an RMA: it might not matter what specific label is attached to contemporary changes in warfare but the issue of whether their effects will be of a magnitude that occurs either once every 20 years or once every millennium matters a great deal. Framing the debate in this way is not simply hyperbole, since it is an accurate depiction of the breadth of understandings of the term that is found in the literature. Setting the definition of RMAs to one side, there is also considerable disagreement over their causes, the conditions that are necessary for them to occur, their consequences for warfare and the international system more broadly and, of course, over whether a particular development does or does not qualify for the label. At the widest level, there is not even any consensus over whether RMA is a useful concept at all, since it risks focussing attention on single episodes rather than the broader processes of evolution at varying speeds.

It is generally accepted that the development of the ends, methods and instruments of warfare has not proceeded at an even pace. At certain times in history either a single innovation or, more frequently, a combination of changes in various fields, transforms the conduct of warfare. This observation has led some thinkers to use the concept of a 'Revolution in Military Affairs'. The term was first used in academic circles as early as 1955, when developments in the sixteenth and seventeenth centuries were referred to as the Military Revolution.[1] During the Cold War period, Soviet military thought devoted considerable attention to RMAs and 'military-technical revolutions' initially referring to the impact of nuclear weapons but increasingly applied to the emerging technology of conventional warfare.[2] The term was borrowed from Western historians and Soviet military analysts to become widely used in US military circles during the 1980s and 1990s to refer to contemporary developments. In the aftermath of the 1991 Gulf War the existence or otherwise of an RMA became a central debate among strategic analysts and the term began to be widely applied retrospectively as early historical examples of the phenomenon were sought. Since the concept began to become fashionable there has been a tendency for specialists to identify RMAs in their own specific period of expertise, which in turn has given rise to concern that the term is as overused as is the broader term 'revolutionary'.[3]

Clearly, the word 'revolution' implies significant and drastic change, a complete turning about or metamorphosis. Whether the revolution concerned is political, industrial or sexual, it involves not mere reform but rather an overthrowing of an established order and its replacement with something fundamentally different, or the transition from one model to a new one. That is about as far as consensus extends, however, because the issue of precisely how much change is necessary to qualify as a revolution, whether in military affairs or in any other field, is a matter of opinion. From here, the areas of disagreement multiply. Does the change concerned have to occur rapidly, or can it be a more prolonged process? Taking the former view would seem to rule out some plausible candidates, such as the introduction of gunpowder or even industrialisation, yet allowing slower change risks blurring the distinction between revolution and evolution. Does an RMA have to be brought about by a single transforming event or innovation, or can a number of incremental changes combine to push the world through a threshold to a qualitatively different era? A related issue is what sort of change is thought to lead to an RMA; is it mainly technological, as claimed in many accounts, or should the term be extended, or even restricted, to phenomena that change society at the broadest level? Some of these issues can be explored, if not definitively resolved, by looking at the contrasting approaches taken by a selection of influential authors.

At the most restrictive end of the spectrum come those who see very few true revolutions, which they define in terms of the broadest type of socio-economic transformation. Perhaps the most influential example of this school of thought would be Alvin and Heidi Toffler, two American gurus of futurology, who perceive three historical 'waves' based on the fundamental character of the prevailing social and economic system. In their view, there have been only two true RMAs, in the transitions from the First Wave (Agrarian) to the Second (Industrial) with the industrial revolution, and from the Second Wave to the Third (Post-Industrial) with the current information revolution. They argue that most so-called 'revolutions' in warfare are greatly exaggerated: the introduction of gunpowder, submarines and aircraft certainly led to profound changes in warfare but did so by adding new elements to an existing game. A true revolution, they contend, changes the game itself. They reserve the term 'revolution' for a new form of civilisation challenging the old and consequently changing all aspects of military affairs.[4] The fact that the authors who are most restrictive in defining RMAs are firm believers that one is currently underway makes the magnitude of their claim all the more striking. An approach such as this has the advantage of focusing on the basic nature of societies rather than the minutiae of military systems. The converse is the disadvantage of over-looking hugely significant changes within their very long cycles. A further risk, of course, is that of exaggerating the importance of the current era by hailing it as one of only two truly revolutionary periods in history.

Another example from the more restrictive end of the spectrum would be Martin Van Creveld. He does not use the term RMA and is generally cautious about referring to an innovation as 'revolutionary'. For example, he notes that although the introduction of iron conferred significant advantages, it represented an evolution, since the weapons made from it were the same types as had previously been made from bronze.[5] Nevertheless, he divides his book on technology and war into four ages, those of Tools (2000 BC to 1500 AD), Machines (1500-1830), Systems (1830 to 1945) and Automation (1945 onwards). It is interesting that he identifies different demarcation lines compared to the Tofflers, notably in breaking up their Second (Industrial) Wave.

A contrasting approach at the opposite end of the spectrum is to be far more permissive in recognising RMAs. For example, Andrew Krepinevich identifies ten revolutions 'since the 14th century' – it is not clear whether this date is simply a starting point for his survey, or is intended to imply that there were none previously. They are: (1) the Infantry Revolution and (2) the Artillery Revolution of the Hundred Years' War; (3) the Revolution of Sail and Shot at sea (sixteenth to seventeenth century); (4) the Fortress Revolution (sixteenth century); (5) the Gunpowder Revolution; (6) the Napoleonic Revolution; (7) the Land Warfare Revolution in the nineteenth century; (8) the Naval Revolution in the nineteenth century; (9) the Interwar Revolutions in Mechanisation, Aviation, and Information; (10) the Nuclear Revolution.[6] One anomaly is immediately apparent: if the land and naval revolutions in the nineteenth century are counted separately, why merge into one the interwar revolutions in different media? James Adams lists eleven revolutions: the bow allowing cheaper and hence larger armies (1340); artillery replacing old concepts of siege warfare (1420); ships beginning to carry artillery (1600); efficient construction methods making fortresses defensible once again (1600); the musket (1600); the birth of modern armies with rationalised equipment and a staff system (1800); the 'naval revolution', with metal hulls, steam engines, long-range artillery, submarines and torpedoes (1850); railroads, the telegraph, rifling and the machine gun (1860); tanks, carrier aviation, strategic bombing and amphibious assault (1920); nuclear weapons (1945); and the microchip (1990).[7] Some of his examples are debatable. For example, the revolutions he includes that affected siege warfare either negatively or positively could equally be seen as part of a single, continuing struggle between attack and defence (as seen in many areas of military technology), though over the slower pace of development that characterised pre-nineteenth century technological evolution. Like Krepinevich, Adams divides the changes brought about by the industrial revolution into naval and land developments and counts the interwar years as a single RMA.

Accepting as many as a dozen RMAs invites speculation that the qualifications for membership of this group have been watered down, perhaps too much. Nevertheless, it is also useful in providing a reminder that there have been many periods of dramatic change even within the long periods identified by the Tofflers. A looser definition than theirs also widens the set of historical cases available to those looking for useful comparisons with the present, particularly if it is judged that current changes are highly significant but not quite on a par with those that characterised the switch from the Agrarian to the Industrial Ages.

The two contrasting approaches identified so far take, respectively, a highly restrictive and a more permissive approach to defining and identifying RMAs. A third approach suggests the possibility of bringing the two closer together by recognising different categories of revolutions. Thus, Colin Gray describes a spectrum from Military Revolution, through RMA to Military-Technical Revolution. He recognises a potential hierarchy in RMAs when he writes that those involving heavy cavalry in the sixth and seventh centuries, infantry in the early fourteenth century and fortifications in the early sixteenth century:

...changed relations among the combat arms. But, none of them carried the promise of a dramatic improvement in performance on the part of all kinds of armed forces operating in every geographical medium.[8]

The latter is the type of claim made by present day RMA enthusiasts (though Gray himself is rather sceptical about the concept). Metz and Kievit offer a useful definition of an RMA as a 'discontinuous increase in military capability and effectiveness arising from simultaneous and mutually supportive change in technology, systems, operational methods, and military organisations.' They also suggest a division between minor and major RMAs: the former are significant technological or organisational changes that contribute to major RMAs, which are broader and based on fundamental political, social and economic change. Thus, they argue that both the division and corps organisation of the Napoleonic period and the introduction of rifled weapons in the nineteenth century were minor RMAs that made up part of a broader major RMA.[9] Williamson Murray distinguishes 'military revolutions' from RMAs; the former are more fundamental, and 'recast the nature of society and the state as well as of military organisations'. He identifies four: (1) the

Table One: Different Classes of 'Revolutions'

	LESSER	$\rightarrow$	GREATER
Metz & Kievit	'Minor RMA'		'Major RMA'
Murray	RMA		Military Revolution
Gray	Military Technical Revolution	RMA	Military Revolution

creation of the modern, effective nation-state in the seventeenth century; (2) the French Revolution; (3) the Industrial Revolution; (4) the First World War. Comparing military revolutions to earthquakes, Murray suggests that RMAs (he provides a list, which he stresses is not inclusive, of 21) can be seen as pre-shocks and after-shocks.[10]

These three approaches, summarised in Table One, are closer to the Tofflers in restricting major RMAs or Military Revolutions to longer-term shifts in the basis of the socio-economic system, and hence help to raise the attention of analysts above technological change alone, yet are more permissive than the Tofflers in recognising that other, less epochal changes can amount to revolutions in their own right. The term 'military-technical revolution' could be used for changes that only become an RMA when fully appreciated and implemented; alternatively, 'RMA' could be restricted to broad socio-economic shifts, rather than those rooted in narrowly military technology. On the other hand, of course, the terms 'military-technical revolution' and 'military revolution' could be dispensed with altogether to reduce the proliferation of contestable terminology that bedevils this subject.

What developments have been suggested as examples of RMAs? Many pieces examining the current purported RMA do not explore the issue of historical parallels in any great detail but rather offer a few illustrating examples of what the author considers to be comparable RMAs. Some authors cite examples of what others consider to be RMAs without explicitly stating their own opinion as to whether they do in fact represent genuine cases. Also, when a writer does not list any innovations before a certain date, it is not always clear whether this implies rejecting the credentials of earlier examples, or if it simply denotes an unspecified starting date for the analysis. Nevertheless, a brief survey of what are considered as RMAs in the literature is revealing because it shows how great the author concerned believes will be the effect of current changes. The list set out in Table Two is not exhaustive but offers a survey of some of the changes identified as candidate RMAs. As a

Table Two: Suggested RMAs

- Assyrian combined arms tactics (from around 9th century BC)
- Cavalry stirrups (5th century AD)
- Persian and Byzantine heavy cavalry (6th and 7th centuries)
- Infantry pikes and longbows (early 14th century)
- Gunpowder
- Cannon (early 15th century)
- Ship-borne cannon (early 16th century)
- French military reforms of 16th century
- Efficient fortress construction methods (1600)
- Musket
- Swedish adoption of massed volley gunfire (16th and 17th centuries)
- British financial revolution
- Social and political upheavals of French Revolution
- Introduction of corps system into armies
- Introduction of the modern staff system to armies
- Railroad, rifle and telegraph (mid-19th century)
- Naval steam engines, metal ships and armour (late 19th century)
- Medical revolution
- Indirect fire and the deep battle (1917-1918)
- Submarine warfare
- Mechanised warfare in the 1930s and 1940s
- Blitzkrieg, strategic bombing, offensive carrier aviation, amphibious warfare
- Nuclear weapons and ballistic missiles (1950s and 1960s)
- Peoples' War
- The microchip
- Cybernetics and automated troop control, 1970s onwards
- The information era

composite from several sources, it cannot be inferred that any particular analyst will agree with the list as a whole.

A number of interesting points arise from consideration of the above list. Aside from the obvious differences in what various writers consider to be true RMAs, there are also divergences in how they classify the specific examples that they recognise. Thus, some authors count the introduction of gunpowder as a single RMA while others divide its effects into hand-held firearms and artillery, or split the latter into applications on land and at sea. Some analysts also split naval and land developments from each other in the nineteenth century and in the period between the two World Wars. Such an approach raises the question of the extent to which a 'revolution' can occur in a single medium: the changes in naval warfare mentioned in Table Two might be seen as a 'naval revolution' or as one element of a broader RMA, rather than forming one by themselves. The issue of the inter-relationship of technological developments is another interesting one. Is the period between the two World Wars best characterised as one RMA or as several? Should its beginning be recognised as during the First World War or afterwards? Was air power one revolution or more, in the form of strategic bombing and also of combined or 'joint' uses with land and sea forces? Were carrier aviation and advances in amphibious warfare in this period two revolutions, a single revolution, merely part of a broader RMA or indeed not revolutionary at all?

While accepting that the literature on the subject includes a wide variety of approaches to identifying RMAs, some generalisations can be made. First, although technology tends to be acknowledged as the principal source of RMAs, it is neither necessary nor sufficient. The existence of a novel technology, regardless of its latent potential, cannot amount to an RMA unless and until it is fully understood and reflected in military doctrine and organisation. Krepinevich defines a military revolution as:

> ...what happens when the application of new technologies into a significant number of military systems combines with innovative operational concepts and organisational adaptation in a way that fundamentally alters the character and conduct of conflict.[11]

This definition helpfully emphasises that new technologies are not on their own sufficient, but depend on developments and adaptations in other related fields. It is a common error, however, to imply that technology is essential to an RMA, which is not invariably the case. The most often cited, and generally accepted, example of an RMA that was driven by social and political rather than technological causes is the period of the French Revolutionary and Napoleonic Wars, which is covered in greater detail in the next chapter. Another result of social, economic and political factors that could plausibly be called an RMA would be the creation of the modern nation-state, which was a critical point in defining the nature of modern conflict.

The picture is further complicated by the fact that many advances in technology might form part of the broader underpinnings of an RMA without amounting to one in their own right. Progress in chemistry and in metallurgy, for example, helped to prepare the way for improvements in artillery in the fifteenth and sixteenth centuries and then again in the nineteenth century. They are just two of many changes in technology that were not narrowly military but nonetheless had important effects on warfare. John Keegan, for example, stresses the importance of the domestication of horses and developments in metallurgy, which together led to chariots and hence helped to bring about the war-making state.[12] Other key non-military advances that had enormous military effects include the wheel, the oxcart, writing (not least in permitting the greater administrative sophistication which fostered the rise of far more powerful states and empires), roads, maps, timekeepers and printing.[13] The net could be spread even wider to include broader developments in society and economics that increased the populations of the major European countries and hence expanded the potential pool of recruits for armies as well as enlarging the supporting financial base. Murray's account of military revolutions is notable for the breadth of contributing factors that he recognises. He accepts the usually cited sources, including technological, operational and organisational, but also adds cultural, social, conceptual, ideological, financial, architectural, tactical, administrative, scientific and political factors. Moreover, he does not believe that all RMAs have the same types of sources; thus, he cites the gunpowder revolution as having technological and financial drivers, while the naval revolution of seventeenth and eighteenth centuries has those two but administrative and social sources as well.[14] RMAs can therefore be seen to have broad and multiple roots rather than resulting from specific advances in technology, however dramatic and eye-catching these might be.

Many such developments, however, could be seen as part of the broader evolution of civilisation and of technology rather than as elements of successive revolutions. The same can be said of some developments in military technology, including the shift from the wooden bow to the composite bow or the introduction of the longbow. Innovations such as these altered the appearance of some armies (not all states imitated the initial beneficiaries) and the tactics with which they fought, offering decisive advantages in specific battles, thus having a considerable though perhaps not revolutionary effect. A further difficulty that emerges from discussions of the development of military capabilities, then, lies in separating discrete 'revolutions' from continuing evolution.

Some writers are sceptical about the very concept of RMAs precisely because they believe that the process is better characterised as evolutionary.[15] Since some technological changes take place over a considerable period of time, it can be difficult to distinguish between an RMA that takes a prolonged period to have its full effect and commonplace evolution or, in particular, a 'rapid evolution'. Many authors, for example, hold that the introduction of gunpowder amounted to an RMA; yet its impact unfolded over many years, with older weapons continuing alongside firearms for a long period. Similarly, sailing ships and galleys co-existed for many decades, with the latter enjoying advantages in some situations and in some parts of the world,[16] so it might be misleading to refer to a 'sailing ship revolution'. Another example that is generally accepted as an RMA but took considerable time to have its full impact can be found in the Industrial Revolution. Its beginnings can be identified in the late eighteenth century, it accelerated during the nineteenth century and arguably extended into the early years of the twentieth century. So it seems to be accepted that RMAs are not necessarily rapid events. In that case, however, how are they to be distinguished from evolution? This question is not merely one of semantics: the current period is variously interpreted as one of continuing, if accelerated evolution, as either the end or the beginning of one long RMA, or alternatively as an RMA in its own right.

One possible answer to the revolution versus evolution quandary would be that 'revolution' should not be used for refinements of an existing model but rather for the creation of a new one. Lawrence Freedman takes this approach, writing: 'Revolution involves more than change, and certainly more than simply change of an incremental variety. It represents a moment of transformation.'[17] This distinction might be difficult to make in practice, however, not least because a sufficient accumulation of incremental changes could pass a 'tipping point' and create a new paradigm. Continuing the biological metaphor suggested by the term 'evolution', in the natural world evolution proceeds incrementally and very slowly but at some point an entirely new species can be discerned. Identifying revolution as opposed to evolution is not a question to which there is a definitive answer, as it finally comes down to the perspective of the individual author. Stepping back to take a broad approach that stresses evolution has its advantages in terms of recognising continuities, yet it is still possible to identify periods of momentous change that seem to merit particular attention – not least for those who believe themselves to be living in one such era.

How much change, and on what level, is required for an RMA to be proclaimed? An innovation could change the appearance or basic equipment of infantry or cavalry or, if it was more far-reaching, it might alter the balance between them. Alternatively, significant improvements in range, or a shift in the balance between attack and defence might be sought. Moving up the scale, the introduction of a new combat arm, such as artillery, aircraft or submarines, could be seen as having more fundamental effects on the nature of warfare, especially if they open up new military-strategic options. At a still broader level, innovations could change the specific characteristics that give states an advantage in the world, such as large population giving way to industrial strength, or the rising and falling utility of sea power. At a still higher level, in a more distinctly political arena, lie significant shifts in the reasons why states fight or even the creation (and, as some would suggest of the contemporary period, the erosion) of the nation-state itself. Where one draws the line for what counts as an RMA will depend on the restrictiveness or permissiveness of one's definition of the concept.

A Working Definition

So, where does this leave us? There are several contrasting approaches that can be taken to defining and identifying an RMA. Although using the concept does involve a risk of understating the continuous evolution in military affairs, on balance sufficient grounds exist for accepting that there are periods of such dramatic change that they merit particular attention. With reservations, therefore, this book will accept that RMAs do occur. Perhaps the more difficult question concerns how liberal to be in conferring the term. Clearly there is no single, generally accepted definition of what constitutes an RMA, hence the huge variation in how many cases are allowed by individual authors. All that the beleaguered reader can do is to keep in mind how each author uses the description and also to examine the implications drawn when it is used. The latter point is crucial: two analysts might agree that the contemporary period represents an RMA yet mean something entirely different in terms of the magnitude and precise nature of the consequences that they are predicting and, hence, disagree on the significance of using the term. Someone who believes that there have been twenty RMAs in history will not expect the same effects as someone who recognises only two.

The definition used here is intended to steer a course between the extremely restrictive interpretation, which rules out plausible examples that offer useful comparisons for the contemporary period, and the excessively permissive, which seems to water down the term too much. The term 'Revolution in Military Affairs' will be used to refer to a step-change in the basic character of warfare. It should not be reserved solely for shifts in historical epoch such as the gradual transition from agrarian to industrial but neither should it be stretched to include developments whose main effects are at the technical or tactical levels of warfare. An RMA should fundamentally affect strategy and the role of military power in the international system, leading to a qualitative shift in what war is and how it is conducted. It should be a period of great acceleration of change that has far greater consequences than routine evolution, and which therefore demands specific attention.

Three additional and important clarifications should be made. First, RMAs are often but not exclusively brought about by technological innovation. Whatever the main sources, they must be thoroughly understood and reflected in ideas and practice, with appropriate adaptation in organisation, doctrine and force structure, to become an RMA. Second, the implications of an RMA depend on, and cannot be understood in isolation from, the political and strategic context in which they occur, which is not merely the background but is rather one of the major influences on what occurs. Finally, as noted above, the vast range of ways in which the term is used in the literature means that calling something an RMA is merely attaching a tag. The implications of using that label can only be made clear when what is meant by RMA is elaborated. Referring back to the changes listed in Table Two, some examples that should be accepted into the august category of genuine RMAs would be the French Revolution and Napoleonic Wars; the Industrial Revolution; the period of the two World Wars; and the advent of nuclear weapons. These cases are the subject of the next chapter, which aims to explore in a little more detail just what is implied when something is called a Revolution in Military Affairs.

Chapter 2
Previous 'Revolutions in Military Affairs'

Chapter One explored different approaches to identifying and defining a 'Revolution in Military Affairs'. This chapter will put a bit more historical meat on the bare bones by looking in a little more detail at four periods that are generally acknowledged in the literature as having featured RMAs: the French Revolutionary and Napoleonic Wars; the industrial revolution in the nineteenth century; the interwar period; and the introduction of nuclear weapons.

The first aim is to provide a little historical background for contemporary events. The cases selected constitute the setting from which recent developments have emerged and are thus important for an understanding of modern events and concepts. The second aim is to provide a number of conclusions that might have some utility for analysing the present day. The small number of cases used and the distinctness of their circumstances make it risky to seek 'lessons' or a formal check list to apply to contemporary affairs. The intention is certainly not to produce any kind of predictive model but rather to offer some general pointers to inform analysis of current events and debates – to suggest some questions that might be asked and possibilities that might be explored. At the very least, this survey aims to challenge the easy assumption that history offers little of value or relevance for the present, on the grounds that current events are so different from previous ones that no parallels can be drawn. It should also help to determine the comparative magnitude of the changes currently underway and thus help to explore the question of whether they truly represent a 'Revolution in Military Affairs', and if so, what that implies.

The French Revolutionary and Napoleonic Wars

The changes in warfare at the end of the eighteenth century are generally viewed as an RMA in the literature.[1] They were also interpreted as a turning point at the time: indeed, a central question for Carl von Clausewitz, the father of modern strategic thought, was whether this new form of war that he witnessed was in fact the same phenomenon as the utterly different form of conflict that preceded it. What makes this period particularly significant in a study of RMAs is that the changes that occurred did not result from technological innovations but rather from broader developments in politics and society. Nevertheless, the effects of these changes were of the greatest significance, transforming how wars were fought and creating the foundations upon which the additional innovations of industrialisation would be built.

Military technology saw few changes in the decades prior to the French Revolution. Although the industrial revolution was in its very earliest stages, it was still some way from truly taking off. Since the introduction of the bayonet in the 1690s, which eliminated the split in infantry between musketeers and pikemen, a single type of infantryman had become standard. Artillery had long been sufficiently light and mobile to find a use on the battlefield rather than primarily in sieges, as had been the case in the early centuries of its existence. Lighter gun carriages and increasing standardisation in production permitted a gradual and relative increase in the importance of artillery but the effect was far from revolutionary. Other than the organisational change of the introduction of the division, which made possible a degree of articulation and operational flexibility not seen since the Roman legions, the armies (and indeed navies) of the 1780s looked much like those of the early 1700s. Wars were generally fought between professional armies for limited goals and hence, because of the expense of such forces and the potentially high casualties inflicted by firearms, they rarely involved major battles. Campaigns often took the form more of attempts to manoeuvre into a superior position, at which point the side finding itself at a disadvantage would concede and withdraw.

There had, however, been gradual but significant changes in non-military areas. The population of the major European states increased significantly on the back of steady progress in agricultural productivity. General increases in wealth combined with better organised states to create more capable government bureaucracies and better national infrastructure, notably roads. More importantly, various political, social and economic pressures began to build that would eventually explode onto the world system. These changes set the scene and established the preconditions for a true RMA.

The various developments of the eighteenth century greatly increased the potential for war of the major European powers. The French Revolution provided the trigger to unleash this potential, thereby having a massive and lasting effect on warfare. It did so primarily by unleashing the novel social, political and ideological force of nationalism, which provided a new source of legitimacy for states (and thus helped to undermine the existing basis of the international system) and a powerful new source of motivation for troops. The energies unleashed by the 1789 revolution, with the levée en masse – not just conscription but rather total national mobilisation – hugely increased the size of the French army and the nationalistic ardour of the troops thereby brought to the colours, giving the French republican leaders and then Napoleon Bonaparte unmatched resources for war. The fact that revolutionary France swiftly found itself attacked by its neighbours compelled it to explore and embrace the new tactical and operational possibilities that were now open to it. French armies were able to fight a series of frequent and costly campaigns and yet always had more troops who were available and eager to fight. Even the volunteers' lack of sophistication was turned to become an advantage, as their lack of formal drill and training encouraged the replacement of the rather rigid linear techniques in general use beforehand with more dynamic and aggressive tactics. Moreover, the introduction of promotion by merit as the norm brought a new stream of talent into the officer corps. The result was new organisation and doctrine, which permitted tactical and operational approaches that were considerably more offensive, allowing the pursuit of more ambitious strategic goals, which fitted well with the aims of the revolutionary governments and of Napoleon, whose rise was itself made possible by the revolution.

When Napoleon came to power he contributed few military innovations (though it is perhaps significant that his rise through the French army began in the artillery: his expertise in this technological arm suggests the gradually increasing significance of firepower on the battlefield).[2] He did introduce the corps system, that is, the combination of a number of divisions into a self-contained miniature army, with its own artillery, logistics and planning staff, as well as infantry and cavalry. The change in organisation that resulted has been described as a 'minor RMA' in its own right,[3] but could equally be seen as an evolutionary step from the division (which was itself a rediscovery of ideas as old as the Roman legions). However, Napoleon is perhaps best seen as embodying, thoroughly understanding and skillfully utilising the changes to which the revolutionary period had given rise.[4] He made significant improvements in administration, overhauling the French state to make it a more efficient servant of his aims. Most of all, he proved brilliantly able to use the new French army to fight a series of bloody and ambitious campaigns, with the aim of vanquishing enemy armies and conquering opposing states in contrast to the more limited aims of eighteenth century wars. He repeatedly shattered coalitions that were more powerful than France, often defeating highly capable enemy commanders, whose forces far outnumbered his own despite mass conscription providing him with around a million men under arms. The new force of nationalism and the way that the armies it inspired were used by Napoleon permitted him to conquer much of Europe and fundamentally changed the place of war in the European system. It is small wonder that the enormous difference between warfare before and after 1789 became the starting point for Clausewitz's investigations. Total war had re-emerged in Europe. Moreover, the growth in state power over the previous decades meant that total wars were now on a considerably greater scale than hitherto. When industrialisation was added to this potent brew, the result was modern warfare.

The impact of the RMA unleashed by France at the end of the eighteenth century could hardly have been more dramatic and its tendency to attract the attention of later would-be military revolutionaries is quite understandable. Yet in 1815 it was Napoleonic France that lay comprehensively defeated, in spite of initiating and leading an RMA. This outcome was the result of a number of factors. First, the transformation initiated by political revolution in France inevitably spread to other countries. While the nationalistic fervour of the French armies allowed them to conquer other European peoples, thereafter it produced a like response in them, reacting against the invaders. Others could be motivated by nationalism to fight against the French, whether in formal armies or as guerrillas. Second, other states were quick to take note of the changes in the French army and undertook reform of their own armies, notably in Britain and in Prussia. As is often the case with innovation in the military field, the first to introduce it reaped impressive advantages but only until others imitated it – and they had little choice but to do so. More broadly, other states and commanders learnt to cope with Napoleon's strategic and operational approach. Third, although the new way of fighting pioneered by the French army initially proved immensely effective in defeating opponents that closely resembled itself, it was notably less robust against dissimilar foes or unfamiliar strategies.

- France was never able to devise a strategy for defeating its most dogged foe, Britain, with its reliance on maritime power. Conversely, Britain succeeded in exploiting its advantage at sea to decisively influence events on the land.
- The disastrous and prolonged campaign on the Iberian peninsula saw the French worn down (Napoleon referred to the commitment there as a 'bleeding ulcer') and then at last comprehensively defeated by a combination of local guerrilla forces fighting in favourable and familiar terrain, regular Spanish and Portuguese armies motivated by their own nationalism, and a small but increasingly effective British expeditionary force, supplied and supported from the sea and commanded by Arthur Wellesley, later Duke of Wellington, which eventually invaded southern France. The fact that Napoleon relied for much of the campaign on subordinate commanders, who often seemed as concerned with manoeuvring politically against each other as with military moves against their enemies was one factor, which is a useful reminder that RMAs cannot do away with human frailty. But the difficulty that French commanders encountered in coming to grips militarily with the operational approach of the opposing coalition, which included elements quite unlike the conventional armies that Napoleon regularly routed, was also a notable factor.
- When Napoleon invaded Russia, his opponents refused to play by the rules as he understood them; instead of capitulating after defeat on the battlefield they withdrew and continued to resist, even after further defeats and even after giving up Moscow. Napoleon was thus drawn deeper into Russia and stayed longer than his original plans had assumed, which stretched the

already meagre logistical system beyond breaking point. The result was the disastrous retreat out of Russia in 1812, which only some ten per cent of the original invading army survived. It was neither inadequate planning nor an unusually harsh winter that defeated Napoleon in Russia but rather his inability to adapt to an unfamiliar and unexpected strategy.

• The strength of France, on the crest of the RMA wave, was immense but it was not enough to achieve Napoleon's objectives against a combination of all of the other great powers, and the lead France enjoyed proved both temporary and inappropriate to different strategies. Less ambitious goals than Napoleon's might have been more achievable, which is a significant reminder of the importance of the political context for how an RMA plays out, yet the very nature of the new military means provided a pressure in the opposite direction to moderation. The failure of the new military system to deal with dissimilar or 'asymmetric' opponents and strategies is also instructive.

Warfare was changed fundamentally in this period, although this was not at the expense of all elements of continuity. A total war would no longer take the form of a single battle but rather of campaigns, fought over a longer period and potentially over far greater distances, by larger and more motivated armies. Battles and campaigns became more bloody. According to David Gates, France alone lost 916,000 dead, which represented 38 per cent of the generation born between 1790 and 1795 (considerably higher than the 24 per cent losses of the 1891-95 generation that fought in the First World War). He further notes that the Napoleonic Wars cost Europe as a whole about five million dead – the same proportion of the overall population as died during 1914-1918.[5] Greater changes would come later with the ability to co-ordinate armies operating far apart from one another. Indeed, it could be argued that continuity was more striking than change in this period, given that methods of command, weapons and speed of advance remained largely constant. Such an argument, however, seems to confine change in warfare to the area of technology. The changes were immense and lasting, and other states had little choice but to take note and follow suit. It is fair to conclude that the French Revolutionary and Napoleonic periods did indeed amount to an RMA.

Perhaps the most significant conclusion to be drawn from this RMA is its political roots. It is no coincidence that the strategic thinker who has done the most to assert the intimate link between warfare and politics was developing his ideas at the time of the French Revolutionary and Napoleonic Wars. For Clausewitz, the political roots of the changes he observed were abundantly clear:

...the tremendous effects of the French Revolution abroad were caused not so much by new military methods and concepts as by radical changes in policies and administration, by the new character of government, altered conditions of the French people, and the like.... Not until statesmen had at last perceived the nature of the forces that had emerged in France, and had grasped that new political conditions now obtained in Europe, could they foresee the broad effect all this would have on war.

As he concluded: 'It follows that the transformation of the art of war resulted from the transformation of politics'.[6]

The longer term effects of the changes wrought by the French Revolution were of great importance for later RMAs. Nationalism played an important role in the developments of warfare in this period and would eventually shatter the stable post-1815 European system. It was thus an important element in the political context for the technological changes that are considered in the next section. While nationalism strengthened some existing nation-states (notably France and Britain), it eventually broke up the Austro-Hungarian empire and weakened the Russian and Ottoman empires, and also created new states in Italy and Germany. The force of nationalism was then harnessed to states that were becoming ever more powerful as a result of the accelerating process of industrialisation in the nineteenth century.

The Nineteenth Century

The changes of the Revolutionary and Napoleonic era reintroduced total war to Europe and generally raised the war potential of the leading powers, so the scale of total war became greater than ever before. Yet these developments took place at a time when industrialisation was at a relatively early stage and military technology in 1815 was not markedly different from that of 50 or even 100 years before. The nineteenth century saw a great acceleration in the industrial revolution, which added significant technological advances to the social and political upheavals of the late eighteenth century. However, these changes took place in what was generally a time of international stability, characterised by a remarkably long period of peace between the great powers. As a result, there were no major systemic wars to demonstrate or test the effects of the host of new technologies. The international political background played an important part in limiting awareness of the possibilities of industrial age warfare, the full impact of which therefore eventually proved a considerable and unwelcome surprise. Yet the nationalism unleashed by the French revolution eventually helped to undermine the stable post-Waterloo system and culminated in a cataclysmic war that both showed in the starkest possible way the full implications of war between industrial states and also ushered in a period of further dramatic innovation in military doctrine.

Many of the principal technological advances of the nineteenth century were not immediately or directly military in origin (though as in other periods, military considerations did play a part in driving some of the innovations forward). The most significant developments, which changed the face of the world and truly revolutionised politics, economics and society, were the invention of steam power and railways, together with the accompanying acceleration of industrialisation, with mass production and great increases in the wealth and populations of the major powers. As well as changing states internally, transforming the make-up of societies and the political balance within them, these developments inevitably had a dramatic effect on warfare. Increasing populations could support larger armies, which could now be equipped with mass-produced and standardised weapons. Railways allowed these forces to be moved far more rapidly and kept supplied over far longer distances than commanders had dreamed of in previous ages. An additional side-effect was the enhanced importance of planning staff to co-ordinate the increasingly demanding tasks of mobilisation, logistics and deployment, so the nineteenth century saw the rapid development of general staffs as well as creating new military specialties in logistics and in engineering. The telegraph meant that the actions of widely dispersed forces could be better synchronised, while political leaders could remain more closely informed of events and could exert tighter control over deployed forces than hitherto. Improvements in communications would also change the nature of the relationship between Clausewitz's 'remarkable trinity';[7] in addition to governments being better informed about the activities of and better able to instruct armies, public opinion began to become more aware, and more rapidly aware, of the military operations being carried out by their political leaders and armed forces. The increasing role of war correspondents in the Crimean War and thereafter marked the beginning of a long process of growing public awareness of, and eventually a voice in, the conduct of war. It is worth noting, in passing, that information was therefore an important aspect of this RMA, as it would also be in the period between the two world wars.

These developments in essentially civil technology had enormous effects on warfare, which were magnified by simultaneous developments in more specifically military technology. Rifled firearms became standard issue for infantry, and muzzle-loading weapons gave way to breech loaders. These changes greatly increased both accuracy and rate of fire.[8] Smokeless powder did much to change the appearance of the battlefield. Firepower was increased still further by the introduction and improvement of machine guns and continued development of artillery, not least with the introduction of rifled barrels. The result was greatly increased casualties on the battlefield, as the volume and accuracy of fire was multiplied many times over, with predictable results. The linear tactics of the Napoleonic Wars, which were themselves more bloody than previous conflicts, now became suicidal and prohibitively costly as the strength of the defensive relative to that of the offensive was greatly enhanced. The change in the balance between attack and defence compared to the previous period was due to the fact that firepower had greatly increased while speed of movement on the battlefield had remained the same, based on a man moving on foot. (The next major change, in the first half of the twentieth century, would be increases in tactical mobility to match the leap in strategic mobility brought about by railways, but this required the refinements of the later stages of industrialisation, particularly the internal combustion engine.) Forces gradually became more dispersed and field fortifications, entrenchment and camouflage became more prominent. The role of the cavalry continued to erode – it had been on the wane even during the Napoleonic Wars – and it was gradually confined to the margins of the battlefield and to the roles of reconnaissance and raiding.

Yet, the effects of all of these changes were not immediately apparent. However earnest the intentions of military planners, they were seriously constrained in their efforts to interpret the new factors by the lack of relevant operational experience. There were simply very few cases of major wars between great powers in which the various developments of the mid-nineteenth century were fully tested. The generally benign international environment of this period that made it genuinely difficult to judge the impact of the new technology might be compared to the present, when there is no serious hostility between the great powers – though without losing sight of the fact that this happy situation did not last, in spite of hopes that a new era of peace had begun. Relatively small-scale wars pitting a great power against either a minor power or a colonial non-state actor that sought a pitched battle tended to flatter the forces of the nineteenth century just as it would today.

There were few major great power wars during the nineteenth century. The Crimean War, in which Britain and France fought Russia, was one exception. It was a curiously old-fashioned and limited conflict, however, and took place before the new technology had become widespread. The 1866 war between Austria and Prussia demonstrated the superiority of breech-loading rifles to the old muzzle-loading variety. The nineteenth century war on which most attention was lavished by European military thinkers was the 1870 Franco-Prussian War, in which the superior Prussian general staff was able to use railways to mobilise and deploy its armies with impressive speed, overwhelming France in a brief and decisive campaign. Two important points emerge from this. First, it was actually France that had made the more impressive early progress in developing railways.[9] However, in 1870 it was Prussia that used them to far greater effect against France, whose initial lead thus proved fleeting. Second, one reason for the major European powers being so utterly wrong in 1914 in their expectations about the nature of a future war was that they confidently anticipated a repeat of 1870. This excessive focus on a single example helped to lead military planning astray.

There was, in fact, one conflict in the nineteenth century that might have provided rather more accurate guidance to the nature of total warfare involving the new technologies: the US Civil War was the first true industrial conflict. Tactically, increased firepower made battlefields far more dangerous and punished the use of Napoleonic frontal assaults (which, nonetheless, would be tried again in 1914). Strategically, the significance of industrial production, railways and the popular will to continue to fight became abundantly clear. Total war had become a matter of attrition, which the increased war-making capacity of a modern great power made a longer drawn-out process. There were some respectable reasons for the European powers not paying greater attention to the US Civil War. The geography and terrain of North America were different from that of Europe and civil wars would always be unlike international great power wars. However, it seems plausible to suggest that there might also have been a tendency to concentrate so much on the Franco-Prussian War because it offered more palatable conclusions. Indeed, even the 1870 war was looked to selectively for lessons: at the Battle of Gravelotte-St. Privat, as at Königgrätz (1866) in the Austro-Prussian War, there were indications of the advantages conferred on the defensive by increasing firepower.[10] Perhaps there was an inclination to seek lessons that supported plans rather than those that would challenge them. Perhaps there was also a tendency to look at the military campaigns to the exclusion of broader elements, such as the wisely crafted Prussian political strategy with its carefully limited aims. This cautionary tale should underline the importance of not focussing excessively on one conflict and cherry picking lessons for force planning and doctrine – particularly when that conflict offers atypically pleasant conclusions – as many analysts have tended to do with the 1991 Gulf War.

A further point that arises from the nineteenth century is that the new technologies conveyed a striking superiority on European armies in colonial wars when fighting conventional battles. The famous quip by Hillaire Belloc rang true: 'Whatever happens we have got, the Maxim gun, and they have not.' The technological superiority of European weaponry was one of the most significant factors in the dramatic spread of their overseas empires.[11] However, this was a lead that was not destined to last as military technology began to spread to extra-European powers and eventually to internal groups who sought independence. Just as nationalism was carried by France to her opponents (and would, in time, spread to colonial peoples), so the new weapons and ways of fighting that were the result of industrialisation would eventually be diffused beyond Europe by the imperial powers themselves. Moreover, even European armies with modern equipment found it difficult to come to terms with opponents who fought in unfamiliar ways. The British army enjoyed initial success in the Boer War when its opponents pursued a conventional strategy but faced far greater difficulties when they resorted to guerrilla tactics. The British learnt the same harsh lessons as their forbears had in North America in the late eighteenth century, lessons that would be taught to several other great powers in the twentieth century. This conflict also saw an additional factor emerge to complicate British policy, namely the constraining influence of domestic and international public opinion. As will be explored in Chapter Seven, asymmetric approaches frequently invalidate the 'Maxim gun' maxim.

Developments at sea

It was noted in the previous chapter that some thinkers split nineteenth century developments in naval warfare from those on land. Although it can be misleading to conceive of naval strategy as entirely detached from what happens on land, there is a case for considering the changes at sea in this period separately from those on land because the technological changes of the mid-nineteenth century did have a very distinct effect on navies. The fleets of 1914 differed from those that had fought at Trafalgar to an even greater extent than the armies on the eve of First World War differed from those engaged at Waterloo; the changes at sea were more analogous in their impact to those wrought on land warfare by mechanisation.[12]

The move from sail to steam as the method of warship propulsion affected navies and naval strategy at every level. Warships were no longer dependent on the presence or direction of the wind and now enjoyed both greater ability to manoeuvre and higher speeds, but these gains came at the cost of dependence on bases for refuelling and being tied more closely to the shore than had previously been the case. Warships were given belts of iron armour, crucial protection for wooden hulled ships against the emergence of guns that fired explosive shells rather than solid shot, and then began to be built with iron hulls, which meant the ships could be larger and heavier and carry a greater weight of guns and armour. Iron soon gave way to steel, which further increased the strength of ships, while armour became thicker and more effective. Guns developed rapidly, becoming larger (in a race with improving armour) and featuring rifled barrels, breech loading and turrets. The pace of technological change itself became more rapid, as warships became obsolescent within a few years of being launched. Gone were the days of Trafalgar, where Nelson's flagship HMS *Victory* was already over 40 years old yet still at the cutting edge of effectiveness. HMS *Warrior*, the first all-iron warship, was invulnerable and invincible on her launch in 1860 but only 10 years later was considered obsolete.

Later in the century further innovations posed increased threats to warships, notably naval mines and automotive torpedoes (as distinct from static naval mines, which had previously been called 'torpedoes' and were what Farragut famously damned at Mobile Bay in 1864), the latter carried on small, fast and agile boats and later in submarines. These innovations gave rise to the first in a long series of premature obituaries for surface warships in the face of novel threats; similar claims continue to this day. Such arguments overuse the term 'revolutionary' and overlook the action-reaction dynamic of technological change. Some late-nineteenth century naval thinkers saw torpedo boats as the ideal counter to battleships, since the large main guns of lumbering capital ships lacked the ability to engage their nimble but deadly new foes. However, the role of battleships, countering the enemy battle fleet to secure control of the sea, still needed to be performed, so responses were found to counter the new threat in the form of adding a secondary armament of quick-firing guns to battleships, and accompanying them at sea with a new class of vessel, the torpedo boat destroyer, which later became known simply as the destroyer. Neither the torpedo boat nor the submarine proved to herald the death knell of the battleship as some had predicted, since they could not replace the battleship in fulfilling its strategic responsibilities and responses were available to the direct threats they posed. The cost and complexity of the modern fleet increased, however, as navies began to take on the combined arms character that had long been predominant in armies. This phenomenon had the effect of increasing the minimum investment needed to fund a first-rank fleet and to stretch the gap between major and minor navies. A similar process would unfold in the middle of the twentieth century with regard to the strategic and tactical challenge to surface warships posed by air power.

Nonetheless, naval warfare changed at every level. Fleets changed, with the addition of destroyers, heavy cruisers, battle cruisers and eventually aircraft, as well as submarines and torpedo boats. Naval battles changed, as engagements could take place at greater ranges, with the threat of torpedo attack becoming an important consideration. Naval strategy evolved, with a recognition that close blockade of enemy bases had become far more risky than in the days of Cornwallis, St. Vincent and Nelson but the emphasis in doctrine on a decisive clash of battle fleets remained. All the major fleets held a similar conception of the role of navies and tended to imitate each other in pursuing modern technology. Thus, when Britain launched the truly revolutionary HMS *Dreadnought* in 1906, the other major navies rapidly followed suit. As was the case with warfare on land there was little solid experience on which to build predictions about the effect of the changes that had occurred. Some ideas turned out to be incorrect, notably the notion that steam power would bring back ramming as a tactic, which resulted from a freak incident in a single battle. If it is possible to speak of a 'revolution' confined to a single medium, then the second half of the nineteenth century can be seen as a naval RMA. Alternatively, these changes could be viewed as one specific application of the broader industrialisation RMA.

One effect of the lack of practical experience of major naval warfare was that the impact of the submarine was generally underestimated and misconceived. It was generally expected to be used against warships, particularly for coastal defence and attacks inside enemy ports. Its use against merchant shipping was not anticipated. Brodie suggests that this was due in large part to the influence of one theorist, Alfred Thayer Mahan, who dismissed the significance of a commerce raiding strategy and did not predict the far greater effectiveness of the submarine in such a campaign.[13] The other reason for overlooking the possible use of submarines against merchant shipping was faith in international law and morality, which from the perspective of the present day looks rather naïve. It was against the laws of war to sink a merchant ship without first removing the crew to a place of safety; a submarine could not do this and could only have a decisive effect if it attacked merchant ships without warning, ergo it could not legally or morally be used against commerce. Julian Corbett, perhaps the most perceptive naval strategist, underestimated the submarine for just this reason.[14] In the First World War, although Germany began with a conventional battle fleet strategy it eventually, and with some hesitation, switched its main focus to an asymmetric strategy of using U-boats against British merchant ships. The principal lesson that might be drawn from this salutary experience is caution in trusting to legal and moral restraints, or to arms control measures, to prevent the use of a new technology, particularly if its use would help an inferior power to blunt a significant advantage of a stronger opponent. Another parallel for the present might lie in the negative influence of the submarine: while it could not establish control of the seas, it could effectively disrupt it, which might well be enough for a power that is not dependent on use of the sea when pitted against one that is. Similarly, a weaker state could in future seek to disrupt the electromagnetic spectrum on which American forces are increasingly reliant, rather than attempting the more demanding task of trying to use it positively for itself.

The broader picture

At the level of the international system, the nineteenth century saw significant changes in what was required to be a great power: population, territory and agricultural productivity remained important but were joined and to some extent eclipsed by new resources, particularly coal and iron production, and industrial capacity. The administrative and organisational efficiency of the state became an increasingly important determinant of its power. At the broadest level, the combination of railways and steam power would over the longer term increase the strength of Land Powers relative to Sea Powers (though changes in the middle of the twentieth century would do much to redress the balance). The great continental states such as Germany and the United States could now realise their enormous potential wealth and power, while the relatively small forces that had typically been deployed by maritime states could rapidly be overwhelmed by troops brought up by rail. Whereas Napoleon had complained that 30,000 British troops at sea compelled him to tie down 300,000 men in garrisons, when Bismarck was asked how he would respond to the British army landing on the Baltic coast of Germany, he famously replied that he would have the local police arrest it. Britain's advantage at sea was also eventually eroded by the switch from sail to steam as the means of warship propulsion, as the industrial might of a hostile continental power could be more easily and more rapidly translated into sea power than had been the case in an era when the difficult skills of handling sailing ships had to be painstakingly developed.

There is no doubt that the nineteenth century saw many dramatic changes in technology that had a massive effect on warfare at every level. It could be argued by those who take the wider historical view of military revolutions that these developments did not represent an RMA until they were fully understood and incorporated into the doctrines and force structures of the major powers. Hence, on this view, the changes brought about by industrialisation represented only a potential RMA that was not fulfilled until after the First World War. The innovations of the nineteenth century could be seen as either a continuation of the social and political changes of the French Revolution or as the precursor to the interwar RMA, or even as both.

Regardless of whether the changes brought on by industrialisation in the middle of the nineteenth century are termed an RMA, their implications were immense. The shape and structure of both armies and navies, as well as how they fought, were fundamentally changed while at home, economies and societies also underwent huge upheavals as a result of industrialisation. Great powers had little choice but to follow suit if they sought to remain leading players in the international system, but it was possible to do this since technology spread rapidly from one state to another, as long as the regime concerned could afford the increasing sums of money that were required. Moreover, the rate of technological change accelerated, with obsolescence coming faster, and the costs of falling behind becoming all the greater. The educational level of a state's population and the robustness of its scientific base became increasingly significant determinants of power. While modern technology proved vital against peer competitors, it conferred a decisive advantage against less developed societies, as long as the latter followed a conventional, symmetrical strategy; yet alternative, more troublesome options were also available.

Once again, the political context of the advances in technology was crucial. The fact that the international system was relatively benign, at least in the absence of major wars between the great powers, draped a cloud of uncertainty around the full implications of the new weapons. This happy situation was not to last, however, as a large and powerful new country was created in the centre of Europe, with great industrial and military resources and highly ambitious aims for its place in the world. The initial peaceful stability and the eventual rise of a powerful and aggressive revisionist great power provided the backdrop against which the technological changes of the century would be played out.

The Interwar Years

The years between the two World Wars saw a wide range of significant innovations in military thinking and practice. Many thinkers consider the developments of these years to amount to an RMA in their own right, although others see in them the culmination of the changes that emerged in the late 19th century. An example of this latter approach is Earl Tilford:

> ...the military-technical revolution that issued from the maturing Industrial Revolution at the beginning of the 20th century did not translate into a true RMA until after the First World War, although all the technological elements were available during the war: the railroad, machine guns, tanks, long-range and rifled artillery, rapid-fire rifles, electronic means of communication, and airplanes.[15]

Jonathan Bailey differs, dating the beginning of what he sees as the only true RMA of the twentieth century (indeed, 'the most significant Revolution in Military Affairs in the history of warfare') to 1917-18, with the advent of indirect artillery fire. By creating the deep battle and adding a third dimension to warfare, he argues, this innovation established the Modern Style of warfare, an RMA that was merely extended by later developments such as armour, air power or information technology, which were its products and complements.[16] Williamson Murray agrees with Bailey, arguing that, 'of all military revolutions, World War I should be regarded as the most revolutionary in military terms.' He continues:

> Perhaps the best way to illustrate this point is to suggest that a British or German battalion commander from the battlefields of summer 1918 would have understood the underlying concepts of the battlefields of 1940, 1944 and even 1991. A battalion commander of 1914, however, would not have had the slightest clue as to what was occurring in 1918: that was how far military affairs had travelled in the course of four years.[17]

Whichever of these perspectives is taken, the conclusion that these years saw revolutionary change in military affairs is generally accepted. The enormous amount of attention devoted to these matters by contemporary analysts and proselytisers for particular concepts and weapons suggests that the magnitude of the developments that took place was well appreciated at the time. Indeed, as will be shown, some interpreters predicted that the impact of the new weapons would be truly revolutionary.

Why did the closing stages of the First World War and the two following decades amount to such a fertile period for strategic thought? First, the scarring experience of the Great War established an evident need to re-think existing ways of using military power. Second, several important new technologies had seen initial uses during the war, some in innovative ways, including the tank and aircraft. Their tentative early use and rapid technical improvement, along with new tactical and operational concepts, was not yet enough during the war to revolutionise warfare but was ample to spark the imaginations of theorists and to give them the inspiration to produce the much needed new approaches. Moreover, the new arms and services that came into being during the war provided such thinkers with institutional bases from which to pursue their causes. Third, the war left an international system that was essentially in a period of respite before renewed hostilities: Germany was determined to overturn the international system and with its experience of recent defeat and its armed forces constrained by the Versailles treaty, had every incentive to look towards innovative concepts that utilised recently emerging technology. Japan sought expansion in its own region, which would require effective tactical air power and new forms of naval power projection, while the US envisaged a future war with Japan, which would require long-range operations across the Pacific. A fourth possible factor, which some analysts identify in the present day, was constrained defence budgets. It is often argued that financial stringency acts as an additional spur to innovative approaches. Not all states embraced change with the same eagerness, however, so it seems safe to conclude that other factors are needed, notably ambitious political goals and military hierarchies that are receptive to new ideas. Britain and France both cut their defence spending between the wars, yet neither took full advantage of the new technology that was available: Britain was a satisfied power that set defence spending on the assumption that it would not fight any great power war in the foreseeable future, least of all in Europe, and against a background of strong pacifist sentiment in public opinion. France made efforts to incorporate new technology but drew what proved to be the wrong lessons from the First World War, assuming that the tactical primacy of the defensive (which in any case fitted in with French grand strategy) still applied. The states that were more enthusiastic in their embrace of new technology tended to have ambitious and revisionist goals or perceived a clear rationale for new types of forces in the form of a particular anticipated opponent in a specific theatre. Without such additional spurs towards innovation, constrained budgets can equally lead to more risk averse and conservative approaches, as well as to intensified inter-service rivalry.

The decades leading up to 1914 had seen an acceleration of technological change, primarily with the introduction of the internal combustion engine, which produced the submarine, the aircraft and the tank. The other key advance, which affected how each of these was to be used, was radio communications. Much interwar military thinking revolved around the strategic possibilities to which these innovations gave rise.

Air power

Air power provides one of the most distinctive schools of thought about the effect on warfare of a technological innovation. It is of particular significance for contemporary debates because it gave rise to a truly dramatic theory, which as early as the 1920s claimed that an entirely new form of warfare had been introduced that would not be added to the old methods but would rather sweep them away. Parallels can be drawn between current predictions about the impact of the information revolution and interwar views about the effect of air power. In both cases a split can be discerned between, on the one hand, those who expect the new means to be added to and to transform the existing ways of fighting and, on the other, those who predict a more radical outcome, with the new means entirely replacing the old system of warfare. This is not to suggest that the progress or outcome of the debate over air power has any predictive value for current disputes over the correct interpretation of the RMA. The aim of the comparison is rather to highlight the nature and the extent of the distinction between the more evolutionary and the more radical approaches, and to emphasise that the more adventurous predictions may not necessarily be the most accurate.

The interwar air power thinkers can be divided into two broad categories. The less ambitious of the two, which will be considered further below, essentially envisaged adding air power to the existing military means, which would evolve and become increasingly effective as a result. The more far-reaching school, represented by such thinkers as Giulio Douhet, Billy Mitchell and Alexander de Seversky, insisted that such a conception of air power was flawed.[18] It represented a dangerous and wasteful diversion from the true role of air power and hence risked defeat, they argued, and it would in any case prove superfluous if air power was used properly. Their preferred approach to air power was truly strategic: instead of using it to batter the enemy's army and navy, it should be used directly and immediately on the outbreak of war to target his vital industrial, economic, political and civilian centres. There could be no defence against such a strategy, either (depending on the theorist) because bombers could not be intercepted or because they would easily muscle their way past fighters. Strategic bombing would lead to rapid and decisive victory, separate from and independently of any efforts by land or naval forces – it is this element that justifies the adjective 'strategic'. To those who held this belief in strategic air power, using aircraft with armies or navies was a misuse, a diversion that could prove costly. Land and sea forces might temporarily retain a minor role but the strategic bombing force should be the only real national priority. Douhet himself was in no doubt that air power was revolutionary: 'the aerial machine is not an improvement; it is something new, with characteristics of its own, and it gives man possibilities he has never had before'. For him, the steps from thrown stones to artillery, or from the trireme to steamships, were nothing more than improvements, but this was not the case with air power: 'It is no longer a matter of evolution; it is revolution.'[19]

In part, of course, the strategic bombing doctrine was a reaction against those sceptics who doubted that air power would have a serious impact on warfare or predicted that it would have at most minor effects and could easily be tacked onto existing structures without any fundamental change.[20] In rejecting the most conservative views, however, the interwar air power enthusiasts went to the opposite extreme; they championed strategic bombing not as one more contribution to victory, however significant, but rather as an independently effective way of winning wars. It is easy to see the attraction of this dream. It promised quick and relatively cheap victories and even very low enemy casualties, since an opponent losing command of the air would have no choice but to surrender before his population was attacked on a large scale. It also offered a clear and compelling rationale for the preservation (in Britain) or creation (in the United States) of independent air forces. It is important to note that 'vested interests' – or 'institutional interests' to use a less loaded term – may exist among those advocating change as well as among sceptics.

However, the interwar air theorists such as Douhet, Mitchell, Seversky and their disciples were largely wrong. It did prove possible to achieve an effective defence against air attack (as, indeed, Britain had managed to do in the First World War)[21] which imposed such attrition on attacking aircraft that the cost of the campaign rose above what the results were worth or the attacker was prepared to bear. Besides, the evident disaster that would clearly befall any state that totally lost control of the skies above it encouraged the major powers to devote considerable exertions to preventing this from happening. Such defences could be worn down but only after a long drawn out process, so command of the air could not be achieved as rapidly or as easily as had been assumed. Second, the air enthusiasts tended to exaggerate the impact of bombing, both in terms of the destructive effect of individual bombs and also in terms of their wider effects against industry and civilian morale, which proved rather more robust than had been assumed. Strategic bombing eventually made a significant contribution to the allied victory in the Second World War, once problems with navigation and bombing accuracy had been reduced, once complete command of the air had been established and once targeting ideas had matured somewhat. It helped to reduce enemy production, to consume his resources in defending against or dealing with the consequences of bombing, and to erode civilian morale (although, contrary to the expectations of many air theorists, never to the extent that the survival of the Axis regimes was jeopardised). However, this contribution was as an additional means of attrition rather than as an independent means to victory in its own right. The air campaign against Germany, for example, was explicitly just one part of a broader strategy: its major contribution lay in preparing the way for Overlord rather than in making it unnecessary, securing command of the air beforehand and then providing tactical support and hindering the movement of German reinforcements.[22] Moreover, an enormous cost was attached to the application of theories of strategic air power. It is possible to question whether its contribution quite justified the immense human and financial cost of the air campaign. Others point to the diversion of aircraft away from other much needed tasks, such as preventing Britain from being defeated by the U-boat campaign.

The single-mindedness of the air theorists also detracted effort and attention away from other uses of air power that made a greater contribution to victory than the strategic air campaigns, notably in combined arms tactics on land and in carrier aviation at sea. This is not to suggest that air power should be 'subordinate' or 'auxiliary' to ground and sea forces (terms which have at times been used to describe genuine misunderstandings of the role of air power, but which have often been used by air power purists to dismiss operations that do not fit their strategic tunnel vision). Many of the most important uses of air power in the war were conducted separately from other arms at the operational level, notably attacks on German fuel supplies, or carrier aircraft knocking out air bases on Japanese-held islands. The conception behind these activities was joint at the strategic level: they were intended to contribute to overall objectives, not to win the war by themselves. Moreover, the air campaigns were fundamentally dependent on the land and sea campaigns for their effect. In Europe, shipping brought in the fuel without which the bombers would have been grounded, while in the Pacific, maritime power seized island air bases within range of Japan. Furthermore, had the Axis forces not had to fight on land (and it is worth noticing in passing that emphasis on the air campaign against Germany does tend to underplay the central role of the USSR in wearing down German power) the attritional effect of strategic bombing would have been far less. The effect of air power on warfare was revolutionary indeed but it was not quite the impact that the interwar air theorists predicted, either in magnitude or in the precise way in which it acted.

There are two principal ways in which air power might be interpreted as having initiated a true RMA. The first would be if it had led to an entirely new, separate and distinct form of warfare, as alleged by the interwar air theorists and their later apostles. Air power did not have this effect; it changed many aspects of warfare but did so by joining and integrating with the other armed services, making them adapt and creating a new entity that might be interpreted as representing evolution rather than a true 'RMA'. This second interpretation of the effect of air power could still be seen as 'revolutionary', in the sense that it introduced a hugely significant new element into warfare, which no great power wishing to retain that status could ignore and to which all existing elements of the armed forces had to adapt. This debate turns on semantic definitions of 'revolutionary' but the main point is that even if the impact of air power is seen as 'merely' on the operational and tactical levels (rather than as a separate, strategic means to win), this still represented an enormous change, which only seems relatively modest in comparison to unrealistically ambitious claims such as those made by Douhet, Mitchell and Seversky.

Tactical air power and land warfare

A striking feature of the interwar military revolution was the way in which it applied to all media of warfare. Theories of strategic air power constitute the clearest, most radical and most lasting (though far from the most convincing) school of thought to emerge from this period but important ideas arose elsewhere, which involved the use of air power in other ways.

Some interwar thinkers, including Basil H. Liddell Hart and J.F.C. Fuller in Britain and Charles de Gaulle in France, applied the new technology to land warfare.[23] They built on the nascent tactical and operational approaches of the Great War to devise a new way of fighting that sought to avoid the mass slaughter and immobility of the Western front. The ideas that eventually emerged from their work and that of others were thoroughly combined-arms in conception. Tanks would enhance firepower and make it far more mobile; mechanised vehicles would restore mobility and protection to infantry; artillery and tactical air power would provide additional concentrated firepower where it was needed. The result would be a far more fluid and mobile form of warfare, concentrating combat power to smash through the enemy front lines and then burst out into his rear areas, spreading confusion and overrunning key operational and strategic objectives, including command posts, air bases and supply areas. The tempo of warfare would be vastly increased, shattering the cohesion of the opponent as much as destroying his forces, and inflicting as much psychological as physical shock and dislocation to hamper his capacity to make decisions as well as the means to carry them out. Such ideas sought to use new technology to permit new tactical and operational approaches, which would have dramatic strategic effects.

One of the key elements of mechanised warfare, singled out by a number of historians, was the use of radio communications for command and control. The forces envisaged by the armoured warfare pioneers would be widely dispersed but could operate as a single co-ordinated whole thanks to radio communications. Creveld notes that the decisive German advantage was the fact that theirs was the only army in which all tanks (rather than just the command vehicles) had radios that could transmit as well as receive messages, which greatly increased flexibility: 'This flexibility, possibly even more than the tanks themselves, constituted the true core of the new style in warfare.'[24] Eliot

Cohen recognises the importance of radios and also of other supporting factors, not least an appropriate doctrine and a decentralised approach to command, writing that Germany:

> ...succeeded not because of material superiority but because they got several things right – supporting technologies such as tank radios, organisation, operational concepts, and a proper climate or culture of command.[25]

Beaumont stresses the importance of encouraging improvisation and initiative in low-level commanders to allow them to cope with an increasingly confusing battlefield, and the way that Germany fused a combination of new and old technologies.[26] These comments usefully underline the broad basis of the interwar innovations, which involved far more than simply using tanks. They also demonstrate once again that military-technical innovations require organisational and doctrinal adaptation to take full effect. Once again, the importance of radios demonstrates the significance of advances in the ability to use information to enhance tactical and operational agility.

It is also significant that although the origins of the new thinking lay to a considerable extent in Britain and, in part, France, it was Germany that applied them to such great effect. Britain had no intention of becoming involved in the type of war that would require the mechanised forces advocated by Liddell Hart and Fuller. In France (and also in Britain) there was a reluctance on the part of those in authority to embrace the ideas of the new thinkers. Germany, which had ambitious goals requiring the overthrow of the international system, had a greater incentive to take up radical ideas. Similarly, in the future it could be challengers to the system, who want to overturn an existing power's military lead, that will prove more receptive to the adoption of innovative approaches.

Some writers caution against reading too much into 'blitzkrieg doctrine', suggesting that it was not quite as well formed and developed as is often implied.[27] There may indeed be a tendency to impose more cohesion on these ideas when looking back at them than actually existed at the time. Nevertheless, the results from the Second World War were striking both in their effect and in the clear contrast they offered with the campaigns of the previous war. Moreover, the vital importance of understanding the full implications of change and of devising appropriate military doctrine to apply it was clearly demonstrated. France had a greater number of tanks than Germany in spring 1940: it was the different way in which the two sides envisaged their use that was to prove crucial. France followed the practice of the previous war by scattering its tanks throughout its infantry units to boost their combat power; Germany, on the other hand, concentrated its tanks into armoured units that, supported by artillery, tactical air power and mechanised infantry, could smash their way through the defence at decisive points and then exploit the breakthrough. The advantage of the offensive, both tactically and operationally, was thereby restored to warfare. Of course, mechanised warfare had by no means reached its peak of effectiveness (for example, the bulk of the German forces that invaded the USSR remained dependent on horse-drawn supply wagons); indeed, as will be explained in the next chapter, some analysts identify the high-point of the blitzkrieg RMA as being Operation Desert Storm in 1991.

However, echoing the fate of Napoleon, the state that pioneered the use of this new form of warfare lost the Second World War. Many of the same factors that thwarted Bonaparte also help to explain this later defeat. Blitzkrieg proved extremely effective against small states, or against states using the old system, or against states using the new system less skillfully. However, Hitler's grand strategic failings led him to take on opponents who did not fall into any of these categories.

Like Napoleon, Hitler could not find a way to defeat Britain and her maritime power, since the RAF and the Royal Navy together prevented him from conducting land operations against her, and the Luftwaffe could not knock out Britain by itself.

Russia's greater size and less favourable terrain (particularly for logistics, given the paucity of good roads) made it a far less suitable location for the German army and air force than areas to the west, not least against asymmetric warfare waged by partisans and guerrillas, which still required large numbers of troops to counter.

The USSR proved not only to be almost incredibly resilient but also to be an adept pupil, and the Red Army became extremely proficient at mechanised warfare in its own right; the greater Soviet industrial capacity simply overwhelmed Germany using a symmetric strategy.

Germany had significant vulnerabilities that could be exploited by a properly targeted strategic air campaign, notably shortages of fuel and important transportation links.

The new methods of warfare were not sufficient to compensate for several pressing strategic problems, including operating in North Africa against opponents who could control the sea, but more strikingly for the decision to fight simultaneously against the British Empire, the USSR and the United States – with Italy as an ally.

Blitzkrieg was immensely potent yet it also had significant shortcomings and vulnerabilities that contributed to Germany's downfall. One important weakness lay in its enormous logistical demands, which became particularly damaging given that much of the German supply effort still remained dependent on older forms of transport. Moreover, when the opposing side was able to conduct effective air interdiction against the German supply chain, blitzkrieg could be brought to a halt. The advances in land warfare between the two World Wars were immensely significant, not least in the fact that they rested on further examining technological breakthroughs that had already occurred and applying innovative thinking to them, and combining them in new ways. The result was certainly an impressive new tool but neither a panacea for all forms of war and all types of opponent, nor something that could compensate for a fundamentally flawed grand strategy.

Naval warfare

Naval forces also saw considerable change between the two world wars.[28] The most visible and lasting innovation was the rise of the aircraft carrier. Early carriers had served in the First World War but their primitive stage of development and the primarily continental nature of the war meant that they had little chance to prove themselves, though the first example of power projection from carriers against the shore occurred as early as Christmas Day 1914. All of the major navies looked to a greater role for carriers between the wars. One of the main themes of the strategic air theorists was that air power posed a particular challenge to navies, both tactically (making them too vulnerable to air attack to play a useful role) and strategically (strategic bombing would win wars independently and rapidly, therefore depriving navies of their former missions). The major counter to this challenge was for navies to take aircraft to sea with them. This innovation provided an important element of defence against the direct threat of air attack and also helped to counter other threats to ships, notably the submarine. Naval aviation eventually proved to be a superior means of performing the vital task of destroying enemy surface vessels, although the major powers were slow to recognise this. There were differences of degree between them but all the major interwar navies expected the battleship to remain the heart of the fleet, with carriers playing an indispensable but supporting part. In the Second World War the increased range and weight of attack made possible by aircraft eventually proved superior to the old battleship broadside in encounters between opposing fleets (with submarines also taking on a prominent role), though the battleship retained important roles well into the post-war period, not least in helping to defend carriers when their aircraft could not fly in bad weather or at night.

Carriers therefore proved able to help fleets in securing control of the sea by meeting old and newer threats and countering enemy surface vessels. For the allies in the Second World War (and for Britain and the US at any time) there was no task more important than guaranteeing their use of the sea, which was a basic necessity for survival and for remaining in the war; the seas had to be secured before any other operations could be contemplated. Carriers made another vital contribution to allied strategy, however, in projecting power against the shore. This had long been a role of warships but now the range and weight of firepower increased from those of naval guns (although these continued to be important) to those of carrier air wings. Carrier aircraft were used against ships in port (pioneered by the British against the Italian fleet at Taranto and then followed more dramatically by Japan at Pearl Harbor), against shore-based air forces (in which role carriers proved far more successful than the air theorists had expected: carrier and shore-based aircraft turned out to have different strengths and weaknesses and to be complementary rather than alternatives) and against a host of other targets ashore.

One important aspect of this power projection role was the support of amphibious operations, which saw such impressive developments in the interwar period that some analysts count it as an RMA in its own right. The failure of the Gallipoli campaign led to a range of conclusions: some thought that it demonstrated that amphibious operations were no longer possible in the industrial age, but others came to the alternative conclusion that it proved the need for more attention to be devoted to specialised techniques and equipment for amphibious warfare. The strategic situation of the United States and Japan meant that both put a high priority on such operations, and hence a great deal of effort was put into improving capabilities during the interwar period, particularly by the US Marine Corps. The result was that purpose-built landing craft, with well trained troops, backed by gunfire support and air cover either from shore bases or, more often, from aircraft carriers, restored amphibious operations as a strategic option. Their success was proved many times in the Mediterranean, Europe and, especially, the Pacific.

Unlike the changes on land and in the air, however, there was a greater degree of choice as to whether individual states embraced the innovations in carrier and amphibious warfare. Some states did not perceive a need for such capabilities and could simply look to disrupting their opponents' use of the sea rather than seeking to assert sea control for themselves. For such states, smaller surface vessels, submarines and land-based aircraft could well prove sufficient to provide the level of naval power that was required. Increasingly, the highest level capabilities in carriers and amphibious warfare would be confined to a small number of powers. (Of course, the same would become true of strategic air power in the post-1945 era.) Japan had led the way in the creation of carrier forces, though, like the other major navies, the Imperial Japanese Navy long continued to view the battleship as the most important element of the fleet. Nevertheless, like Germany, Japan found itself fighting an opponent who proved better able to use the new means of warfare at sea and in the air, and who had far greater economic and industrial power with which to wage total war. If there was a naval RMA, then, it proved to be one that many states could simply opt out of, as well as one in which the initial pioneers were swiftly relegated to an inferior position.

The changes that can be seen in navies between the wars were in their own way every bit as striking and significant as those that affected the air and land forces. One reason not to hail them as a separate RMA in their own right, however, is that doing so could obscure one of the principal features of the interwar developments, which still endures: that is, the degree to which they required an integrated approach. It was proved many times in the 1939-1945 war that tanks on their own could be vulnerable to a number of counter-measures, so mechanised warfare involved a combined approach, unifying the efforts of tanks, infantry, artillery and tactical air power as well as engineers, signallers and so on. Air forces could not rely on bombers alone but also required fighters as well as specialised aircraft for reconnaissance and damage assessment, to say nothing of their enormous sea and land transportation requirements for logistical support. Naval forces also became a mixture of heavy ships, aircraft carriers, destroyers, frigates, submarines and aircraft (based both ashore and on ships), in addition to supply and replenishment vessels, marines and amphibious craft. Each of the services became an increasingly combined arms team. A similar story was repeated with the three services at the strategic level. The Mediterranean and Pacific campaigns were the clearest but not the only demonstrations of the ever closer link between land, sea and air warfare. This tendency was to increase in the years after 1945 with the increasing pace of developments in electronics and missiles: when a cruise missile launched from a submerged submarine can hit a target far inland, the accuracy of any strict separation of land, sea and air forces is doubtful.

In sum, the changes that can be identified in the period of the two World Wars can plausibly be seen as an RMA (or, on another view, as several minor RMAs which together and with other, broader changes, amounted to a major RMA). The experience of the Second World War suggested that the cluster of developments described above had wrought radical change on the tactical, operational and strategic levels of warfare, and had altered strategic geography for good. An alternative approach, taking a longer-term perspective, might conclude that the key fundamentals still applied, notably the continuing importance of attrition in a total war between the great powers. The improvement, if that is the right word, in how they fought was merely a matter of means, not ends. Perhaps a true RMA might better be sought in a technological development that had a more fundamental effect after its emergence in the closing stages of the Second World War.

The Cold War Period: Nuclear Weapons

The period since the end of the Second World War is of particular interest to this study not only due to the fact that it saw the birth of the term 'RMA', but also because one or possibly two strong candidates for the label have been identified during it. The first, the advent of nuclear weapons, is one of the few generally accepted RMAs that is so narrowly based on technological change.

The second is the RMA that is the main subject of this book, the roots of which can be found in the Cold War period.

It is difficult to think of a more dramatic entrance on the world stage for a development in military technology than the debut of nuclear weapons. The Second World War was a conflict of unprecedented scale, fought literally all over the world, causing a number of deaths that dwarfed any previous war, and involving a host of new weapons used over land, sea and air. It took quite a finale to top what had gone before but the use of atomic bombs against Japan did just that. Neither the type of target nor the number of casualties was new – far more people had died in the 'conventional' bombing of other cities, such as Berlin and Tokyo. What was new with Hiroshima and Nagasaki was that in the case of each city, a single bomb had caused such devastation. Yet the weapons used against Japan were far from the peak of destruction that this new technology could offer: the later development of thermonuclear weapons, the H-bomb, provided warheads with a destructive power several orders of magnitude greater than the Hiroshima bomb.

A detailed account of the developments of nuclear weapons and nuclear strategy would be well beyond the scope of this book.[29] The sheer bulk of the literature on nuclear strategy – the RMA will have to remain a fashionable term for a very long time to make anything approaching a challenge for library shelf space – is one indication of the grip that it exerted on strategic thought and policymakers during and since the Cold War. In terms of spawning a vast amount of debate and writing that sought to comprehend its effects, in terms of the creation of new doctrines and institutions (such as US Strategic Air Command – motto: 'Peace is our Profession' – and the Soviet Strategic Rocket Forces, as well as a host of think-tanks) and compelling existing structures and ideas to adapt, in terms of radically changing how the major powers viewed war, and in terms of depth of impact on public opinion and popular culture, nuclear weapons do seem fully to justify the RMA tag. One distinctive feature of the nuclear RMA is the extent to which it rested on a small number of specific technological advances, namely the weapons themselves and their means of delivery (particularly ICBMs).

Clearly the debate over the impact of nuclear weapons is an immensely controversial one in which a general consensus would be sought in vain. One widely held view interprets them as having had an effect unlike that of any other major weapons system, namely making war between the great powers much less likely. The idea of a deterrent was not new. It has been suggested that, to take one example, one significant effect of the Royal Navy in the nineteenth Century was to intimidate the other great powers, thus preventing any challenge and underwriting the Pax Britannica.[30] As suggested above, of course, much of the nineteenth century was a period of self-restraint by the great powers, none of which sought to revise the system; this observation could be interpreted as either making the deterrence hypothesis impossible to prove or, alternatively, as supporting it. The deterrent effect of nuclear weapons is an even more convincing claim and all the more striking for occurring during a period of intense and prolonged rivalry between the world's greatest powers. It could be argued that nuclear weapons were superfluous for this effect; even with conventional weapons, the Second World War showed that total war between modern industrial powers was too destructive to contemplate. Yet suggesting that the US and USSR would have been equally careful to avoid direct confrontation with each other in the absence of nuclear weapons seems to be placing a great deal of faith in the ability of policymakers to weigh up costs and benefits, in conditions of great uncertainty and with very high stakes, and to avoid a gamble. What nuclear weapons, twinned with appropriate delivery systems, did was to make the destructive effect of total war both too enormous to contemplate and utterly unavoidable; there was far less chance of a government being able to delude itself that the costs of a major conflict might be acceptable. The result was that direct war between the major powers became far less likely: the motto of SAC was quoted above not to mock but rather because there is considerable truth in it. As so often, Winston Churchill put it well, when in 1955 he suggested to the House of Commons that 'it may well be that we shall by a process of sublime irony have reached a stage in this story where safety will be the sturdy child of terror, and survival the twin brother of annihilation'.[31]

A huge range of theories and concepts was developed to try to understand the potential impact of these weapons. It is important to point out that not all proved to be correct. For some in the first wave of thinkers, nuclear weapons finally provided a means that would allow strategic air power to fulfil the hopes of its interwar enthusiasts. Yet they did not follow the logic of their arguments to its conclusion and failed to appreciate that when the level of destruction reached a certain level – and spread to both sides – the weapon could become more a deterrent than a warfighting tool (though there was no shortage of tracts trying to find ways of making it the latter). Others believed that nuclear weapons might make conventional forces redundant on land and at sea, though none of the major powers found this to be plausible despite the evident attraction of any suggestion that promised to save so much money. The impact of even the nuclear RMA, then, was subject to some limits and many predictions about it proved to be exaggerated.

The sheer range of issues that nuclear weapons threw up and the breadth of opinions about them in the literature are yet further reminders of the difficulty of evaluating all the effects of an RMA while it is underway. Nuclear weapons did not make all war obsolete, there were reactions to the US and the Soviet nuclear capability, in terms of imitation as well as proliferation, and continuation of lower-intensity conflict – which also become a useful tool by which the leading powers could use proxies to challenge each other. There were vast debates over the ideal balance between counter-force and counter-value targeting, the possibility of limited nuclear war, the controllability or otherwise of escalation and the impact of 'tactical' nuclear weapons for battlefield use, let alone the New Look, the Pentomic Division (one idea about how conventional forces might evolve for the nuclear battlefield), the neutron bomb, the Strategic Defence Initiative, arms control, MIRVs, MAD and the desirability or otherwise of nuclear proliferation. Of course, the full impact of nuclear weapons on warfare and international politics is still unfolding, with their proliferation well beyond the 'big five' of the Cold War.

One striking feature about the nuclear RMA is that, unlike some of the other cases referred to above, there was a full realisation from the outset of the magnitude (if not the precise nature) of its effect on warfare. It was also the first development to be referred to by contemporaries as a 'Revolution in Military Affairs' or 'military-technical revolution', initially in the USSR. It was not, however, the only development to which Soviet analysts applied this label.

The first signs of the 'current RMA'

The idea that the world might be approaching a new RMA based on conventional weapons was closely linked to nuclear strategy. For some years, military thinkers on both sides of the iron curtain believed that a war in Europe would inevitably be nuclear from the start. There had always been some dissenters who believed that there could be a European war that was fought, at least for a time, solely with conventional weapons. Eventually the official doctrine of both sides came to accept this possibility, though it was still thought likely that the nuclear threshold would eventually be crossed.

Soviet acknowledgement of the possibility of a conventional phase to war in Europe led them to increase dramatically the size of their conventional forces and also to look to innovative concepts, such as the 'Operational Manoeuvre Group', which aimed to exploit a breakthrough into the rear of NATO forces, and thus make any Western use of nuclear weapons, against forces on their own territory, far more difficult to decide upon as well as to carry out. Such developments, of course, elicited a reaction from the West.[32] The major NATO states, particularly the US, were painfully aware that the rapid quantitative and qualitative improvement of Soviet conventional forces threatened to undermine the credibility of the Western deterrent. The fear grew that NATO faced being rapidly overwhelmed by successive waves or echelons of Soviet armour, leaving no option other than the apocalyptic step of nuclear first use. As a result, the US began to look to emerging technology that could target Soviet forces well beyond the front lines. Crucially, this technical research was accompanied by a great deal of new thinking in the American military, in part due to the stinging experience of defeat in Vietnam.[33] The reaction of the US Army, in particular, to the debacle of Vietnam was immensely healthy, taking the form of a determination to re-think its basic doctrine. This self-examination resulted in a very creative period for new ideas and concepts, which some commentators fear is currently being lost as the generation of Army officers with Vietnam experience disappears from the service. Similarly, at sea the growing threat of attacks by sophisticated Soviet anti-ship missiles, to be launched from aircraft, submarines and surface vessels in numbers that threatened to swamp the defences of individual warships, compelled new thinking in air defence that culminated in raising the existing concept of the battle group to new levels of integration. The weapons systems and ideas that began to emerge drew on many of the technologies that had been developing rapidly during the Cold War period, pushed on by the superpower rivalry, notably electronics, guided missiles and new types of sensors.

Awareness began to spread that the combination of these developments could represent a fundamental change in military affairs.[34] In the 1980s, a group of Soviet military theorists led by Marshal Nikolai Ogarkov (at one time Chief of the General Staff) began to write about a military-technical revolution. New military systems approaching the effectiveness of nuclear weapons in striking power and range would, they predicted, extend future battles deep into rear areas. These new systems would link target acquisition, command and control, and long-range weapons to create 'reconnaissance-fire complexes' and 'reconnaissance-strike complexes'. Initially there was concern in the West that this debate portended a Soviet drive to prepare to win a non-nuclear war in Europe but realisation gradually spread that the Soviet armed forces saw the changes as to their disadvantage, as they threatened to neutralise their considerable advantage in heavy armour.[35] Among the important sources of these Soviet ideas was the growing attention being devoted by the US to the potential of emerging military technologies, culminating in doctrinal concepts such as 'Follow On Forces Attack' and 'AirLand Battle'. Introduced in 1982, the latter concept included the use of longer-range fire to disrupt second and following Soviet echelons, creating gaps which could then be exploited by manoeuvre. It also placed a greater emphasis on joint action by the different services, as its name suggested; thus new Army surface-to-surface missiles would target enemy air defences to enhance the ability of combat aircraft to strike Soviet second echelon forces.[36] From the Soviet point of view, emerging technologies threatened to raise the US armed forces to a new level of effectiveness. New systems and ideas affected the Army, Navy and Air Force; the programmes initiated in this period culminated in many of the weapons systems that proved themselves in the 1991 Gulf War. The USSR attempted to keep up with these new arms races, not to mention the Strategic Defence Initiative (or 'Star Wars') but the strain that they caused the Soviet economy, together with the growing awareness that the effort to keep pace with American technology was unsustainable, contributed greatly to the internal collapse of the Soviet system and hence to the end of the Cold War.

The 1970s and 1980s therefore saw the emergence of a set of interrelated technological and conceptual development that some interpreted as promising revolutionary improvements in the effectiveness of conventional weapons. It was these weapons and ideas that would burst onto the wider consciousness in the Persian Gulf in 1991.

Conclusion

All of the cases studied in this chapter have been broadly accepted in the literature as either RMAs or, at least, as periods of unusually significant change. The changes of the Napoleonic period were clearly perceived as a watershed at the time, compelling the other great powers to reform and to imitate French innovations. The impact of the changes of the nineteenth century was also clear but they took effect over a longer period. Contemporary analysis of interwar military developments most closely resembles today's debate over the existence of RMAs; this is in large part due to the acceleration in the pace of technological change which has been a feature of the last 150 years or so. Both nuclear weapons and the changes now underway have been widely interpreted by contemporaries as RMAs.

In each of the three pre-1945 cases examined, the changes that were considered provided significant advantages in fighting: (a) similar opponents using a symmetrical strategy but lagging behind in incorporating the new developments; (b) similar but weaker opponents who used the new methods, but less effectively; (c) dissimilar and less developed opponents who sought, perhaps unwisely, to use a symmetrical strategy. However, the innovations proved far less effective against asymmetric strategies, or against very different opponents. Moreover, the advantage provided against symmetric competitors proved to be transitory as the innovations concerned were partially blunted by imitation, by adoption of counter-measures, or by some combination of the two. It is striking that the state initiating a new way of fighting could very rapidly find itself confronting a more skilled proponent of the same art: German blitzkrieg found an enthusiastic and adept pupil in the USSR, and while Germany initiated the bombing of cities against Guernica and Rotterdam they would soon, as Arthur Harris promised, reap the whirlwind. In each case, the new techniques or technology tended to spread to other states fairly swiftly, though acquisition of the major naval capabilities proved to be more a matter of choice for individual states.

What was required to be a great power changed over time but the particular states that were great powers remained quite constant, suggesting a fairly strong ability to adapt. An increasing gap can be discerned between the capabilities of major and medium powers, and between medium and minor powers. This gap did not always prove decisive, however, and applied mainly to symmetric strategies. Successive revolutions therefore tended to widen the overall range of capabilities as the leading edge of military power increased at a more rapid pace than the trailing end. In the Tofflers' terminology,[37] First and Second Wave capabilities and even armies are likely to co-exist with Third Wave ones, though the latter will not necessarily prevail against less sophisticated foes. The minimum investment required to be a major power became higher, as did the penalty for attempting to fight a superior opponent with a conventional, symmetrical strategy; yet asymmetric strategies were usually available and offered a greater chance, albeit no guarantee, of success.

No clear conclusion emerges about what made states more receptive to innovation, though states that seek to revise the system seem more likely to embrace change than those that seek to support it. The former have in a number of cases introduced major innovations but then suffered defeat due to pursuing excessively ambitious objectives, which does suggest that an RMA might tempt a state into peril by encouraging an escalation in the ends sought. It also seems that the perceived existence of some form of opponent or threat, at least potentially, has generally been required to force the pace of adopting new ways of fighting. If accurate, this observation makes the current enthusiasm for the RMA in the United States, a status quo power and by far the leading military power, all the more striking – it is perhaps tempting to point to a society and a military that is peculiarly technophile as an explanation.

There was a considerable variation in the accuracy of how the impact of new doctrine and technology was assessed: some predictions were good, many were bad and some were indifferent. It should be emphasised that over-estimation of their effects seems as prevalent as under-estimation, particularly in the more modern cases. In some cases, important elements of continuity were evident and the new means co-existed with the old. The leading edge of military capability became more combined-arms and more 'joint' in character, with the various elements of the forces becoming more interdependent. Weakness in or failure of any one of several key elements could prove disproportionately damaging. The most capable forces also became increasingly expensive and complex, with greatly increasing support needs (which took a growing proportion of service personnel).

The political context was a crucial factor in all RMAs, both for the extent to which innovations were adopted and for the context in which they were used; that is, relating to what states fought for, where they fought and possible restrictions on how they fought. Other broad factors not directly connected to the changes under consideration had a huge effect, which makes it all the more difficult to draw comparisons across the ages. Thus, World War I was marked by offensive military doctrines, which were partly the result of prevalent ideas in European society rather than depending exclusively on analysis of the state of military technology. Similarly, it is widely acknowledged that there is today in the major Western powers a distinct unwillingness to risk casualties: this phenomenon could result either in refusal to engage in high-risk action or in a more energetic pursuit of technologies that promise to reduce the risk to personnel.

One of the most important points to take away from this survey is that novel technologies and concepts, even if they amounted to an RMA, did not prove sufficient to compensate for serious errors on the political level. The failings of Napoleonic France or Nazi Germany are not to be found at the tactical or even operational levels, but rather in their disastrous grand strategies. One could even suggest that, on the contrary, an over-estimation of the potential of the new military capabilities might have encouraged them to pursue suicidally ambitious policies by giving them the delusion that their inflated political aims were achievable. Far from allowing them to square the circle of objectives and resources, their enthusiastic embrace of an RMA might have hastened their march down the path to ruin. As will be argued at greater length below, even if an RMA is truly underway at the beginning of the twenty-first century, it will not necessarily fulfil all the hopes that rest upon it and all the claims that are made on its behalf.

Any or each of the cases examined above could be interpreted as an RMA. Alternatively, the first three (or perhaps the second and the third) could all be seen as part of a single RMA, though the long period of 'revolution' identified by this latter view would seem to raise doubts about the advantage of the RMA concept over a more evolutionary understanding of change. Significant elements of continuity and evolution link the three cases with each other and also with developments since 1945. The continuing development of combined arms thinking on land, the addition of missiles to land, sea and air forces, and the growing importance of electronic warfare to all of them could be seen as part of an on-going process of evolution in military technology and military art that began in the nineteenth century and is still underway. Indeed, many contemporary debates over the role of air power or the growing potential of operational manoeuvre with properly inter-linked ground forces have some similarities to ideas first raised in the interwar years. Maybe analysts of the present can find more useful material in the recent past than is sometimes recognised.

Chapter 3
The 1990-91 Gulf War and the RMA

Something occurred in the night skies and desert sands of the Middle East in 1991 that the world had not seen for three hundred years – the arrival of a new form of warfare that closely mirrors a new form of wealth creation.[1]

The 1990-91 Gulf conflict occupies a prominent place in analyses of contemporary conflict and trends in military technology. It is easy to see why. The crisis occurred at a crucial time, just after the end of the Cold War, when the Western powers were considering how to reshape strategy, procurement and military doctrine for a world without a single, dominant focus for defence policy. The invasion of Kuwait poured cold water on euphoric predictions of an end to major conflict and showed that the Western armed forces might still have to conduct large scale, high intensity, warfighting operations. Moreover, as this conflict was for a long time the only major regional inter-state conflict to have taken place since the end of the Cold War, it tended to be over-represented in analyses of warfare. Although it has been cited in support of many different, often contradictory conclusions, on its own it represents a rather narrow basis on which to rest predictions about the future of warfare. Nevertheless, the nature and course of the conflict were both crucial in driving the debate on what some came to see as the current 'Revolution in Military Affairs'.

The most striking initial impression of the conflict was the great success of American military technology. The 1980s had seen the introduction into service of various new weapons systems, as well as novel ideas about how best to use them. Yet the operational performance of US forces had not always lived up to expectations, albeit that the interventions in Lebanon and Grenada, or limited military action against Libyan or Iranian forces, did not quite fit the model for which these capabilities had been designed. In contrast, the 1990-91 Gulf conflict provided an impressive showcase for new technology that appeared to have been dramatically successful, just when major questions about the future shape and composition of the armed forces were being examined. The war appeared to vindicate the hopes of those who put their trust in advanced military technology that promised a new level of effectiveness. Furthermore, it hinted at an even greater revolution to come. One influential American think tank concluded:

...the Gulf War documented the emergence of a challenging new era in conventional warfare. The effect of high technology – in weapons, command and control systems, intelligence, and other areas – has revolutionised the nature of war.[2]

According to one writer, a leading Soviet commentator was persuaded that a new generation in warfare had begun by a single television image, namely the footage of one Precision-Guided Munition (PGM) blasting a hole in the wall of a building, through which a second PGM then entered.[3] This revolution seemed to apply particularly to the United States and promised significant benefits:

American combat effectiveness in the Gulf War suggested that a historic revolution in military affairs (RMA) is underway, possibly solving many of the strategic dilemmas the United States faces in the post-Cold War world.[4]

Such views were not confined to military analysts but also extended to politicians. According to Richard Cheney (then Secretary of Defense, later Vice President), 'This war demonstrated dramatically the new possibilities of what has been called the "military-technological revolution in warfare".' William Perry (later Secretary of Defense under President Clinton) wrote, 'a new class of military systems…gave American forces a revolutionary advance in military capability.'[5] The conflict in the Persian Gulf was therefore the most significant single factor in promoting the idea that a Revolution in Military Affairs was underway.

An enormous literature exists concerning the war in the Gulf.[6] The conflict has been repeatedly and minutely dissected from various points of view and marshalled in support of a variety of arguments. This chapter will not retell the basic story of the conflict, which is covered well in a number of accounts.[7] Nor will it seek to provide a comprehensive account of all the detailed conclusions drawn and lessons learned. Its aim is the more limited one of assessing certain broad schools of thought about the implications of the conflict for the development of warfare. Does the Gulf War suggest that a revolution in warfare is underway or imminent and, if so, what sort of RMA is it?

Can broad conclusions be drawn from the Gulf War?

There are always pitfalls in seeking to draw broad lessons from single cases. The more unusual the case, the less widely applicable are the conclusions drawn from it, and the greater risk there would be in assuming that the scenario will be repeated. The question of the wider applicability of conclusions arises with any single case but is particularly relevant here; any conflict is unique but the Gulf War had more unusual features than other recent conflicts. Particular care must therefore be taken in basing predictions upon it. This warning applies all the more because the Gulf conflict was unusually favourable to the American style of warfare – a danger thus exists of drawing conclusions that are excessively comforting, fostering complacency. The contrast with other post-Cold War operational experience emphasises that the Gulf War was unusually conducive to the type of intervention that Western states, and the United States in particular, are most willing and best able to conduct. Basing force development too closely on the Gulf campaign would risk creating armed forces only capable of handling the most favourable situations and which would struggle in the conditions that would more usually be expected. Moreover, such a tendency could be exacerbated by raising excessively optimistic expectations among decision-makers and in public opinion over military success and low casualties in intervention.

In what ways was the 1990-91 Gulf conflict exceptionally favourable for the Western powers? The answer lies in a combination of political and military factors. Politically, the initial cause of the conflict made it easy to unite international opinion against the Iraqi regime and to form a coalition with agreed political objectives. The fact that the initial cause of the crisis took the form of an unambiguous invasion of one state by another, followed by its occupation and annexation, greatly facilitated the creation of a consensus against Iraq. The clearest possible breach of the most fundamental principle of international order and international law (that force not be used to change borders) was combined with a clear and serious threat to one of the most important interests of the major world powers (the supply of oil from the Gulf). It was therefore relatively easy to create a coalition with the United States fully committed from the outset and the vast majority of the international community – including the USSR and most Middle Eastern states – in broad agreement. United Nations Security Council consensus, overflight rights and ample host nation support were therefore readily secured. The very different course of events surrounding the conflicts in the former Yugoslavia or the post-1991 containment of Iraq (both of which saw a rather more surly Russia and considerably less co-operative regional states) demonstrate just how unusual, and how helpful, these political factors were.

Militarily, the form of the Gulf conflict was particularly conducive to the preferences and advantages of the major Western powers. Conventional, high-intensity warfare by a regular army has generally proved far easier for them than guerrilla warfare or low intensity conflict waged by sub-state actors. Even among conventional, major regional conflicts, the 1991 war looks relatively benign. In contrast to the conflicts in Korea or Vietnam, operations in the Gulf were not constrained by a need to avoid the risk of escalation that could bring other great powers into the war on the opposing side. The terrain in which the war was to be fought was equally appealing to the West: the flat desert environment, with few natural obstacles or civilians and with enemy forces out in the open at the end of long and vulnerable supply routes, was ideal both for air power and for armour-based, manoeuvre warfare. Indeed, the very name of the operation was revealing: it was a great deal easier than 'Mountain Storm', 'Jungle Storm' or 'City Storm' would have been – if such operations would ever have been attempted. The weather, while generally described as worse than usual for the area,[8] was far better that could be expected in Korea or Europe, which greatly assisted air power, sensors and weapons guidance systems. The timing of the conflict could not have been better: the Cold War had just ended so Western armed forces were free to be re-deployed from Europe (and a small part of their total force was able to call on a far greater proportion of their support, base networks and transport assets) but had not yet been whittled away in search of a peace dividend. The region was also ideal in terms of host nation support, as the Persian Gulf in general and Saudi Arabia in particular were unusually well provided with high quality ports, roads and airfields, many of which had been designed to support the very military systems in use by Western forces. Ample fuel was available. The Coalition also enjoyed a long and uninterrupted build-up period, which allowed it to make the elaborate preparations needed to fight its ideal form of war.

Finally, it would be difficult to conceive of a more attractive opponent than a regular army, embracing conventional strategy and tactics, using precisely the equipment and doctrines that the West had spent the Cold War training to counter, though doing so far less effectively than the USSR and with technology at least a generation behind. A large part of the Iraqi army was poorly trained and low in morale, much of its officer corps had been purged in recent years and many of its best units were held back to ensure the internal security of the regime. It had some advanced weapons systems but lacked the ability to use them effectively, and in certain key areas its capabilities were either primitive (such as ballistic missiles and reconnaissance assets) or non-existent (notably satellites, anti-satellite systems, submarines and – perhaps narrowly – nuclear weapons). Moreover, the Iraqi leadership compounded these weaknesses by pursuing an inept political and military strategy, uniting nearly the whole world against itself, utterly conceding the initiative to the Coalition and allowing it the luxury of a six-month period in which to build up ample forces and their enormous support needs, as well as to acclimatise and train them and to gather intelligence. This combination of factors added up to an exceptionally attractive opponent.

The combined result of all these flattering circumstances is that a scenario couched in such terms would have been dismissed as quite unrealistic for use in a crisis exercise. It is generally recognised that the Gulf conflict was exceptional and that it cannot be assumed that the next international crisis will be similar. Yet this acknowledgment often seems to be somewhat rote and tends not always fully to permeate the accompanying analysis. This is not to say that no lessons can be drawn from the conflict, or that no useful pointers to trends in warfare may be found in it. Rather, it demands a great deal of honesty in explicitly identifying the ways in which this experience was unusual and hence some caution in proposing any lessons. In the Gulf, military technology, doctrine, political and military objectives and strategy were all in harmony (and operated in suitable terrain, against an opponent that was ideal rather than merely suitable). It is easy to overlook some of the links in this crucial chain of happy circumstances.

Initial reactions

Early interpretations of the war were strikingly, even overwhelmingly, positive. The tone of these views stemmed in some part from relief that the Coalition had not only won but had done so with remarkably few casualties: it should be recalled that before the ground campaign reputable analysts with strong track records had predicted several thousand American deaths. The impressive performance of US military technology, doctrine and personnel strengthened this reaction, especially when seen in the context of previous, less successful military interventions. The most obvious of these was Vietnam, memories of which loomed over the Pentagon and the White House throughout the conflict and which provided the formative experience of many of the American commanders involved. Other less ambitious operations in Lebanon, Grenada, Panama and the attempt to rescue American hostages in Iran had generated fairly low expectations of US military performance. As Freedman and Karsh put it, there was an impression that the American armed forces had a 'tendency to be muscle-bound, riven by inter-service rivalry and obsessed with technological gimmickry'.[9] That this picture was hugely exaggerated is irrelevant; it was generally held to be accurate. As a result, the impressive performance of the US military in the Gulf was all the more striking.

The conflict therefore appeared to be a convincing vindication of post-Vietnam developments in US military doctrine and training as well as confirming the potential of various new technologies introduced during the late 1970s and 1980s. There had been a great deal of scepticism surrounding these expensive weapons systems,[10] but in the Persian Gulf they succeeded 'beyond our wildest expectations'.[11] Reactions were not wholly complacent and many lessons were drawn about weaknesses that could and should be remedied. It was accepted that more aircraft should be equipped to use precision-guided weapons, for example, and that the US Navy should pay more attention to countering naval mines. Broadly, though, the first reactions tended to be euphoric, bordering on the hubristic. The US, now the only superpower, strode the world like an invincible colossus, its military technology guaranteeing an almost casualty-free intervention capability.

Predictably, the initial euphoria soon began to fade. First, a degree of political disillusionment set in. Doubts grew over whether the war had been quite the success it had initially seemed, since Saddam clung to power, ruthlessly suppressing the internal revolts that some in the West had hoped would finish the work of the Coalition. Moreover, he continued to defy his adversaries and resisted, with some success, the efforts of UN inspectors to unravel his weapons of mass destruction programmes, succeeding in fracturing the international consensus against him. He was still secure in power on the tenth anniversary of the invasion of Kuwait and two years after that was once again the focus of a major and politically divisive international crisis. A distinction must be drawn between, on the one hand, the explicit objectives of liberating Kuwait and reducing the Iraqi conventional and non-conventional forces as threats to the region and, on the other, the desirable but not explicitly sought aim of securing a more amenable regime in Baghdad: the latter was not itself an objective in 1991 even though it became one subsequently. At the very least, this point should serve as a reminder of the limitations in the political objectives that even high-tech military intervention can achieve.

Second, revised estimates of the performance of some weapons systems in the war, and of air power in particular,[12] threw into question the technological triumphalism of the war's immediate aftermath. One example of this was the changing evaluation of the success of the Patriot missile system. At first, the accepted view was that it 'was successfully used in its new anti-ballistic missile role',[13] 'destroying perhaps 94% of engageable targets'[14]. Subsequent analysis reduced the claimed success rate to 80 per cent for the missiles based in Saudi Arabia and 40 per cent for those based in Israel; others suggested the figure was even lower.[15] Regardless of the fact that the weapon was performing a role (area rather than point defence) against a target (ballistic missiles as opposed to aircraft) for which it had not been designed, this deteriorating picture characterised the disillusionment with some of the systems used in the conflict, as did reduced claims for accuracy of PGMs and the acknowledgment that there was no evidence that air strikes had destroyed even a single mobile Scud launcher in spite of extensive efforts.

Third, further experience of post-Cold War military intervention, especially in Somalia and the former Yugoslavia, brought home just how favourable the circumstances of the Gulf conflict had been. It proved far harder in these subsequent crises than it had been in 1990 to forge international consensus and to agree on what the problem was, let alone set political goals or military objectives. The use of military power in these conflicts was also far more difficult because many or even most of the favourable elements mentioned above were absent. The heightened attention focused on the peculiarities of the Gulf conflict made it clear that many conclusions drawn from it might well not apply in other situations.

Nonetheless, many analysts continued to argue that the Gulf War demonstrated that an RMA was either imminent or underway. Perhaps the most prominent and distinctive of these schools of thought, certainly the most vocal, took the form of yet another reprise of strategic air power theories.

A Revolution in Air Power?

Naturally, the most convincing confirmation of the revolution in war was seen in the application of air power in the air campaign.[16]

The previous chapter explained the interwar theories that vaunted strategic air power, popularised by thinkers such as Douhet, Mitchell and Seversky. They claimed that strategic bombing would, on its own, be sufficient to win wars by directly attacking the political, economic, industrial and military centres of enemy power. Striking these critical targets was the proper role for air power, they argued, not the mere 'auxiliary' tasks of co-operation with land and sea forces, which would become increasingly marginalised and obsolete. Although the experience of the Second World War largely refuted the essence of these ideas – the contribution of strategic bombing was both less in degree and quite different in kind to what was predicted – they proved resilient and reappeared periodically during the Cold War period.

It is striking that not only did the Gulf War lead to a resurgence of claims that strategic bombing could win wars independently, but many of their proponents explicitly referred back to the interwar theorists. United States Secretary of the Air Force Donald B. Rice wrote that 'Air power did exactly what air power visionaries said it could...technology caught up with theory.'[17] For Major General Charles D. Link, USAF, the war showed that 'the dreams of the early air power prophets were not in error but merely postponed'.[18] Another USAF officer concluded that Douhet 'was right all along.' Indeed:

Air power was the decisive element, with land and sea forces in largely supportive, though important, roles....The vindication of Giulio Douhet lies in the fact that air power had finally been decisive in a war....This is the essence of Douhet's concepts: air power so powerful that it alone could defeat an enemy. It happened in Desert Storm.[19]

Blackwell (unusual in this company as a former army officer rather than an airman) asserted that the campaign plan 'vindicated the theories of air power advocates from decades past', citing Douhet and Mitchell in support of the approach of cutting off the enemy from command and supply and then out-manoeuvring him with smaller ground forces.[20]

What, then, did this school of thought believe that air power had achieved during the course of the Gulf War? Meilinger asserted that it proved Giulio

Douhet right about the dominance of air power:

> ...the overwhelming Coalition victory in the Gulf War is an example of what Douhet predicted airpower could accomplish. Specifically, his formula for victory – gaining command of the air, neutralizing an enemy's 'vital centres', and maintaining the defensive on the ground while taking the offensive in the air – underpinned Coalition strategy.

The Iraqi army still had to be defeated, 'for psychological reasons', but 'in this case airpower was able to do so with incomparably greater efficiency and at lower risk.'[21] Colonel John Warden, the principal intellectual mentor of the air campaign, subsequently claimed that, '[Iraq] lay as defenceless as if occupied by a million men. For practical purposes, it had in fact become a state occupied from the air.'[22] For Luttwak, Alexander de Seversky was also rehabilitated: 'at least it may be said that after 70 years the old promises of "Victory Through Air Power" were finally redeemed in 1991 in the skies of Iraq'; and, 'the final ground offensive of Desert Storm was not offensive at all but rather an almost unopposed advance'.[23] He concluded that although it appeared to be conducted by balanced forces, Desert Storm, 'was in fact an air war that might have ended with Iraq's surrender in a few more weeks, but which was concluded by a ground advance that turned out to be almost administrative in character.'[24]

It was therefore argued that after many years of trying, this conflict finally saw air power achieve what had long been promised but had not hitherto been feasible in practice. Due to a combination of advances in technology and high-level acceptance of its potential, air power was able to accomplish all that had been promised by its early proponents. This debate was not of merely historical interest: the proclaimed success of air power in the Gulf gave rise once again to suggestions that US strategy should rely far more upon it. A 1993 RAND study concluded that 'the calculus has changed and airpower's ability to contribute to the joint battle has increased', and recommended that although the other services would continue to be necessary, their budgets should be cut to fund modernisation of the US Air Force.[25] Faith in strategic bombing underlay later American pressure for air strikes against the Bosnian Serbs and also led to a bombing-only strategy over Kosovo. In both cases, it was confidently expected, air power could deliver swift and low-cost political success without the contentious and potentially risky deployment of ground forces. This school of thought, if accurate, would truly amount to a revolution in military affairs.

The claim that a strategic air campaign won the Gulf War is poor analysis, however, and a policy resting on it would be dangerous. Air power was undoubtedly of enormous importance in achieving the low-cost success of the Coalition campaign. However, it did not win the war alone and the role it played was quite different from that envisaged and advocated by the interwar thinkers. Several analysts who cite them do so in very general ways, presenting their argument as if it were merely that air power is important or that command of the air should be gained and then exploited. These uncontentious statements are far less than was argued by Douhet, Seversky and their colleagues – if they truly represented the essence of the strategic bombing theory, it would have been banal – and yet another demonstration that they were accurate would not be sufficient to establish that a revolution in warfare had occurred. The interwar air theorists conceived air power in a very specific way, operating quite independently of ground and maritime forces, winning war on its own by direct attacks on the enemy's vital centres to destroy his will and ability to continue resisting. Attacks on his armed forces in the field or air support of one's own land and sea forces would be superfluous, irrelevant and a dangerous diversion of effort.

The plan for the air campaign

There were different views as to how air power should defeat Iraq.[26] Some thought it should be used against the enemy armed forces, isolating and then destroying them. This approach would have been totally rejected by the interwar thinkers cited above, who saw the enemy forces in the field as a false objective. Many air planners in 1990 followed their line and sought a truly strategic approach, aiming to win the war through direct pressure on Iraq's leadership and infrastructure. The initial air campaign plan, devised by Colonel Warden and his team in Washington, rested on the hope that attacks on such strategic targets as leadership, command and control, petroleum and electricity systems, infrastructure (especially transportation), weapons of mass destruction and the Republican Guard might force an Iraqi retreat without the need for a bloody ground campaign. The 'Instant Thunder' plan – the name being deliberately chosen to distinguish its approach from the more incremental 'Rolling Thunder' plan carried out in Vietnam – envisaged a six-day campaign against 84 targets to disable or fatally weaken the regime.[27] The Gulf War Air Power Survey quotes a USAF operations order of 2 September 1990 as predicting that the strategic attacks would lead to 'the progressive and systematic collapse of Saddam Hussein's entire war machine and regime'.[28] It is doubtful that a mere six days of air strikes against only 84 targets could have achieved such an ambitious political objective. In any case, this approach was rejected by US Central Command, not only by General Schwarzkopf, the overall allied commander, but also by his theatre air commander, Lieutenant General Charles Horner (USAF). They assumed from the start that a land war would be necessary and insisted that, first, air strikes would precede a ground attack and not replace it; and, second, that direct attacks on the Iraqi forces deployed in the desert would be an important part of the air plan. From its outset, the campaign was to be thoroughly joint, albeit with air power taking the lead in the first stage. Air power was never intended to be strategically independent in the Gulf, achieving victory on its own.

The campaign failed to achieve the more ambitious objectives of air force planners: the regime did not collapse, nor was it fatally weakened in the longer term.[29] The inclusion of the Iraqi leadership among key targets was, according to the Pentagon's Final Report to Congress, the main difference between this campaign and previous strategic bombing campaigns,[30] but in fact relatively few strikes were aimed at the regime's administrative structures.[31] It could, of course, be argued that a true air campaign, as advocated by the interwar theorists and intended by Warden, was never really tried, whether due to ignorance, resistance to new ideas or inter-service politics. Without the commitment of some of the air effort against the Iraqi forces in the field, air power could have concentrated on strategic targets and secured a withdrawal from Kuwait without a ground campaign. Luttwak, for example, blames the 'diversion' of the air effort away from strategic strikes to the Iraqi ground forces for the fact that the WMD programme was not fully destroyed.[32]

This line is unconvincing. There were good reasons why such a campaign was not tried – not least, the fact that there were grounds for scepticism that it would work. Damage to civilian targets could make life less pleasant and more dangerous for the population of Iraq but there were severe limits on its capacity to change the policy of the Baghdad government. Merely increasing civilian suffering would not result in a change of policy, even if it had been politically acceptable to Western public opinion, its Arab allies and the wider world. Indeed, although the civilian casualties inflicted were remarkably low by historical standards, they were enough to cause significant political problems for the Coalition. Saddam Hussein retained sufficient coercive power to suppress any rebellion, so the effect on the population was one of low-level but prolonged suffering rather than creating an impetus to revolt. It may well have been true, as Luttwak wrote, that the population of Baghdad was deprived of electricity, telephone and water services,[33] but it is rather difficult to see how this contributed to victory – or how a more intensive effort in this direction would have done so. Moreover, many voices in the West, let alone the Middle East, found even this impact on the civilian population to be legally and ethically unacceptable. Bombing has never enjoyed success in turning a population against a dictatorial regime to the extent that it is overthrown, even though it was explicitly used to this end against Germany and Japan in the Second World War, and more recently against North Vietnam, Iraq and Serbia. It was the Iraqi regime that had to be convinced to change its position. This government could shield itself from the direct effects of the bombing just as it had in the face of economic sanctions, and its will to continue its policy remained resilient. Solely targeting the will of an authoritarian government to compel it to change its policy would have been to gamble on a mechanism that has never succeeded; the better option lay in targeting its means to resist.[34] Such an approach gave air power a significant role but as part of a broader strategy involving ground and maritime forces rather than as the sole means to victory.

The results of the air campaign

The success achieved against the critical objective that was Iraq's weapons of mass destruction programmes was limited, mainly due to incomplete intelligence.[35] You cannot destroy something if you are unaware of its existence or location. The post-war UN inspection regime was far more effective than the air campaign in rolling back this programme, though still well short of complete success, and it is unlikely that this system would have been put in place without the pressure of the ground campaign. A similar problem arose with efforts to destroy Scud missiles, which posed a serious political problem for the Coalition, if not a huge military threat. A combination of mobile missile launchers, effective Iraqi tactics for launching missiles and then departing the area, and impressive use of decoys meant that even with a huge commitment of reconnaissance and strike aircraft, only limited success was attained.[36] The limited success of air strikes against the WMD programmes and the elusive mobile Scud missile launchers were a timely reminder that intelligence and targeting still impose limitations on air power even when other conditions are remarkably favourable.

The initial phase of the air campaign did have a dramatic impact, however, in reducing the combat effectiveness of the Iraqi forces in the Kuwait theatre, which made it a significant complement to the direct tactical strikes on front-line and reserve forces. First, the Iraqi air force and its integrated air defence system was eliminated, ensuring air supremacy for the Coalition. It could therefore use the air freely and with remarkably low losses while Iraq was unable to use aircraft, other than fleetingly and at considerable risk, for either offensive operations or for reconnaissance (which ensured that it remained ignorant of the 'left hook' through the desert). The Iraqi armed forces' command and control system was severely disrupted, though not destroyed and the leadership was still able to receive information and send out orders. The Iraqi ground forces were seriously weakened by aerial interdiction of their supplies which, combined with the strikes directly aimed against them, also eroded morale to the point where many soldiers were simply not willing to resist the Coalition advance. The Republican Guard had been included as a 'strategic' target, due to its importance as a protector of the regime, as well as the theatre reserve for Iraq's land forces.[37] Some of the other results of the purely strategic campaign were of less obvious utility for the ground offensive. Iraq's power generation and oil production industries were extensively damaged: the former was useful for denying electricity for military purposes (while also affecting the civilian population), though the latter did not have a significant military effect due to the short duration of the war.

The strategic air campaign overlapped with direct tactical attacks against the Iraqi forces (especially armoured vehicles and artillery) in the Kuwait theatre, though the latter gradually took up an increasing amount of the air effort. This element of the campaign inflicted severe losses on the Iraqi forces: on the eve of the ground war, US Central Command estimated that the Iraqi forces in the theatre had lost 39 per cent of their tanks, 32 per cent of their APCs and 47 per cent of their artillery pieces, though the CIA and Defense Intelligence Agency estimates were lower.[38] Other accounts have suggested that these figures overstate the overall losses (many of which were, in any case, inflicted during the ground campaign)[39] but even if that is true and the actual statistics were only partly as impressive as was stated at the time, the fighting strength and effectiveness of the enemy had clearly been hugely reduced, directly by destruction and also indirectly, in disrupted logistics and reduced morale.

The air campaign's mixture of strategic and tactical strikes therefore established the conditions in which the Coalition ground campaign could win a decisive victory with low casualties. However, it is quite inaccurate to characterise Desert Sabre as a mere unopposed advance: some units, particularly from the Republican Guard, did offer stiff resistance.[40] The US Army's official account of the conflict argues that on the eve of the ground campaign, the Iraqi forces had been battered by air strikes and artillery, but 'had not been defeated, much less destroyed':

Despite 41 days of almost continuous aerial bombardment, the Republican Guard remained a cohesive and viable military force able to fight a vicious battle and survive to fight insurgents in northern and southern Iraq.

Bombing did not destroy the will of the best Iraqi units, nor stop them responding to the Coalition's left-hook manoeuvre, nor prevent them from evacuating many units in the closing stage of the war.[41]

Nevertheless, some advocates of air power have suggested that the ground campaign was superfluous. For Lieutenant Colonel Jones, cited above: 'Perhaps the key question remaining from Desert Storm is "Did we need a ground operation at all?"' The Coalition would have met all its political objectives with two more weeks of bombing, he argued, though ground forces would still have been needed to clear up and secure Kuwait.[42] Such assertions are unconvincing. It is not clear how more of the 'strategic' strikes would have put any greater pressure on the Baghdad government. The clear defeat of, and inflicting significant losses on, the Iraqi army were crucial objectives, and a ground campaign was necessary to achieve them. It is also doubtful that Iraq would have accepted – even to the limited extent it did – all of the UN Security Council Resolutions, including those relating to its weapons of mass destruction, without the defeat of its forces on the ground and the occupation of a large area of its territory by Coalition forces. It is perhaps significant that when post-war efforts to force Iraq to disarm were backed up by the threat of air power alone rather than by renewed ground action, the regime resurrected its WMD programmes with considerable success.

The contribution of air power to the Coalition victory in the Gulf was enormous. In fact, it is difficult to identify a war in which air power played a more significant role – perhaps the Israeli campaign in the 1967 Six Day War comes closest. Moreover, although some shortcomings were apparent, this contribution was achieved with what were by historical standards a very high degree of accuracy, almost incredibly low losses of Coalition aircraft and low collateral damage and civilian casualties. Other significant new elements included the use of stealth technology, the large-scale use of precision weapons and the very large number of targets that were hit simultaneously across the depth of the theatre. The air campaign in the Gulf therefore demonstrated the great advances that had been made in both the technology and effectiveness of air power.

The only reason for caution in hailing the success of air power lies in the fact that some of its advocates have claimed even more on its behalf. Air power did not win the war alone but was one element of a joint force. It depended on ground forces to defend Saudi Arabia and its vital ports and air bases, to compel the Iraqi forces to take up static defensive positions in which they were vulnerable to air attack (this situation can be contrasted with the Kosovo campaign, when the early use – or even the threat of the use – of ground forces was publicly ruled out and the Serbian forces could disperse in towns and wait out the bombing) and to complete the victory with an offensive thrust into Kuwait and Iraq. Ground forces also contributed directly to the 'air campaign', reinforcing the idea that warfare is becoming increasingly joint: attack helicopters destroyed many armoured vehicles and artillery pieces, special forces on the ground were a vital part of the hunt for Scud missiles and, as envisaged in the Air-Land Battle doctrine mentioned in the previous chapter, Army missile systems were used to destroy Iraqi air defences.[43] Air power also depended on maritime forces, the contribution of which in the Gulf War tends to be greatly underestimated,[44] for the vast bulk of the huge logistical effort that the air and ground forces required. Naval assets also played a significant role in the air campaign, particularly carrier-based aircraft and Tomahawk land attack missiles, and in an operation conducted in less favourable circumstances might have to bear even more of the burden. It was not only naval aircraft that contributed to the air campaign, as Army attack helicopters also proved effective: Air Force officers all too often confuse 'air power' and 'Air Force'.

The Pentagon report to Congress offered a judicious conclusion:

> ...the decisive character of our victory in the Gulf War is attributable in large measure to the extraordinary effectiveness of air power....On the other hand, air power alone could not have brought the war to so sharp and decisive a conclusion....In sum, while air power made a unique and significantly enlarged contribution to the decisive Coalition victory, the combined effects of the air, maritime and ground offensives with important contributions from many supporting forces were key.[45]

Moreover, the specific way in which the air campaign contributed to victory was utterly different to that predicted by the interwar theorists and their later apostles. Its contribution lay not in independently pressuring the Iraqi population and leadership as the sole tool of strategy, but rather as one among several means of directly and indirectly weakening the Iraqi armed forces and their ability to resist. This point is not merely a matter of politics or semantics, over whether air power had *a* leading role or *the* leading role, nor simply a matter of judgement about how important its contribution was. This issue goes far deeper and relates to the basic conception of how air power contributes to achieving political objectives. The Coalition air forces were far from mere auxiliaries supporting ground and maritime forces (which was what the interwar theorists and later airmen feared they might become); yet nor were they an independent means for victory. To repeat a point made in the previous chapter, this assessment of the contribution of air power in the Gulf War looks modest only in relation to the inflated ambitions of the Douhet-Mitchell-Seversky school of air power supremacists.

Finally, the Gulf War was an ideal showcase for air power. The various reasons why the conflict was exceptional have already been set out, and they apply most of all to air power. The availability of so many well supplied air bases and the long and uninterrupted build-up period; the political isolation and technological inferiority of the enemy; and the conventional shape and vulnerability of the enemy forces in the desert, far from civilians, all made this conflict the most flattering scenario for air power that has ever been seen. Other, subsequent conflicts have been far less favourable to the exercise of air power and make it clear that although its relative contribution in the Gulf was perhaps the greatest it has been in any war, it would be rash to hail this as amounting to a revolution in military affairs in its own right. It may more accurately be described as a good example of what modern air power can achieve in extremely conducive, even ideal, conditions. It would be foolish to assume that such favourable circumstances will be repeated in the future. Indeed, the very success achieved by the Coalition means that future opponents are certain to make great efforts to avoid presenting the West with such an easy scenario – a point that will be returned to below.

A Brave New World?

Suggestions that the Gulf conflict demonstrated the existence of a Revolution in Military Affairs do not rest solely on claims relating to air power. Many analysts look more broadly at the various technological advances, of which air power was just one element, which when combined with effective doctrine and well-trained personnel enjoyed dramatic successes in the Persian Gulf. The picture they paint represents a wider and rather more plausible contender for the title of RMA.

Although PGMs had been used before, the Gulf conflict saw their first use in such a significant campaign.[46] Although PGMs amounted only to about 10 per cent of the weapons used by the Coalition, their direct effect of greater accuracy (though still not quite meeting the elusive goal of 'one bomb, one target') had significant indirect effects. By decreasing the number of aircraft sorties required to achieve a hit, they allowed more targets to be struck by a given number of aircraft and increased the rate at which they were attacked, hence intensifying the dislocation inflicted on the opponent. The widening use of precision weapons promised still better accuracy and greater strategic impact in the future, and one of the major lessons drawn was the need to modify more aircraft to use them. There was a 'down side' associated with their use, however, in the form of serious deficiencies with damage assessment, which proved unable to keep pace with advances in the weapons used and thus limited their effectiveness.[47]

Possibly even more impressive than the eye-catching weapons themselves were the less obvious developments in intelligence gathering, targeting and battlefield management that lay behind them. Unmanned aerial vehicles (UAVs) and the JSTARS (Joint Surveillance and Target Attack Radar System) aircraft, rushed into service before it was formally ready, provided major steps forward in knowledge of where the enemy was and what he was doing, and extended the depth of the battlefield. According to the authors of the US Gulf War Air Power Survey, JSTARS 'proved enormously capable of identifying the path of attacking or retreating columns or Iraqi equipment and provided both battlefield intelligence and targeting information,' especially during the Iraqi attack against Al Khafji.[48] The satellite-based Global Positioning System (GPS) provided Coalition forces with accurate information of their location, even in featureless desert areas or at sea. The war was also 'the first conflict in history to make comprehensive use of space systems support', with the Coalition able to call on 64 satellites of 23 types, for intelligence gathering (imagery and electronic), communications, meteorology, navigation, missile launch warning and weapons guidance.[49] The combined effect of these information systems and more accurate weapons was impressive. Although most attention is devoted to air power, artillery also benefited from the new systems: GPS provided precise knowledge of the individual battery's own position, UAVs and various other reconnaissance systems revealed the location of the enemy and corrected fire, which was also aided by computer analysis and radar for counter-battery fire. Multiple-launch rocket systems (MLRS) and the US Army Tactical Missile System, together with improved munitions, offered greater firepower and range; indeed, the author of the US Army's official history of the campaign refers to artillery undergoing a 'quantum jump in precision and lethality'.[50] Air power advocates often tend to understate the significance of artillery, which recent developments have enhanced to a considerable degree and which complemented the activities of aircraft. Other incremental improvements to the effectiveness of land and sea forces, such as thermal sights or rounds tipped with depleted uranium, or improvements in military doctrine and training of personnel, are even more significant when seen in the wider context of the information umbrella that unfolded above them.

The striking performance of the various new technologies in the Gulf promoted the idea that a revolution in military affairs was either underway or imminent. As the previous chapter explained, the concept was already present in some military and academic circles during the 1980s but the Gulf War did a great deal to popularise it. One of the best books on the conflict suggested:

> The Persian Gulf War is without precedent in the annals of warfare. It was the dawn of a new era in which high technology supplanted the bayonet, a war in which one side had a clear picture of events while the other foundered deaf, dumb and blind.[51]

The claim was that information technology was leading to a transformation in warfare that was broader and more dramatic in its impact than the air power school of thought considered above. Thus, Alan Campen called his book on the conflict *The First Information War* and wrote that the Gulf War 'differed fundamentally from any previous conflict...the outcome turned as much on superior management of *knowledge* as it did upon performances of people or weapons'.[52]

A Revolution *in Military Affairs?*

The performance of the various information capabilities deployed in the Gulf was far from perfect. After all, the Iraqi invasion of Kuwait was itself a surprise (despite the region being a major focus for intelligence efforts), as was the Iraqi army attack on Al Khafji during the air campaign (despite the concentration of large numbers of intelligence gathering assets in the theatre). Difficulties were encountered in disseminating intelligence from national and theatre systems to operational and tactical commanders,[53] different systems often proved unable to share information even if both were American (let alone the difficulties surrounding connectivity with allies), many sensors were severely constrained by poor weather, cloud and smoke, and PGMs were not always reliable and in any case only represented about 10 per cent of the weapons used in the conflict. Moreover, as the limited effect of the air campaign on the Iraqi WMD programmes showed, 'smart' weapons are in truth only as intelligent as the targeting information that supports them. Some claims about current capabilities are simply wildly fanciful and quite untrue: Campen, for example, quotes a USAF Lieutenant Colonel saying: 'A lethality system appears to exist that can provide continuous, instant, almost 100% probability of kill or anything that moves.'[54] Such implausible assertions do little to support claims of an RMA.

However, no one argues that the war saw the final version of the new technologies: what it did, rather, was to show how much had been achieved while hinting at greater things to come.[55] Thus, as is frequently the case with new technology, it left much to the inclinations, judgement and imagination of those assessing it. The gap in overall knowledge of the battlefield between the Coalition and Iraq was immense, while the various technologies that were used by the former were highly accurate compared to previous conflicts. Iraq was initially unaware of the huge western flanking movement conducted by VII Corps; its air defence systems were blinded and its air force rendered ineffective; its large and heavy ground forces were devastated by air strikes, long range artillery, attack helicopters and tank fire that used target acquisition and aiming systems that could destroy Iraqi tanks before their crews were aware of a threat. Both the discrepancy in the level of information enjoyed by the two sides, and the practical effects of this gap, were historically unprecedented. Given the newness of some of its elements and inevitable teething problems, if the incomplete system of systems could achieve this, what capabilities might a more advanced version offer?

Others deny that the Gulf War truly represented a wholly new model. On this interpretation the Gulf War is seen as one more step forward; either as the peak of effectiveness of the old style of warfare before the genuine transformation begins, or as a 'minor RMA' before a far more significant 'major RMA'. As Metz and Kievit put it, 'American combat effectiveness in the Gulf War suggested that a historic revolution in military affairs (RMA) is underway', but, alternatively, 'it could be argued that American effectiveness in Desert Storm represented superior training during the last phase of the blitzkrieg RMA'.[56] Adams takes the latter line, describing the Gulf conflict as 'the last hurrah of the armed forces and generals who had trained on the legacy of the second world war'; some new technologies had been used, but 'the tactics had remained essentially evolutionary and revolved around the application of mass on the battlefield'.[57] Thus, PGMs offered considerable advantages in the Gulf War but were still fired from large and expensive manned platforms such as aircraft or warships, or depended on human guidance. In future they could be fired from far greater distances or from unmanned platforms, or be entirely autonomous, seeking their own targets. UAVs were used for many purposes but essentially remained an adjunct to old-style forces. In future, they could operate more extensively and autonomously and take on a far greater range of roles, including precision strike. The possibility of a full or major RMA does not, of course, mean that it must be grasped: according to Harknett, the Gulf War showed that the US forces could incorporate information technology and derive huge benefits from it without undertaking the enormous and potentially risky organisational changes urged by the more enthusiastic RMA proponents.[58]

Even if there is a potential RMA in the near future, not all states have the luxury of fully embracing it. American choices will largely define the cutting edge of future military technology and the rest of the world is likely to cherry pick a selection of fruits from the entire orchard of technological possibilities. In some ways, then, the debate over whether the Gulf War supports proponents of a minor or a major RMA is rather semantic for any country other than the US. Many of the conclusions about the conflict apply only to the United States: debates over the effects of the strategic air campaign or the contribution to it of carrier aircraft, as well as lessons about strategic lift and strategic intelligence systems, are of limited relevance to other countries, which could never aspire to capabilities on the scale of the sole military superpower. Nevertheless, the experience of the war still offered a great deal of useful guidance for other states, particularly relating to the importance of the changes brought about by information technology.

Just as many of the lessons of the Gulf conflict drawn by the US apply to other states such as the UK, so do some of the warnings. It may well be true that the advanced technology demonstrated in the Gulf will have the effect of greatly increasing effectiveness and raising the relative 'punch' of small forces. However, forces of the highest capability and readiness cannot be maintained on the cheap. Rochlin and Demchak make a highly persuasive case that the attention lavished on the high-tech weapons systems used in the Persian Gulf has not generally been matched by equivalent emphasis on the enormous and costly support structures that they require in the form of training, maintenance, supply and stocks.[59] It is precisely these less visible and less high profile, yet essential support elements that always seem the first to suffer when the Treasury is on the prowl for savings in the defence budget.

The Other Side of the Hill...

Perhaps the least comforting school of thought relating to the Gulf War begins with an emphasis on the striking victory achieved by the Coalition and argues that the very magnitude of this success ensures that it is unlikely to be repeated. The other approaches considered above seek to draw lessons from the perspectives of Coalition members, specifically the major Western powers. Yet others can also draw conclusions from the conflict, and the results of their analysis could prevent such a favourable outcome in a future confrontation. In the Gulf War, the Coalition enjoyed certain advantages and pursued certain strategies, while Iraq suffered certain shortcomings and made certain errors, which need not be repeated – especially given the inevitable proliferation of advanced military technology

Some of the errors made by Iraq could have been avoided. Politically, it was unwise to invade the whole of Kuwait rather than just seizing the disputed oilfields (taking which would have increased the oil reserves under Iraq's control as well as applying coercive pressure on the rump of Kuwait and Saudi Arabia through the implicit threat of further military advances). Alternatively, Iraq could have agreed to a partial withdrawal from Kuwait, as a 'sign of good faith' in response to the diplomatic good offices of a friendly power. Such a move would have complicated the political elements of Coalition strategy, denying it such an easy *casus belli* and potentially even fracturing the international consensus. Certain diplomatic blunders could have been avoided, notably using foreigners as hostages, attacking embassies in Baghdad and displaying mistreated prisoners of war on television. Another aggressor could also make more effective use of his own people as human shields (which occurred by default when the Coalition restricted attacks on Baghdad following the civilian casualties inflicted in the Al Firdos bunker attack). There were signs that Iraq had begun to exploit such scruples, with reports suggesting it had started to park combat aircraft near mosques and schools, on the assumption that they would not be attacked in such areas. Iraq made many attempts to influence regional, Western and world opinion – what some would call 'information warfare'. These efforts happened to be crude, unsuccessful and generally counter-productive but that does not mean that a future opponent will not be more subtle or more successful.

One of the greatest errors made by Iraq lay in allowing the Coalition a long, unhindered build-up phase. Either Iraq itself or a sympathetic state could have mounted attacks on the long sea lines of communication, perhaps anonymously, with naval mines, or from an merchant ship under a false flag. Even a few such attacks would have compelled the diversion of considerable resources to protect vital shipping, complicating and drawing out the build up, and would have hindered the process of chartering ships and greatly increased insurance rates, thus raising the costs of the operation. Alternatively, or in conjunction with harassment of shipping heading for the theatre, terrorist, special forces or air attacks could have been launched against Gulf ports and air bases, or against the forces themselves, when they were at their most vulnerable before they were fully established in situ. One widespread fear among Coalition commanders was of a terrorist attack on recently arrived troops while they were still concentrated in a small number of buildings, similar to the 1983 bombing of the US Marine barracks in Lebanon.[60] A bloody attack of this sort, carried out by a government rather than a terrorist group could have had the effect of firming up Western public opinion against the Baghdad regime but could equally have achieved the Iraqi goal of shattering the fragile US domestic consensus on involvement in the conflict. In the warm afterglow of victory it was often forgotten just how much domestic opposition to the war there was in the US, not least in the Senate where the resolution backing the use of force passed only by the narrow margin of 52 votes to 47, despite the relatively favourable conditions of the Gulf crisis.

A future challenger could draw other lessons from Iraq's experience in 1991, by seeking certain niche capabilities that could frustrate American strategy or provide an asymmetric response to it. Air operations would be hindered by more effective air defences, especially using more infra-red or optically-guided weapons, which are harder to suppress than radar-based systems. Recent experience in Yugoslavia shows that small, hand-held anti-aircraft missiles exert a considerable deterrent effect at the level of the political leadership, let alone on the pilots themselves. Many of the advantages that the West enjoyed in the Gulf are unlikely to remain its monopoly, especially as Russia and China began to pass on advanced weapons explicitly to counter what they regarded as a worryingly unipolar world. Proliferating systems include precision strike weapons, cruise missiles, navigation and weapons guidance based on GPS,[61] improved electronic warfare, including GPS jammers, and satellite reconnaissance capabilities (from commercial as well as national sources). Systems could be designed to interfere with key Western capabilities, such as satellites, AWACS and JSTARS aircraft, which could hinder its efforts to pursue its preferred strategy. The West can expect to continue to enjoy a lead in most if not all areas of military and information technology but the erosion of the monopoly it had in 1991 would represent an important and detrimental development.

Future challengers could also present a greater ballistic missile threat: it is true that Patriot and other ballistic missile defence systems will improve but so will the threat, in terms of range, accuracy, load, and counter-measures against defences.[62] These or other delivery systems could have been matched up with weapons of mass destruction, which were the greatest single 'dog that did not bark' in the Gulf War. Iraq possessed chemical and biological weapons, and had used the former both against Iranian forces and Kurdish civilians, but did not turn them on the Coalition. Iraq was also said to be close to a nuclear capability:[63] what would have been the effects on the international reaction to the Iraqi invasion of Kuwait if the operation had been preceded by a successful nuclear test? A frequently cited reflection on the Gulf War is that one of the principal lessons of the conflict was not to confront the US without nuclear weapons. Since 1991, of course, a number of states have achieved that status and others will no doubt follow. A low cost and relatively unsophisticated system could be designed, based on satellite information for targeting and GPS guidance, carrying a nuclear or chemical warhead on stealthy cruise missiles or long-range, accurate ballistic missiles, fired in salvoes together with several decoys. A credible threat of use of weapons of mass destruction against local ports and airfields, let alone cities, could well deter regional states from offering the lavish host nation support provided during the Gulf War or could deter non-regional powers from sending in their forces – especially if the threat were extended to their own territory. The deterrence model used by the West during the Cold War would not necessarily apply against such opponents: their aim would not be to threaten Western homelands directly, but rather to provide their own deterrent against Western counter-intervention, as an umbrella beneath which regional aggression could be safely conducted.

Other forms of asymmetric response (which are covered in more detail in Chapter Seven) could lie in the use of irregular or guerrilla forces in challenging terrain rather than reliance on conventional forces in terrain ideal for the use of air power and armoured forces. Such an approach might be a matter of deliberate choice but could equally result from the circumstances of a conflict being different to those of the Gulf. Other possibilities raised by some analysts include 'information attacks' on critical infrastructure or terrorist attacks against US or other Western states, which could be deniable for the perpetrator and highly damaging to the victim. The clear lesson of the Gulf conflict for any state that might be tempted to challenge the West is to avoid letting it pursue its ideal strategy. The Gulf War offers the example of several errors committed by Iraq and a number of useful ideas not fully exploited. Combined with strategies used by other opponents in subsequent conflicts, there is plenty of food for thought for those who might challenge the West.

It is unlikely that any one or two of the actions outlined would have been sufficient to reverse the result of the Gulf War but a combination of them could well provide the essence of a strategy with a reasonable chance of success. One lesson of Vietnam and Somalia is that an opponent does not need to aspire to the military defeat of the United States on the battlefield, but should rather seek to deny it its ideal form of intervention, complicate its strategy, foment and exploit political divisions at home (in public opinion, in Congress and within the administration) and with its allies. The best way to defeat the US would be to frustrate its strategy and prevent it from becoming militarily involved in the first place.

Conclusion

The Gulf War was undoubtedly a striking success for advanced US military technology and conclusively demonstrated that information technology has opened up many new possibilities. However, the evidence it provides could support a range of conclusions regarding the existence of an RMA.

First, the whole case could be dismissed as too idiosyncratic to allow any broader conclusions to be drawn about the nature of warfare; however one-sided the victory in these unique circumstances, it could not be interpreted as revolutionary. Alternatively, the 'lessons' that the US and its allies might draw from the conflict could be seen as devalued by the reaction of future challengers to the irresistible American advantage in conventional weapons, even without a new RMA.

Second, it could be argued that the Gulf War was simply part of the on-going evolution of military effectiveness. After all, many of the weapons systems and concepts used in Kuwait and Iraq had far earlier roots and amounted to incremental improvements on what had gone before.

Third, the new techniques exhibited in the Gulf could be seen as part of an RMA, but as the closing stages of the one initiated in the First World War and the interwar period. On this long view, a revolution would have to be sought elsewhere.

Fourth, Desert Storm was hailed by some as proof that the long heralded revolution in strategic air power had finally appeared.

Fifth, it could be argued that the Gulf conflict did mark a new departure, and hence the beginning of a new RMA, in the increasing role and impact of information on the battlefield. This perspective could be further divided according to how radical the eventual effects are held to be; that is, whether they will greatly change current force structures (which some would see as a 'minor RMA') or, in time, replace them with something entirely new.

Whatever the precise conclusion drawn, the Gulf War clearly thrust the concept of Revolutions in Military Affairs into the mainstream of strategic studies and military planning. It played a key role in spreading the debate over the existence and nature of a contemporary RMA, to which we will now turn.

Chapter 4
The Current 'Revolution in Military Affairs'

During the 1980s, many innovative concepts and technologies were considered by and introduced into the United States armed forces. The Gulf War of 1991 convinced many analysts that a revolution in military affairs was underway that was comparable to previous cases such as those brought about by the French Revolution and Napoleonic Wars, Industrialisation and the developments of the interwar period. These claims, together with the counter-arguments raised against them, gave rise to perhaps the most intense debate in strategic studies and military affairs since the advent of nuclear weapons. This chapter explores the debate surrounding the current RMA. It looks first at the arguments of those who believe that a revolution is underway, asking what they think is happening and what effects they expect it to have. Various reasons for scepticism are then considered, which suggest that the claims of the RMA proponents may be exaggerated. Finally, this chapter identifies a number of distinctive perspectives on the RMA. These provide a means by which to understand different reactions to whether one is underway, the form it takes and its implications. This framework will be used in subsequent chapters to help investigate specific issues such as information warfare and the applicability of the RMA to different forms and intensities of conflict.

In addition to new technology and new doctrine, another major driver of change in military affairs can be found in international politics. Indeed, many thinkers suggest that here is where the true revolution is to be found; changes in military technology may be significant but they are dwarfed by recent developments in the international political context for the use of force. Lawrence Freedman offers the ideas of a 'Revolution in Strategic Affairs', which he interprets as 'the consequence of the long-term effects of decolonisation combined with the short-term effects of the end of the Cold War and the growing impact of globalisation'.[1] Chapter One suggested that the rise of the nation-state might be considered as an RMA. Currently, there is speculation that the increasing blurring of borders and diffusion of political and economic power is eroding the nation-state and displacing it as the principal foundation of the international order. Clearly if this were the case, it would truly be a revolutionary, even epochal development, fundamentally changing who fights whom, and for what reasons.[2] Anyone who is baffled by the range of views to be found about the impact of modern technology on the use of force will find it an island of certainty in comparison to the debate over its effect on the nation-state and politics more broadly. Predictions range from the utopian (a means of peaceful interaction between peoples), through the optimistic (dictatorship and even authoritarian government becoming untenable), the functional but benign (better delivery of services, improved communications between government and governed), the malign (the collapse of the welfare state and the rise of the 'big brother' state – in the sense of George Orwell rather than reality television), the pessimistic (global chaos) and even the apocalyptic (a genetically engineered virus wiping out humanity or tiny robots turning the world into grey goo). It is not necessary to go quite that far, however, to accept that political issues are of great significance. One example of an important social-cultural factor would be the increasing casualty aversion of the Western states; one from the political field would be the deep impact of the September 11 2001 attacks on the US, not least the subsequent embrace of pre-emption in national strategy. Both of these examples could well create more fertile ground for some of the claims made on behalf of the RMA, since they seem ideally suited to meet this sort of concern. Equally, of course, it could be argued that emerging military capabilities will feed and exacerbate such political imperatives. The relationship between changing technology and military capabilities on the one hand, and broader political factors on the other, is as close and reciprocal as is the connection between supply and demand in economics.

It has already been argued that the political context is fundamental to the course and implications of an RMA; the two are inextricably linked. Taking political factors into account does make the subject more complicated, since it leaves those designing or studying defence policy in a situation comparable to aiming at a target that is not merely moving but also constantly changing its shape. However, doing so is essential if war is to be properly understood. As Clausewitz pointed out, many factors that make a theory untidy and complicated cannot be omitted without leaving it quite unrelated to reality.[3] Even if political factors are not held to constitute the current revolution, an awareness of their influence must permeate any analysis of it.

The Current RMA: the View of the Proponents

The current RMA is generally seen as being driven primarily by technology. As with earlier cases, this is not military technology narrowly defined but rather a broader historical phenomenon, namely the rapid development of information technology. As Cebrowski and Gartska put it:

Network-centric warfare and all of its associated revolutions in military affairs grow out of and draw their power from the fundamental changes in society. These changes have been dominated by the co-evolution of economics, information technology, and business processes and organisations.

It is striking that they define the RMA in such broad, Tofflerian terms and yet they still assess the result as 'a revolution in military affairs (RMA) unlike any seen since the Napoleonic Age...it will prove to be the most important RMA in the past 200 years.'[4] One significant element of the current debate is that, like the Industrial Revolution, the current changes are widely perceived as being driven by advances in the civil rather than the military world, fitting in with the idea of an RMA being a broad social and political phenomenon. The central claim of the would-be revolutionaries is that just as computer-based information and communications technology is changing the political, economic and social aspects of life it is also changing military affairs.

As the previous chapter explained, the 1991 Gulf War forced the RMA debate up the agenda. The weapons systems at the heart of the RMA have undergone rapid development in the past decade. UAVs, for example, were used in the 1980s by Israel but saw their first widespread use by the United States in Desert Storm in 1991. Since then, more advanced types have been used more extensively, by the US and other countries, in Kosovo, Afghanistan and Iraq, as well as in lower intensity conflicts. The next logical step has already been taken of arming such systems to provide Unmanned Combat Aerial Vehicles, able on command to act on the information they are gathering with their own precision strike capability.[5] Current models such as the Predator and the Global Hawk (which has a range of 14,000 miles and the ability to loiter for 24 hours) will in turn be superseded by UAVs such as the Dark Star, which is designed to be stealthy,[6] and these successors are likely to take on new roles such as suppression of air defences. Precision-guided weapons have also come a long way since Germany used a radio-controlled bomb to destroy an Italian battleship in the Second World War. Laser-guided weapons were used extensively in the US air campaigns in the later stages of the Vietnam War, well before their profile was so greatly increased in Desert Storm. It is worth recalling that less than 10 per cent of the air weapons used in that conflict were precision-guided, the other 90 per cent being simple freefall weapons (albeit with their accuracy greatly enhanced by computerised aiming and modern navigation systems). By the Kosovo air campaign at the end of the decade, this ratio was reversed, with more than 90 per cent of weapons being PGMs. Moreover, by the end of the 1990s, laser-guided weapons were beginning to look distinctly *passé* and were giving way to satellite-guided weapons, such as the US Joint Direct Attack Munition (JDAM), that were less susceptible to unfavourable weather or battlefield conditions, and did not require designation of the target by the launch platform or forces on the ground. Already 'smart' weapons are expected to be followed by 'brilliant' weapons: the former strike accurately the target they are programmed to, while the latter autonomously locate and identify targets for themselves. These examples show the advances made in just ten years.

It is easy to focus on individual items of technology or weapons systems. A B2 stealth bomber is significantly more capable than a B-52, while the list of capabilities of an Apache Longbow helicopter is impressive indeed, as are concepts such as arsenal ships, medium-weight armoured vehicles and 'brilliant' weapons. Yet focussing so narrowly on what are small parts of a far bigger phenomenon misses what is genuinely new about the current RMA. The heart of the emerging model is the linking of these weapons systems with each other and with sources that gather and use information; however accurate a precision-guided weapon, however long its range, it is of little use without knowing what to target and getting that knowledge to the user. Moreover, these related technological advances are themselves combined with new concepts and organisations for their use. The microprocessor has led to ever more powerful and more compact computers, which in turn have permitted the creation of a host of extremely effective military systems. Each of these is far more effective than its predecessors but what truly makes them stand out is their integration.

There are three main elements in the perceived RMA. First, numerous types of sensors, operating in multiple spectra and on both manned and unmanned platforms, deployed in space, air, land, sea and sub-sea, permit an unprecedented level of effectiveness in gathering information about the battlespace and the dispositions of friendly forces, enemy troops and non-combatants. Second, computerised information processing and command and control systems allow this vast amount of data to be rapidly analysed and distributed for use. Third, this knowledge of the battlespace can then be put to devastating use with strikes by precision strike capabilities, which include increasingly accurate, long-range weapons, smaller but more effective land forces and also 'non-lethal' options such as computer attack and information warfare. These three types of systems – sensors, command and control, and precision strike – are thus integrated into what has been termed a 'system of systems', the whole of which would be far greater than the sum of the parts (see Figure One).

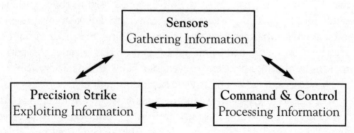

Figure One: The 'system of systems'

The individual most closely associated with the concept of the 'system of systems' is Admiral William Owens, sometime Vice-Chairman of the US Joint Chiefs of Staff. He explains the idea behind the system of systems as follows:

This concept depicts war as a deadly contest in which the side that best understands the battlespace and can best transfer that knowledge among its own elements to apply force faster, more precisely and over a greater distance wins.[7]

The effect on warfare of these developments is, according to the proponents of the RMA, dramatic. Digitised forces will be linked through a computerised network to each other, to sources of information and to distant fire support, reliance on which will allow them to be more lightly equipped. They will become smaller, more mobile and more dispersed, yet still operating as a single co-ordinated whole by virtue of the network that binds them together. Lighter supply needs will be met by more efficient and less physically extensive logistical support systems. Emerging intelligence and surveillance capabilities, with their associated command and control systems, will provide friendly forces with an accurate, real time picture of the entire area of battle, or greatly improved 'situational awareness', from the tactical to the strategic levels of war. Meanwhile, the opponent's ability to gather information will be degraded, disrupted and deceived. The result will be 'dominant battlespace awareness', a situation in which one side has near perfect knowledge while its opponent is denied accurate information. This disparity, when combined with increasingly accurate and long-range firepower, as well as other forms of precision strike capability, will allow post-RMA forces to manoeuvre, rapidly concentrate and then disperse again, and to overwhelm larger conventional forces, which will be deprived of accurate information, shattering their cohesion and ability to act, almost literally running rings around a blinded, immobilised opponent. Increased tempo and lethality will make the battlefield a far more dangerous place for the side that is inferior in information. The RMA will permit combat forces to be lighter and more easily sustainable, which is also a requirement since traditional logistic structures involving large fixed rear bases and vehicle convoys will become prohibitively vulnerable. It will also facilitate the high level of training that will be essential, through the increased use of simulation at all levels, from individual platforms all the way up to large-unit operations. At the broader level, warfare will become less linear and the battlefield will become deeper as simultaneous precision strikes are carried out across its whole area. This 'parallel warfare' will reduce the traditional distinction between the close, deep and rear battles, and blur the difference between the tactical, operation and strategic levels of warfare.

The new technologies will both require and facilitate changes in the ways in which armed forces are organised, with flatter command structures and more authority delegated downwards, as well as changes in the composition of the force. Thus, Arquilla and Ronfeldt predict that military organisations will come to be made up of smaller, more dispersed actors operating as one: 'interconnected networks rather than separate hierarchies'.[8] Owens envisages 'information-empowered, dominantly knowledgeable forces', which call for 'flattened, less hierarchical organizations', with lighter logistics structures and less need for close air support or for tactical and operational reserves that exist to deal with the unexpected (which, significantly, he expects to disappear).[9] The shape of armed forces will have to adapt, as Cohen argues, with more emphasis on long-service professionals and including more specialists in computers, missiles, space systems and electronic warfare.[10] The very character of warfare will change, according to Steven Metz: with the rise of precise, stand-off strikes, 'The RMA could relegate the close-quarters clash of troops to history.'[11]

According to the seductive vision of the RMA proponents, force will become more precise and more effective, more discriminate and less costly in human and financial terms, reducing casualties among one's own troops, non-combatants and even enemy forces. The RMA might even remove the need to deploy troops on the ground to control territory, because that physical control will no longer be necessary to achieve desired military or political effects. These developments will square various political-strategic circles, allowing smaller and cheaper forces to achieve ambitious political and military objectives effectively and efficiently. These forces will also meet the political imperatives of low casualties (on all sides), rapid deployability and reduced need for permanent basing in regions where this might be undesirable or unattainable. It is thus easy to understand the appeal of the RMA. It promises the ideal answer to the strategic dilemma faced by the United States during the 1990s, which has been sharpened since September 11 2001, of how to sustain an increasingly ambitious defence policy, at an affordable cost, and with casualties low enough to be politically acceptable.

Network Centric Warfare

One key RMA concept is that of 'network centric warfare' (NWC). This term was coined to contrast with 'platform centric warfare', that is, an approach that emphasises individual platforms, such as armoured vehicles, warships or aircraft. Network centric warfare, on the other hand, focuses not on individual assets but rather on the inter-connected whole. As a first stage, information technology enhanced the performance of each platform, as well as the sensors and weapons systems it carries; in the second stage it has linked them into a network. A diagram of the force would not take the form of individual dots but rather of a web. A parallel here can be found in personal computers: initially, individual PCs improved the user's ability to perform such tasks as work processing, number crunching and desk-top publishing. More dramatic changes have come about when these PCs, their processing power and capabilities still advancing all the time, have been linked into networks, either within the organisation concerned or externally.[12]

An early prototype of NWC can be seen in the Gulf War, where the JSTARS battlefield surveillance aircraft proved able to locate an enemy convoy, then computerised command and control would allocate targets to whichever asset was best suited to respond from artillery (gun and rocket), tactical aircraft and attack helicopters. Assisted by GPS and computerised fire control and aiming, they were able to fire swiftly and accurately, and then to move off before the enemy could return fire. As argued in the previous chapter, conditions in the Gulf were favourable but the system was at an early stage. Already, more advanced and capable versions have seen service in former Yugoslavia, Afghanistan and (again) in Iraq.

A further example of NWC can be found at sea in Co-operative Engagement Capability (CEC). As with other recent innovations, the roots of this programme lie in the Cold War period. Navies had been organised in task forces for many decades, using the complementary capabilities of different warships for mutual support. The ever growing threat to US carrier battle groups from the diverse Soviet force of submarines, surface warships and land-based maritime strike aircraft, all armed with cruise missiles, threatened to overwhelm the defences of any single warship or even a balanced task force. The solution was to integrate the task force, linking individual warships into a computerised network. They would share sensor information with each other, also drawing on data from other sources such as satellites, aircraft and under-sea sensors, to create a common tactical picture that would be of sufficient quality for weapons launch and direction. That is, one ship could detect a threat and another could engage it. The whole force therefore in effect acts as a single entity.[13] The naval example of CEC is significant for a number of reasons. First, it is no mere distant aspiration but is already at an advanced stage. Second, it is not confined to the US Navy as the Royal Navy, to name but one, is also working towards it. Third, and more broadly, this sort of model is often used by RMA enthusiasts to describe what they expect all warfare to resemble. The picture emerges of vehicles and even individual soldiers becoming platforms in their own right, operating over a wider area with highly lethal and longer-range weapons, linked into a network that includes separate sensors and fire support. There are good reasons why the sort of capability represented by CEC has been applied to navies first of all, since they operate in a far less cluttered environment than land forces. Clearly, CEC represents an enormous step forward in capability, whether or not one chooses to interpret it as indicative of a revolution. The aspiration of applying a similar network to land warfare demonstrates the ambitious aims of the RMA proponents.[14]

The RMA is not confined to new hardware integrated into a network but also encompasses innovative concepts. Many of these have a long intellectual pedigree, drawing on the ideas of some of the interwar thinkers mentioned in Chapter Two such as Fuller, Liddell Hart, Douhet and Mitchell, as well as more recent analysts such as John Warden and, of course, the de rigueur references to Sun Tzu. The argument would not be that these ideas themselves are novel but rather that digitised networks mean that what could previously be nothing more than strategic aspirations can now be achieved. One concept often used in the literature is that of the 'OODA Loop', for 'Observe, Orient, Decide, Act' (see Figure Two). Coined by USAF Colonel John Boyd in analysing air combat during the Korean War, it sought to describe the decision-making process of working out what is happening and then taking appropriate action. The aim of the commander is to 'get inside the opponent's OODA loop', which means that the latter is continually confronted with a new problem before he has understood and responded to the previous one, leaving him on the back foot and preserving the initiative for oneself. The aspiration for the RMA is that it dramatically shortens one's own OODA process while simultaneously stretching and complicating that of the opponent. As Cebrowski and Gartska put it: 'The "Observe-Orient-Decide-Act (OODA) Loop" appears to disappear'. For them, the essence of the RMA's potential is not simply the number of enemy targets that are knocked out but the speed with which they are destroyed, which creates all the more shock and shatters his strategy.[15] The OODA process does not need to be reduced to zero to have a dramatic result, only to be dramatically shortened. The equivalent would be a game of chess in which you take two or even three moves for every one your opponent takes.

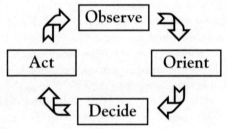

Figure Two: The 'OODA Loop'

Other RMA theorists agree about the importance of how strategy is conceived in addition to the utility of new pieces of kit. That is, just as in previous periods the most effective innovation married technological enhancements to better ways of thinking about warfare, so current RMA proponents believe that emerging military capabilities and new strategic concepts will be mutually supporting. Metz and Kievit, for example, suggest that the RMA 'may see the transition from concern with centres of gravity to a less mechanistic and more sophisticated notion of interlinked systems.'[16] Arquilla and Ronfeldt suggest: 'The organisational and psychological dimensions may be as important as the technical', and use the example of the Mongols' style of warfare to show that 'cyberwar does not depend on high technology, but rather on how one thinks about conflict and strategic interaction'. They suggest the possibility that at best the US will be able to defeat an opponent not by physically destroying his forces, but rather by hitting his systems of knowledge, information and communications.[17] Other concepts that take a similar approach include the concept of 'effects-based warfare', which focuses on the product of the use of force rather than the means used, and involves a more subtle understanding of an opponent as a complex system, which has key points of vulnerability that can be targeted to produce disproportionate effects.[18] Of course, even someone who was sceptical about the RMA as a whole could still find something of value, albeit as an incremental rather than revolutionary improvement, in attempts to consider the use of force in more imaginative ways.

Yes, But... Questions and Caveats

The previous section outlined the claims made on behalf of the Revolution in Military Affairs by its proponents. If they are correct, its impact will be impressive indeed; it would be hard to deny that changes such as those outlined would indeed be revolutionary. There are, however, many grounds on which the arguments, claims and predictions along the lines of those explored above are open to criticism. It is important to consider reasons for doubt about some of the claims made on behalf of new ideas and technologies. There is an unfortunate tendency among their proponents to attack the legitimacy of such scepticism by denouncing it as conservative or narrow-minded. However, previous cases of RMAs suggest that accurately assessing the potential impact of technological and doctrinal change is genuinely difficult and also that exaggeration of the effects of innovations is as common as underestimation. This section of the chapter will investigate some of these reasons for caution, scepticism or outright disbelief. They represent various factors and limitations that tend to be either underplayed or even overlooked in much of the RMA literature. Some of them will be explored at greater length in later chapters. The questions to be discussed are: Will the promised RMA emerge? Is it desirable? Will it be restricted to the US? Will it work in practice? Will it be usable? Are there counters to it? Is it relevant to contemporary problems? Finally, is it actually 'revolutionary' at all?

Will the RMA emerge?

One key question is whether or not the envisaged capabilities will actually become reality, not for technical reasons but rather for political, economic and bureaucratic reasons. RMAs are sometimes depicted as an objective element of reality that can no more be ignored than can gravity. More generally, however, they are understood as being sources of innovation that are only potential revolutions until accepted and understood at all levels, and married to appropriate organisational and doctrinal change, which requires a great deal of political will. Some go further to express doubts that the necessary impetus to accept such innovation is present in today's United States. Truly radical and painful change becomes appealing, it is argued, only in the aftermath of a major defeat, or when there is a revisionist grand strategy or at the very least a possible peer competitor. In the absence of any of these factors, why should the US make the leap to RMA?

There are inevitable difficulties in funding such expensive programmes, since defence budgets are tight even for the sole remaining superpower. This dilemma is sharpened by the fact that the existing armed services (which even the most enthusiastic RMA proponents acknowledge will continue to be needed for some time) need to upgrade or replace some major platforms and systems that are approaching obsolescence. Times of financial stringency might seem likely to provide fertile ground for radical ideas that promise to achieve greater capabilities with smaller forces and at less cost but they also exacerbate inter-service rivalry to maintain programmes as budgets shrink. Redistributing budgets inevitably involves losers as well as winners. Admiral Owens notes that 'reallocating resources in favour of the system of systems means starving programmatic pets in order to nourish the new arrivals'. Nevertheless in 1995 he was optimistic, noting that, 'Funds allocated for the programs that will give us the system of systems are growing at rates considerably higher than the overall DOD budget.'[19] His contentment did not last, however, and by 2002 he was suggesting that the RMA had entered its 'Thermidor', that is, a period of counter-revolution comparable to that following the initial period of the French Revolution. He saw evidence of reaction in the decision of the Pentagon, 'that the less unsettling term transformation should replace the revolution in military affairs', and in the fact that the *Joint Vision 2010* paper was replaced by *Joint Vision 2020*, 'pushing operations contemplated for 2010 out another decade'. The figure who might justly be seen as the Robespierre of the RMA therefore urged an acceleration of the revolution.[20]

There is an inherent problem in such an approach, however: it attacks the motives of anyone who dares to question any claims made by RMA proponents by attributing all criticism to dark motives of conservatism rather than to proper analysis that produces a different conclusion from one's own. Counter-attacking rather than refuting criticism has often been a tendency of the disappointed enthusiast, as shown by the readiness of strategic bombing devotees to blame strategic myopia on the part of senior decision-makers for the failures and impracticalities of their theories. Moreover, for each commentator who points to institutions stubbornly resisting change, another can point to countervailing bureaucratic incentives to seize on big ideas that promise greater budgets or personal advancement (those who agree with me represent experienced expert opinion; those who agree with you are vested interests). For every example of the military being slow to embrace new technology, there is another case of it leaping too eagerly for a technological solution.

There is evidently considerable high-level institutional support for the RMA in the Pentagon, in each of the armed services and in Congress. Proponents of the RMA like to portray themselves as a brave, persecuted minority of conceptual insurgents, battling against the indifference or hostility of a united and conservative hierarchy. Yet this is a group that includes Admiral William Owens (Vice Chairman of the JCS, 1994-96) and Andrew Marshall (director of the Office of Net Assessment in DOD), as well as a host of supporting Senators and academics, many officers ready to recognise a movement that could carry them up the promotion ladder and a number of large and powerful defence manufacturing companies with deep pockets for campaign contributions. The Clinton administration seemed keen on the RMA and its successor even more so, with Donald Rumsfeld generally perceived as being appointed Secretary of Defense (and Paul Wolfowitz as his deputy) with an express mandate for change very much along the lines advocated by RMA enthusiasts. This tendency was only increased by the attacks of September 11 and by the experience of subsequent campaigns in Afghanistan and Iraq, while the considerable boost to US defence spending in the aftermath of 9/11 made it financially more achievable. Even Owens, in his 'Thermidor' piece, noted what he saw as the optimistic factor of the appointment of retired Vice-Admiral Arthur Cebrowski as 'Director of Force Transformation', the gradual progress through the ranks of a generation of officers infused with RMA ideas and the movement of concepts such as 'dominant battlespace knowledge' from rhetoric to budgetary decisions.[21]

There is some scepticism in parts of the US defence establishment over the wilder claims made on behalf of the RMA (indeed, several of the doubting Thomases cited in this chapter are from within the US defence community), yet all of the American services are undertaking extensive and costly experiments and projects that go considerably beyond merely paying lip service to a fashionable concept. Programmes such as the US Army 'Force XXI' and the US Marine Corps 'Sea Dragon', for example, envisage smaller, lighter, more mobile, dispersed units calling in fire from distant, non-organic support systems. The US 'Land Warrior' digitisation programme (and even the less ambitious British Future Integrated Soldier Technology (FIST) system) seeks greatly to increase the capabilities of individual soldiers by providing each one with a computer that provides a link into the data network. The US system will provide information about the battlefield, including a map of the area, one's own location and those of friendly and opposing forces, and allow the sending and receiving of secure data. Aficionados of the RMA no doubt feel that such moves are proceeding agonisingly slowly but at least many of their favourite projects have a real chance to prove themselves.

Some predictions may be made reasonably safely: many of the envisaged systems will emerge while several will not, whether because funding is denied or because the technology required simply proves too demanding; and there will be much squabbling, with RMA proponents being criticised for wasting money on pointless flights of fancy and its opponents condemned for starving promising projects of resources. There could be several reasons why the RMA might not emerge, including the problems highlighted below. If it does not happen, however, it will not solely be for reasons of bureaucratic opposition, innate conservatism or lack of imagination.

Is the RMA desirable?

At least some of the capabilities associated with the RMA, then, are likely to emerge for the United States. The next question to which this conclusion gives rise is whether the RMA is in fact desirable. There are some American heretics, not quite an imminent schism, yet neither a persecuted, nearly invisible sect, who suggest that energetic pursuit of the RMA may not actually be in the interests of the USA. Harknett and his co-writers, for example, warn that the benefits of a truly transforming revolutionary shift might not be worth the associated risks and costs, when the alternative of a more evolutionary approach is available. They describe RMA ideas as 'dangerously misguided' and suggest that for the US to 'pursue a revolution that challenges the basis of the very system it currently dominates' would represent 'a major and unnecessary gamble'. They fear that the RMA will not solve many current problems, would create significant vulnerabilities, and risks provoking a reaction against US foreign policy by current allies as well as foes.[22] They make an interesting and cogent case that is rarely put.

The experience of previous RMAs gives some grounds for concern. As Chapter Two showed, the RMAs epitomised by Napoleon and Hitler were swiftly countered and copied, and did not work to the long-term benefit of either leader or their respective state. Similarly, the Industrial Revolution at first boosted British power but in the long term helped to undermine it. Why should the US embrace large-scale and risky change when it already enjoys such a marked military superiority over any challenger? Indeed, would not any attempt to extend this lead elicit the suspicion of, say, China and Russia, or even France, whose leaders have already expressed concern at the unconstrained American 'hyperpower'? There is already evidence of unease surrounding such concepts as 'full spectrum dominance'. Other problems will arise in accordance with the law of unintended consequences. There must be a danger that new military capabilities will give rise to new sources of vulnerability, as well as producing new threats that could be turned against the West. Extending the military uses of space, for example, could well bring about disadvantages for a state so dependent on the use of potentially vulnerable satellites if it provides an incentive for others to invest in anti-satellite systems.[23] An American leap to an entirely new model of intervention could also pose difficulties for operating with allies who are politically vital if not militarily essential. In addition, the RMA will also change the nature of command, the internal organisation of the armed forces, perhaps even their relationship with society. Could the RMA be a Pandora's box that the US would be best advised to leave well alone?

There are two possible responses to this argument. The first, provided by the RMA proponents, is to insist that the new capabilities will both deter potential peer competitors and also prove effective for the new challenges.[24] The second response would be that the new technologies are going to emerge anyway, so the question is more accurately phrased as whether or not to take up a position on the crest of the RMA wave as opposed to running the risk of another actor gaining a technological edge.[25] This counter-argument leads to the next question.

Will it be solely an American RMA?

The debate about the RMA has been disproportionately dominated by American analysts, which for some only reflects reality. It could well be seen as something that has relevance only for the United States; indeed, it is often referred to as 'the American RMA'.[26] The challenges posed by the ambitious technologies involved and the sheer level of resources required might be seen as restricting the new capabilities to the United States alone. Clearly it is predominantly the US defence establishment that will determine the pace and the extent of the RMA. It would be rash to assume that the US will be the only country to embrace it, however. The idea that the RMA could be solely American seems to be wishful thinking.

The experience of previous revolutions suggests that innovations spread, and the more successful they are, the more widely and rapidly they will do so. By definition, no current or aspiring major power can ignore a true RMA. Furthermore, as has been argued, much of the pace of IT development is being set in the civil sector, leaving some key elements of technology outside the control of any single state; civilian and military technology seem to proliferate both faster and more widely today than hitherto. Many of the systems and capabilities referred to by proponents are based on current technology. As *The Economist* put it, the basic elements of a revolution already exist: 'It is a matter of making existing equipment fit together and adding a few innovations.'[27] No single state would be able to slow down the RMA, let alone to monopolise it. Still, there could be many potential benefits to be had from leading the process. To return to an example mentioned above, the fact that the Industrial Revolution had a long term effect of eroding Britain's relative power does not mean that she was wrong to pursue it, since she could not have prevented it from happening and to remain aloof would only have meant foregoing potential benefits from change that was going to come regardless of her own actions.

The RMA is at the moment primarily American. Owens acknowledges that all states could acquire many of the core technologies but argues that American assets in each area are far more capable and only the US is comprehensively building the larger system of systems that emerges from integration of the three individual elements.[28] His acceptance that the RMA could benefit others is not always a feature of American writing on the subject. Nye and (the same) Owens accept that some other states could match what the US could achieve, if not as soon, but go on to claim that there is no reason for other states to seek to imitate the US system of systems unless they feel threatened by it.[29] This is dubious, to say the least, and looks like wishful thinking, as is suggested by a comparison with the US nuclear umbrella. Despite American preferences, allies are likely to be wary of complete dependence on the US (just as the UK and France saw it necessary to develop national nuclear forces during the Cold War). Russia and China will seek their own capabilities, albeit less advanced than those of the US, so as not to remain inferior; and various regional powers that do not share American interests or ideals will seek to acquire particular RMA capabilities.

The US is unrivalled in the resources that it is able to devote to the RMA. It has the financial luxury to deluge a host of concepts with money, people and time, and then to select those that work best. No other state can do this; instead, they will conduct research into specific, narrower areas of the RMA, and will watch developments in the US with great interest to see what offers the best prospects for imitation or the most promising vulnerabilities to target. Other states will not be able to choose from the whole menu available to the US but neither will they need to: they will be able to select a few appealing items, putting together their own *à la carte* option. The RMA is particularly American but will not be solely American. Where there is scope for choice for the US is in just how fast to force the pace.

One example other than the US of a state that is taking on some of the concepts associated with the RMA is the UK. Its programmes began in the late-1990s with the 'Joint Battlespace Digitisation' initiative, aiming 'to achieve integration of information systems across the whole battlespace in order to enhance operational effectiveness, which is somewhat short of the United States' desire for full spectrum dominance.'[30] This integration, it was hoped, would greatly improve the tempo and operational effectiveness of British military operations. More recently, other concepts have been added, including 'Effects-Based Warfare' (which emphasises outcomes sought rather than the capabilities used to bring them about) and 'Rapid Engagement'. The UK aspiration has perhaps become more ambitious over time yet it remains considerably more modest than that of the Pentagon. Whilst the Americans speak of 'Network Centric Warfare', the British refer to 'Network Enabled Capability'. The British vision still involves the 'system of systems' triad of sensors, information processing and precision strike, and is expected to provide dividends in rapidity and effectiveness of the use of military power and also in force protection. Yet it still seems to display a bit of British pragmatism and scepticism towards the more rosy predictions of total battlespace awareness.[31]

Will it work?

The tantalising image of future warfare presented by RMA enthusiasts involves a quantum leap in military effectiveness, which is to be achieved via an intricate 'system of systems' that both provides and requires an exceptional level of knowledge of the battlefield. The claim to be 'revolutionary' must rest on the promise of very substantial improvement. For example, Shukman suggests that due to satellite navigation: 'For the first time in history, military units can be certain of their own locations and destination of their weapons';[32] the latter claim in particular seems somewhat premature. Owens and Nye suggest that sensors 'will give real-time continuous surveillance in all types of weather over large geographical areas', and that 'the United States will be able to prevail militarily, whether the arena is a triple-canopy jungle, an urban area, or similar to Desert Storm.'[33] This vision requires that uncertainty, or 'the fog of war', and 'friction' (Clausewitz's eloquent term for the tendency of military endeavours to go wrong) can be dramatically reduced or even eliminated. Owens refers to 'the profound challenge which the American RMA posits to the Clausewitzian idea of war, the notion of the "fog and friction" of conflict'. His prediction, he insists, is only that fog and friction will apply far more to one side than the other, denying any claim 'to be able to completely dissipate the fog of war nor fully eliminate the friction of conflict'.[34] Even if disavowed, however, the RMA view of future warfare often implies and requires that uncertainty, chance, human or mechanical error and even the harmful effects of enemy action can be erased. If pressed, an RMA enthusiast will naturally deny this belief, yet if these factors do remain, the result could be that warfare will not change as much as is claimed. The detrimental effect of friction and the fog of war on post-RMA forces could be significant.

The 'system of systems' envisaged by many RMA enthusiasts is, to say the least, technically challenging. There must be questions over whether it will really work as advertised on the battlefield, where there are inevitable problems such as dust, smoke, bad weather, accidental damage, imperfect knowledge, human frailty and stress, all of which are exacerbated by the action of the enemy. It could be argued that far from reducing the potential for friction, the envisaged systems involve greater possibilities for it to occur. The more numerous and complicated are the elements in a system and the links between them, the more scope there appears to be for failure – and the more serious the implications of such a failure. Proponents could retort that their envisaged system takes the form of a web or net rather than a chain, and therefore will include a considerable degree of redundancy. Still, a key element of the system could be knocked out by a mechanical or software fault, human error or enemy action. The greater the reliance on the new technology, the more serious the potential consequences of any failure, and the worse the shock experienced by personnel who suddenly find themselves without the promised advantages. This argument is not to dismiss the potential value of the 'system of systems' but rather to introduce a note of caution and modesty to predictions of the perfectibility of 'battlespace awareness' and hence the practical implications of the RMA. Planners should be cautious in assuming that perfect information will ever be available in complex modern conflicts, especially as a competent opponent will seek to disrupt and deceive the system. The idea of the 'OODA Loop' was mentioned above, in the context of the claim that the RMA promises to minimise or even eliminate the decision making process; it is worth pointing out that the Boyd model was devised from the study of air-to-air combat, which is a far more symmetrical and straightforward form of warfare than many recent interventions.

New technologies can eliminate some of the problems associated with the systems that they replace but may do so at the cost of introducing different problems. Thus, word processors have eliminated many of the difficulties peculiar to typewriters, while photocopiers have removed those associated with hand-operated duplicating machines; yet anyone who has ever had cause to curse Microsoft or Xerox will be sceptical of any suggestion that they remove friction entirely. Moreover, they still suffer from some of the old, familiar problems, not least their dependence on the quality of information and analysis of the material that they are used to propagate. For users of complex machinery, experiencing technological failures is simply a matter of time. What university, company or government department is able to keep hundreds of computers working all the time? How much computer software does exactly what its manufacturers claim? Every computer user has experienced an errant e-mail not reaching its intended recipient, a draft chapter vanishing into the wastelands of cyberspace or Microsoft Word clinging stubbornly to its own idiosyncratic opinion as to where footnotes should be placed. Moreover, for armed forces, the likelihood of mechanical or technological failure is all the greater, given the existence of opponents actively seeking to cause confusion and disruption, and the possible consequences of any glitch or failure are far greater. The more that deployed forces become lighter, relying on non-organic fire support and 'just in time' logistics, the greater the risk that a network not working could result in a computerised Arnhem-style 'bridge too far' or a digital Dien Bien Phu.

Operational experience provides a host of salutary lessons to suggest that technology is a very long way from eliminating the tendency of things to go awry. The 1991 Gulf War saw numerous failures and errors, such as hitting the wrong targets (or striking buildings or other objects that had been mistakenly selected as targets), the difficulties of the 'Scud hunt', and the failure to identify all the constituent parts of Iraq's WMD programmes. The last is a particularly serious problem: however accurate a strike system, it cannot destroy a target that is not known to exist. Moreover, the favourable conditions of the Gulf War masked other weaknesses. The air campaigns in the former Yugoslavia demonstrated the continuing impediments caused by weather even for many PGMs. Numerous unintended civilian casualties were inflicted and significant collateral damage was caused, even though the proportion of PGMs used was far higher than in the Gulf. Erroneous 'information' can still pass through the system, as shown by the politically costly attack on the Chinese Embassy in Belgrade, where the pilot hit the target he was instructed to, only to find that the building was not what the

CIA had believed it to be. In Afghanistan, there were several cases of 'friendly fire' and collateral damage, as well as suggestions that the US strategy was fundamentally flawed, with inadequate information about the opponent allowing the majority of al Qaeda fighters to escape and slip across the border into Pakistan. More broadly, experience in the Gulf, Yugoslavia and other conflicts such as Somalia provides a series of stark reminders that imperfect understanding of local conditions and of the viewpoints of participants in a conflict will continue to limit the effectiveness of a military intervention, regardless of the technology used to carry it out. Many aspects of the 2003 Iraq intervention were both innovative and impressive but it would be difficult to sustain the argument that the operation was characterised by a lack of friction or freedom from the fog of war.

There seems to be as aspiration on the part of many RMA proponents to turn warfare into something orderly, stripped of all the things that make it unpredictable, complicated and untidy. The urge to simplify warfare (or the theory of warfare) is understandable and even commendable, but hardly new. Clausewitz criticised some of his contemporaries for neglecting the unappealing realities of war, and gave a central place in his analysis to the constant factors of friction, chance and the interaction between thinking and reacting opponents. As Beyerchen argues, readers often find Clausewitz confusing precisely because he recognised the nonlinearity of war, that is, its unpredictability and complexity, and the tendency of small causes to produce disproportionately large effects.[35] Many of the claims made on behalf of the RMA suggest, either explicitly or implicitly, that these factors can be relegated to military history. Basing future force structures and concepts of operations on this assumption does involve a considerable risk. One brave US Navy Commander suggested that there is so little evidence that the much-heralded RMA was achievable, that 'the *revolution* in military affairs is better referred to as a *religion* in military affairs. You have to take so much of what the RMA promises to achieve on faith.'[36] There is every likelihood that individual elements of the system will not always function exactly as hoped, with grave implications for the success of any operation.

Will it be usable?

The previous section raised doubts concerning whether RMA capabilities will work as well in practice as their advocates hope. A related question is whether they will be permitted to work as envisaged. It is not only technical issues that tend to be overlooked by RMA enthusiasts but also other restrictions and constraints. When attacks are contemplated that might have a devastating impact on civilians in addition to hostile decision makers or armed forces, political, legal and moral questions are inevitably involved. The use of some military capabilities against Serbia and Iraq (in both 1991 and 2003) was in some cases limited or even prevented due to concerns in domestic, allied and world public opinion. The advances in Western military capabilities since the 1970s have coincided with ever tighter ethical and legal restrictions, partly due to the higher expectations fostered by modern capabilities but also because of the sort of 'wars of choice' that the Western powers have recently conducted. Ethical constraints on warfare cannot be ignored as they have significantly and increasingly affected Western states in recent operations. Political and public dismay surrounding the media presentation of the Basra road 'highway of death' in 1991 (a rather emotive term for what had occurred) was a significant factor in the early end to the ground campaign of Desert Storm, even though the casualties were enemy combatants who had murdered, looted and raped their way across Kuwait City. The changing ethical and legal context must be taken into account by military planners just as much as the political and strategic context. Given the increasing restrictions on recent operations, which show no sign of fading away, emerging strategic concepts that ignore these constraints must be of questionable utility: there is little point in advocating challenging new ideas that will be ruled out for political reasons.

In a limited conflict, will it really be politically acceptable to launch an all-out attack on information systems? Aside from the ethical issues involved, proponents of strategic information attack seem to skate over the escalatory character of such action. Some powerful states that are occasionally suggested as possible future opponents, notably Russia and China, would have the ability to escalate a conflict in response to any effective information attack. Ironically, weakness could become a strength if their inability to match the US in advanced conventional weapons and information warfare capabilities led to their increased reliance on nuclear weapons. Consequently, the use of such techniques against them would be severely restricted on political grounds. Even if a conflict does not directly involve nuclear-capable great powers, there could be political considerations concerning relations with them, or with allies, which might restrict the usability of some RMA capabilities against other opponents.

Charles Dunlap is one of the few authors to consider many of these points, including the difficulty of distinguishing between combatants and non-combatants, the legitimacy of targeting dual systems and the undesirable future precedents that such action might set.[37] Stephen Blank also notes that the United States could come to regret setting a precedent that the whole of a state, civilian sectors as well as military, is a legitimate target in a conflict.[38] Several authors predict future technologies such as, in the words of Metz and Kievit, 'Psycho-technology to manipulate perceptions, beliefs and attitudes'. They note that use of such a capability domestically within the US would be deeply controversial.[39] Somewhat surprisingly, though, they do not address whether its use in a foreign country would be deemed ethically acceptable by American, allied or neutral world opinion. Conventional aerial bombing, like artillery bombardment before it, offered many military options that have been eschewed in practice due to considerations of ethics, law and politics, let alone the more pragmatic desire to avoid retaliation in kind or escalation of the conflict. Any concept for the use of air power or artillery that ignored these issues and blithely assumed that they would not apply would be dismissed as unrealistic. Advocates of the RMA rarely consider the potential effect on their pet projects of similar limitations.

Are there counters to the RMA?

One clear lesson that emerges from the history of attempts to interpret technological change is that there is a tendency to underestimate the probability and the impact of reactions to innovation. Any development in military affairs elicits a reaction, which may be technological, organisational, tactical, strategic or some combination of these. The more successful an innovation and the greater the potential benefits flowing from it, the greater the effort that is devoted to the reaction, which consists of some combination of imitating it and devising counters of various sorts. The question therefore arises of whether the capabilities promised by the RMA could be partly or wholly negated. Success in such endeavours could have serious implications for the willingness and ability to intervene of a United States that had become reliant on its high-tech arsenal for the low cost, short duration intervention that seems increasingly to be demanded.

Some responses could be based on simple technology. The air campaigns against Serbia and Iraq, for example, were hindered by remarkably effective use of decoys, deception and camouflage. Alternatively, a challenger could opt for a form or tempo of warfare to which Western forces were quite unsuited. Such responses will accompany higher-technology approaches. The latter might take the form of targeting new vulnerabilities that the RMA could open up. The known dependence of the US armed forces on satellites would be an example, and affordable GPS jamming systems are already available; the aim would not be to seize control of space but rather to frustrate or reduce the benefits of its use by the US and its allies.[40] It has already been argued that the RMA will not be confined to the US. A hostile actor, whether a state or some other entity, could procure some elements of the new technology, if not the whole 'system of systems' planned by the Pentagon. Emerging weapons could, for example, provide options for offensive information warfare or various niche capabilities that could confer superiority over regional rivals, help to deter or frustrate Western intervention, or simply pose a threat to the homelands of Western states. The United States in particular and the West in general are often seen as particularly vulnerable to information warfare or attacks on critical social, economic or military infrastructure. Martin Libicki, for example, notes that a hostile state could construct a cheap and basic 'system of systems', which could make use of increasing commercial services in collection and processing of information.[41] Commercial satellites already offer intelligence that a few years ago would have been the sole preserve of the US and Soviet militaries. Besides, by the end of the decade significantly more states will have their own space programmes, with all of the military advantages that flow from them, than was the case at its start. Some authors express concern that the political system of the United States could allow others to seize the initiative, selecting and prioritising particular specialised areas.[42] There is also the danger that 'rogue' states or hostile non-state groups could be less restrained in using any new capabilities, particularly with regard to inflicting casualties or targeting civilians.

Responses to US advantages could be broadly symmetrical, imitating elements of new technologies and doctrines. Perhaps more likely are asymmetric counters to RMA capabilities. As mentioned above, some states could opt to escalate a conflict if faced by strategic-level information attack. In a powerful critique of RMA proponents who, he claims, consider the operational level of warfare alone, Stephen Blank stresses that a Russia that faced defeat due to successful information attack could well resort to nuclear weapons.[43] It is indeed dangerous to assume that a state whose conventional military capabilities were paralysed would necessarily accept defeat. The mere possibility of a nuclear response would drastically restrict the use of systematic information warfare against nuclear-armed states. Moreover, since one of the widely noted lessons of Desert Storm was the foolhardiness of confronting the United States without a usable WMD capability, the American embrace of the RMA could well create a powerful incentive for potential challengers to make greater efforts towards proliferation. Future intervention would be hugely complicated by the mere possibility of nuclear, biological or chemical weapons use, whether overtly or covertly delivered, against US troops, regional allies and forward operating bases, or even against the territory of the United States itself. At best, of course, the RMA could provide counters to WMD or their likely delivery systems, but trusting it to do so would represent a considerable risk that the US or its coalition partners (especially those within the region concerned) might not be willing to accept.

Other asymmetric responses might seek to deny the US its favoured form of warfare. This approach could involve exploiting techniques and environments that have proved challenging to US military intervention (notably urban warfare, guerrilla or terrorist strategies).[44] Alternatively it could involve targeting US psychological and ethical self-limitations, threatening civilians or using them as human shields, or using environmental warfare (as with Iraq in 1991 setting fire to oil wells or releasing oil into the Gulf), or even conceptualising warfare, victory and defeat in unorthodox ways. Either way, the aim would not be to inflict a battlefield defeat on the US but rather to reduce its willingness to intervene or to complicate its strategy if it did become involved. The asymmetric challenge to the United States is likely to be diverse, with some opponents taking a high technology and others a lower technology approach, thus presenting simultaneous challenges at both ends of the spectrum of conflict. Asymmetric warfare is covered in more detail in Chapter Seven, so for now it must suffice to point out that even in 1991 it was evident that an opponent seeking to play anything resembling the game favoured by the US will find itself hugely out-classed. The inevitability of this conclusion suggests that a thinking opponent will therefore try something different.

Is the RMA relevant?

RMA proponents tend to concentrate on medium- to high-intensity conventional warfare. Many visions of future conflicts and capabilities seem implicitly to envisage new ways of defeating a Soviet armoured thrust into western Europe or, alternatively, finding ever more effective ways to re-fight the 1991 Gulf War. This is already something the US is very good at. Even without great technological leaps forward, confronting the US with its ideal form of warfare will prove a serious and costly mistake for any country. The sole remaining military superpower has an enormous qualitative advantage in every element of conventional forces (and a quantitative lead in many key areas), as well as in the systems integrating and supporting them, even before taking into account the fact that several of the next most effective military powers are not only unlikely to be adversaries but are close allies. It is difficult to conceive of a true peer competitor in the near future; even Russia or China would hardly fit the bill, while other suggested enemies such as a unified Europe or united Arab world belong in the realms of fiction. Major regional conflicts are more plausible, though even in this category it is difficult to identify a major shortfall in US capabilities other than the risk of being over-stretched by too many simultaneous commitments. The argument is certainly not that inter-state warfare is a thing of the past or that conventional operations will not be required in the future. Rather, the concern is that conventional warfare between states is not the most likely problem to be faced – and it is a problem that the US forces are well able to handle even without an RMA.

Far more likely is intra-state conflict, which post-Cold War experience suggests is very much more challenging than the sort of conflict seen in 1991. Indeed, the Gulf War offers few transferable lessons because it was so unique; other experience since the end of the Cold War has pointed to very different conclusions. Bosnia, Somalia, Haiti, Rwanda, Kosovo, Afghanistan and the post-combat phase in Iraq (2003) seem more representative of post-Cold War conflict than Kuwait. They posed different sorts of problems and have been far less conducive than Iraq's ill-planned action to the strategic advantages and preferences of the US and other Western powers. They were fought within rather than between states, took the form of irregular warfare (guerrilla or paramilitary forces rather than conventional armies with obvious and vulnerable command and logistical structures) and occurred in far less favourable terrain and weather than Desert Storm. There is a risk that the less comforting experience of these conflicts will not modify the conclusions drawn from the Gulf War but will rather lead to an increasing concentration on the more pleasant, appealing sort of conflict, and to a reluctance or even inability to intervene in crises that do not resemble this ideal type. As Freedman suggests, it will, 'hardly be a revolution in military affairs if it leads those who embrace it to avoid most contemporary conflicts, and only to take on those that promise the certain and relatively painless victories.'[45]

Many of the systems vaunted by RMA enthusiasts seem optimised for operations similar to Desert Storm and would have less relevance for the types of conflict that are more likely to occur. This suggests a possible degree of mismatch between the capabilities that the RMA is likely to provide and the capabilities that are needed in the new strategic environment. It would be wrong to exaggerate this problem, however. Some of the experiments conducted by the US armed forces (particularly the US Marine Corps, which is proving more realistic and down to earth than some of its sister services) have not shirked the more difficult scenarios and have examined the problems of, for example, operating in urban environments. Attention is being given in research and development and in doctrine to 'operations other than war' (OOTW) and their requirements. Some RMA and information warfare capabilities will be useful in contingencies other than conventional, regular warfare; this issue is the subject of Chapter Six. The concern here is simply that the RMA is optimised for problems other than those that are most pressing, so too single-minded a pursuit of the RMA could lead to a distorted and inaccurate view of contemporary conflict, and hence produce a policy and a force that were ill-adapted to it. Current and future conflicts will form a broad spectrum: neither this fact nor its implications are fully incorporated into the RMA literature, which concentrates disproportionately on the higher-intensity conflict for which the RMA is best suited.

Are the envisaged changes 'revolutionary'?

Chapter One explained that there are significant differences in just how dramatic change must be for an author to consider it an RMA and, consequently, in how many cases are acknowledged as RMAs. If a particular analyst concludes that an RMA is underway, it is important to know whether it is seen as one of two in history or one of twenty. As this observation suggests, there is considerable disagreement over whether the current changes are revolutionary or merely evolutionary – and, if the latter, whether or not they suggest that a genuine RMA is just around the corner.

Some analysts predict that the effect of the 'system of systems' will be to change existing forces radically, raising them to a new level of effectiveness and requiring considerable adaptation in their structures and practices. Current major platforms (such as armoured vehicles, manned aircraft, surface warships) will be integrated with each other and with various new assets, including unmanned systems, but will remain the heart of the future force.[46] Information operations will be added to the current model, supporting traditional forces directly at the tactical level, or more indirectly at the operational level where they function separately but aim towards the same campaign goals. It is possible to describe a step forward of this sort as an RMA, although this would assume a definition of the term from the more permissive end of the spectrum.

Other writers question whether such developments are in fact 'revolutionary', or whether they rather constitute *evolutionary* change, albeit rapid, incrementally building upon and improving current capabilities. Many 'new' elements are in fact developments of age-old factors in warfare. It has long been important in warfare to gather information while denying it to the enemy, and capabilities for doing so have gradually improved over a long period. Command and control systems have undergone incremental change since the introduction of radio and IT merely continues this trend. Primitive guided weapons appeared during the Second World War and their accuracy and range have gradually improved since. Any doctrinal adaptation to these developments has been evolutionary and is only to be expected. Although the means used, in terms of the elements that compose armed forces and the ways in which they operate, have changed, military strategy continues to revolve around a combination of manoeuvre and attrition to reduce the ability of enemy armed forces to resist, which has long included attacking their cohesion and targeting their rear areas. Thus, in a rejoinder to Martin Libicki's article suggesting that the RMA would reduce the importance of geography, Colin Gray suggests that the alleged 'RMA' is not truly revolutionary: 'Is Libicki's subject truly an RMA, or is it but the current manifestation of the perennial quest for information dominance?'[47]

Other believers in the general concept of RMA agree that limited incorporation of IT into current force structures would not amount to a revolution; the real leap forward will come with the realisation that the ends and means of wars will change, rather than just having another element added to them. This school believes in RMAs but holds that one has not quite yet begun. Thus, Adams describes the Gulf War as 'the last hurrah of the armed forces and generals who had trained on the legacy of the Second World War'; it looked new but in fact, 'the tactics had remained essentially evolutionary and revolved around the application of mass on the battlefield.'[48] Such thinkers suggest that the immediate result will be a mere transitional period before a far greater change when information becomes the heart of warfare, a means and even an end in its own right. This would change the very nature of warfare and its role in world affairs, and would undoubtedly be a revolution – or, if one chooses the additional distinction, would represent a 'major RMA'. Arquilla and Ronfeldt suggest that the initial, first level effects of new technology tend to improve the efficiency of current practices while later, second level effects transform the social system.[49] Whereas the tactical and operational incorporation of information warfare might not be a revolutionary development, creating an entirely new form of strategy would genuinely merit this description. As the next chapter shows, some theorists believe that information warfare promises just that.

Other writers emphasise a more far-reaching cluster of technological changes that, if they do come to fruition, would amount to an RMA in the most restrictive sense of the term. Steven Metz, one of the leading American RMA analysts, argued in 2000 that this second phase was about to begin:

> Increasingly, technological and, more important, social, political, economic, and psychological changes suggest that the RMA may be moving into a second, more radical phase. In it, both the nature of war and the way in which war is fought may be transformed.[50]

Some of the technological advances envisaged by this school of thought make current ideas such as Network Centric Warfare appear to be distinctly modest in comparison. One theme of current doctrine is using force to influence indirectly the perceptions of opposing leaders; 'psychotechnology' would involve directly affecting the perceptions of targeted individuals. Another current area of research is that of 'Micro-Electro-Mechanical Machines' (MEMs), which could result in tiny robots that might be used for reconnaissance or to disable enemy vehicles and facilities, known as 'fire ant warfare'. Such advances could go even further with 'nanotechnology', which refers to engineering on the scale of atoms and molecules (a 'nanometre' is one thousand-millionth, or 10^{-9}, of a metre). Other areas highlighted by those who are rather more sparing in their use of the term 'revolutionary' would include greater use of robotics and automation, 'brilliant' rather than merely smart weapons, high energy radio frequency (HERF) weapons, particle weapons, cyborgs, artificial intelligence and genetic weapons.[51] It could be suggested, then, that a true RMA is on the horizon but will be manifest only when more futuristic technologies of this sort emerge, not merely when the Desert Storm model armed forces become even more efficient.

Current developments therefore are seen by some as being revolutionary. Others, though, see them as more evolutionary. Some of those who take this view might be sceptical in general about the notion of RMAs. Alternatively, they might accept that RMAs occur but simply feel that current developments do not merit that label. Some of this latter camp would go further and say that although the current innovations are not yet an RMA, they could herald one in the near future.

Conclusion: Perspectives on the RMA

This chapter has set out the claims made on behalf of the RMA and explored some of the grounds on which they can be questioned. From this survey, it is clear that a variety of strikingly different perspectives can be identified concerning whether there really is an RMA and, if so, the form it is taking and the implications that it will have. It might be helpful to draw out a few schools of thought that epitomise the different approaches to the RMA. Doing so will both help to summarise the arguments of this chapter and also provide a tool to assist the analysis of later chapters. A few caveats must first be emphasised. First, some readers might quibble with the labels used, questioning whether the 'Radical' view truly merits that description, or wondering whether 'Visionary' is intended as a compliment or a criticism (in fact, as with the other labels that follow, it is meant as neither: the use of rather loaded terms such as 'techno-maniac' or 'reactionary/traditionalist' has been eschewed for precisely this reason).[52] Setting out these perspectives is intended to help explore the various questions rather than to resolve them, and not too much weight should be attached to the names used for them. Each of the views defined offers some useful observations and none is intended to be a mere straw man. Second, dividing an extensive literature into a few schools of thought risks overlooking some of its nuances. There are inevitably several shades of opinion within them as well as some degree of overlap between them. The following are not offered as formal 'models', nor can individual writers necessarily be slotted unambiguously into a single one. They are rather broad approaches to the subject, which are set out to show currents in the understanding of the RMA and to allow different viewpoints to be explored. The perspectives that emerge are the Radicals, the Visionaries, the Sceptics, the Moderates and the Pessimists.

The Radicals accept that major changes are currently underway that amount to an RMA (they tend to have a relatively permissive definition of what constitutes an RMA, identifying many examples in history). The new technologies premiered in the Gulf War showed that if they were properly grasped, fully exploited and matched up with appropriate developments in force structure, organisation and doctrine, the result would be a great leap forward in the capabilities of the armed forces concerned. Information technology, digitisation, improving sensors, longer-range and more precise weapons, computer warfare and innovative new concepts will be added to the national armoury and will result in a transformation of the shape and methods of the armed forces. Major weapons platforms will continue to form an important component of force structures but they will adapt, changing significantly and being increasingly supplemented and interconnected with unmanned systems, sensor networks and long-range strike capabilities, as well as with other major platforms.

The Visionaries concur with some of the analysis of the Radicals, recognising the existence of the trends and developments they identify, and seeing their incorporation as important and useful. However, they deny that these truly amount to an RMA, seeing them as at most a 'minor RMA' or a 'Military Technical Revolution', the latest stage of twentieth century mechanised warfare rather than a true paradigm shift. It is a mere transitional stage, a precursor to the true revolution that will occur not when current forces are merely transformed but when they are superceded by a whole new paradigm of warfare and major platforms are replaced by entirely new means of intervention, such as the exploitation of information as a weapon in its own right, computer warfare, entirely unmanned weapons, nanotechnology and other futuristic options. The real RMA might involve not simply new ways for one's own armed forces to defeat those of the enemy but rather an alternative to defining military success in such a way. This would amount to a true revolution, according to the most restrictive definition of the term. This school tends to the more restrictive in terms of how many historical RMAs are recognised and would interpret the Gulf War as the high-point of twentieth century warfare rather than as the gateway to the future.

The first two schools described accept that an RMA is either underway or is possible in the near future. Not all thinkers go along with this. The Sceptics are dismissive of the concept of RMA, both in general and for the current period in particular. They see the current debate as more of a revolution in defence industry salesmanship, spawning a mass of fashionable terms to which defence planners (or, to be more accurate, 'defense planners', since it is largely an American obsession) must pay rote obeisance or which they embrace for bureaucratic political reasons. They argue that RMA proponents tend to exaggerate the importance of developments of their own era and focus entirely on change to the exclusion of any recognition of continuity, rushing to overlook history in their quest for a new post-Cold War 'grand theme' that will sell new-fangled concepts, expensive weapons systems or impressively-titled books. The Sceptics tend to stress continuity over change, suggesting that information has always been rather significant in warfare, and in the case of the Gulf War would point to the uniqueness and favourable circumstances that so flattered the coalition, as well as expressing doubts that this form of conflict is terribly relevant for current and future defence planning.

Compared to the Sceptics, the Moderates are less scathing in their criticism of the concept of RMA. They are open minded over whether or not RMAs exist in general, while for the most part being suspicious of claims that one is currently underway. They tend to stress gradual, evolutionary change rather than revolution, interpreting contemporary developments as the combination of many influences and the culmination of many factors that have been operating for years or decades. Whilst they would accept that current developments in information technology, sensors and long-range precision-strike systems have the potential to offer some very useful advances, whose benefits they are keen to exploit, they see these as incremental rather than revolutionary or even transforming in their effect. This approach might be criticised for lack of imagination but its adherents would defend themselves either by pointing to conceptual doubts that pour cold water on grander claims, or by pragmatically noting financial, technological and practical constraints. They tend to draw particular attention to the context of the international system and the political, legal and ethical constraints that are likely to be a feature of all future operations.

The Pessimists are perhaps the most challenging to those who believe in the RMA, since they share the basic acceptance that one is underway. Where they differ, however, is in rejecting the rosy view that the RMA will benefit the West.

On the contrary, they fear that the combination of political and technological changes currently underway will be greatly to the detriment of the Western powers, creating a devil's brew of new problems and vulnerabilities – that the alleged new opportunities are powerless to solve. The destabilisation of the international system will multiply the threats faced by the West in the form of rogue states, terrorists or disaffected individuals. Meanwhile, developments in technology will provide these actors with a range of deeply unpleasant new options to attack a particularly and increasingly vulnerable West. The new actors may well have fewer scruples about using computer attack, chemical and biological (even genetic) weapons against a West that finds itself divided politically and hamstrung by self-imposed constraints. The Pessimists also fear that the RMA offers pitfalls into which some in the West are all too enthusiastically tripping. They see its (largely American) enthusiasts as being seduced by elaborate and costly military capabilities that are not hugely relevant for the emerging security environment and, worse, that permit actions and interventions that are deeply unwise and will have disastrous consequences, not least in provoking reactions by hostile actors.

The Radicals believe that an RMA is underway that will produce a quantum leap in the effectiveness of current forces, which will evolve dramatically. The Visionaries believe that if the right choices are made, the current precursor period can develop into a fully-fledged RMA that will produce entirely new means of intervention and an entirely new model of forces. The Moderates doubt that emerging capabilities amount to an RMA but accept that they will offer many benefits and significantly increase the capability of current forces. The Sceptics believe that there is no RMA, just hype, self interest and misunderstanding. The Pessimists fear that an RMA is underway that will vastly increase the dangers faced by the West.

There is some value in each of these perspectives and it is quite possible for a single analyst to accept claims from more than one of them. As a very rough approximation of how the schools of thought relate to government policy, the prevalent view in the UK might best be placed largely in the Moderate camp, with some elements of the Radical school, though with a healthy leaven of Sceptics. The mainstream US view would best be situated in the Radical camp, with a sizeable and influential Visionary element. Both states contain plenty of examples of thinkers who would fit into each of the schools.

The different perspectives will be used in the remainder of this book to help explore specific aspects of the RMA debate. The following chapter considers information warfare and hence overlaps to some extent with this one. Chapter Six looks at how the RMA applies across different parts of the spectrum of conflict, while Chapter Seven discusses the effects of asymmetric warfare. Finally, Chapter Eight examines the implications of the RMA for alliances.

Chapter 5
Information Warfare

The collection and use of information have always been fundamental elements of warfare. Many analysts argue that information has recently taken on even greater importance as the technological means to exploit it have advanced and therefore place it at the very heart of the Revolution in Military Affairs. For some, 'Information Warfare' (IW) is a synonym for the RMA; information is the revolution, as it forges a new economic system and era of civilisation, transforming the very nature of international politics.[1] Some analysts believe that information holds the promise of a new form of warfare in its own right, in which it becomes both a target and a weapon. Others see it as a central element of a broader RMA, revolutionising warfare by providing an ever more significant and usable resource that will transform the existing armed forces. Others again interpret it as a useful addition to planning and conducting operations, though not quite revolutionary in its impact. From a sceptical point of view, IW might well seem to be the most exaggerated and misunderstood aspect of the whole literature. Of course, referring to 'information warfare' or 'information operations' does not necessarily imply a belief that either is revolutionary in effect or even that a Revolution in Military Affairs is underway at all. Even those who are sceptical about RMA and who rather point to evolutionary change can still attach importance to IW. Whatever conclusion reached about it, information is so central to the debate about the RMA that it deserves a chapter devoted to it.

The principal difficulty in writing about Information Warfare is the sheer breadth of concepts and activities that the term is used to cover: 'Information warfare has as many meanings as it has proponents, detractors and observers'.[2] Like the broader concept of RMA, it has become a fashionable term, the strategic flavour of the month. Many disparate ideas and proposals are lumped together under the conceptual umbrella that this term provides, with the result that it is frequently watered down and debate about the implications of the ideas offered is hindered. Approaches vary from the broadest (which can tend to lose meaning) to the narrowest and most technical. Indeed, the term is sometimes used simply to refer to high-tech warfare.[3] Some interpretations of IW do not, in fact, refer to anything new but rather represent long-standing elements of warfare – though in some such cases, the author concerned believes that one familiar activity has now come to have far greater importance than it previously had. Other analysts make more substantive claims that can genuinely be seen as identifying something new but they often exaggerate what exists or what might emerge, or underestimate practical limitations and problems that would reduce the impact of IW. This does not, however, mean that the term entirely lacks meaning or utility. There is some substance in it, alongside a great deal of exaggeration and confusion: the wheat must be separated from the chaff before attempting any judgement concerning the value of specific claims and prescriptions.

Perhaps the most significant distinction between the different approaches to IW is the level or levels of strategy on which the concept is located. The levels of strategy recognised by NATO and the UK are, from the top down: (1) Grand Strategic, the broadest level of national policy; (2) Military Strategic, where military instruments are applied to achieve broad goals; (3) Operational, the planning and conduct of campaigns and major operations; (4) Tactical, the planning and execution of engagements.[4]

Figure Three: The Levels of Strategy

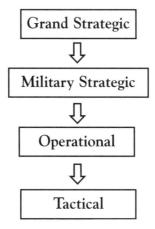

The impact of IW is variously understood on each of these levels of warfare, or on various combinations of them. The distinction is useful because it reveals a great deal about how far-reaching the intentions of the writer concerned are and explains just how the factors identified are expected to take effect. There is a parallel that may help to explain the importance of the level of analysis on which concepts of IW are pitched. Considering interwar theories of air power helps to show how this issue matters and also clarifies some questions to ask about information warfare. It therefore justifies a digression.

A Parallel: Theories on the Impact of Air Power

During the interwar period, some thinkers who were considering how air power might affect warfare concentrated on the tactical or operational levels, identifying ways in which aircraft could be used in co-operation with ground and naval forces. Herein lay the roots of blitzkrieg and of carrier warfare which, as Chapter Two explained, are often interpreted as RMAs in their own right. The more vocal and ambitious among the first generation of air power theorists, however, concentrated on the military strategic level of warfare and claimed to be offering something totally new. These thinkers advocated strategic air power in the true sense, that is, they conceived of bombing not as one more contribution to victory but as capable of winning wars on its own, independent of and separate from the other services. Strategic bombing would directly attack the heart of the enemy's power and his population's will to resist, thereby achieving victory without the need to fight on the ground or over the seas. Throughout the interwar period, during the Second World War and to some extent during and since the Cold War too, there has been a tendency for advocates of air power to look down on tactical or operational uses of air power as merely 'auxiliary' or subordinate, and as diversions from its proper use.

The interwar theorists were not simply arguing that air power was important (though they are sometimes cited today to back this uncontentious assertion). They were arguing for a specific type of importance, namely pre-eminence over the other services, and seeking to establish a specific way of fighting wars, which envisaged air power being not only necessary for victory but also sufficient. There have been numerous attempts to use air power in a truly strategic way – that is, where the hope and intention is that bombing alone will achieve the military and political objectives of the campaign – in World War II, Korea, Suez, Vietnam and the former Yugoslavia, and similar ideas have heavily influenced other interventions, including the 1991 Gulf War. For various reasons, the claims made on behalf of strategic air power have never been fulfilled: the results achieved have often made a significant contribution to victory, but one that was neither of the extent nor of the precise nature predicted by the interwar air enthusiasts and their later disciples. Air power has had its best results not when it acted as a strategically separate arm, fighting its own war, but rather when its efforts were co-ordinated and its effects interweaved with those of the ground and naval forces. It was enormously important in all of these conflicts and its use was not confined to 'auxiliary' tasks of directly supporting ground forces. Yet in no case did it win the war alone.

More significant than strategic bombing was the use of air power in direct support of land and naval forces, which received scant attention in interwar theoretical writings (and, indeed, has been much under-valued in later air force doctrine) but which proved its worth time and again. The close co-ordination of land, sea and air forces has become such a familiar feature of modern warfare that it is seldom remarked upon, but it is worth noting that such uses were explicitly scorned and rejected by Douhet, Mitchell and Seversky.[5]

One other category of uses of air power that has proved particularly significant lies between the other two; that is, activities that were conducted separately from the other branches of the armed forces at the tactical or even operational levels of war but were what would now be termed 'joint' in intention and effect at the military strategic level. That is to say, even if the actions were carried out by a single service, their effects blended together with and complemented those of operations by the other services. One crucial effect of the World War II strategic bombing campaign against Germany, for example, was that it secured for the allies command of the air, without which any invasion of the continent would have been prohibitively costly. Similarly, in the run-up to and immediately after the D-Day landings, Allied air power made the vital contributions of attacking German transport links to hinder the deployment of reserves and targeting fuel production and supplies to reduce the effectiveness of German forces. Neither of these actions would have had a useful effect other than in conjunction with an invasion. A parallel from the maritime campaign (which was particularly misunderstood and under-rated by 'Bomber' Harris and other senior RAF commanders) lies in the use of land-based aircraft for anti-submarine patrolling and for laying mines. Each of these tasks was conducted separately from the other services but aimed towards a common and joint aim. Even if the impact of air power is seen as 'merely' on the operational and tactical levels (rather than as a separate, strategic means to win), this still represented an enormous change, which only seems relatively modest in relation to the unrealistically ambitious claims made by the air power enthusiasts mentioned above.

There are several ways in which air power might be interpreted as having initiated 'revolutionary' change. The first would be if it had led to an entirely new, separate and distinct form of warfare, replacing the older armed services. A result of this magnitude, at the grand strategic and military strategic levels, would in its own right have justified the title of 'RMA' and would have been a change of the order identified by the perspective that the previous chapter labelled the 'Visionaries'. Air power did not have that effect. It changed many aspects of warfare but did so by joining and integrating with the other armed services, making them evolve and creating a new entity. These changes were primarily at the tactical level, in direct co-ordination with land and naval forces, and the operational level, with some military strategic roles as well, though the latter have not amounted to bombing being able to win wars by itself. This second interpretation of air power still conceives of it as transforming warfare but in a way that incorporated elements of the previous paradigm rather than making them all obsolete. This effect could still be seen as 'revolutionary', in the sense that it introduced a hugely significant new element into warfare, which no great power that sought to retain its status could ignore and to which all existing elements of the armed forces had to adapt. It would therefore correspond to the 'Radical' school of thought defined in Chapter Four. The introduction of air power does therefore tend to be seen as an RMA – though different definitions of the terms could result in it being classed as a 'minor RMA', a 'military technical revolution' or even as merely an evolutionary development within the broader era of industrial age warfare.

As will be shown below, there is a comparable debate about the impact of IW. Some see it as a useful tool that carries some benefits at the tactical level but little more. This view would be that of the Sceptical approach to the RMA. Others, corresponding to the Moderate school of thought, see it as being both tactical and operational in its effect, making it a significant but not revolutionary development. More ambitious still would be the Radical perspective that would see IW as having tactical, operational and military strategic implications that make it truly revolutionary, though transforming rather than entirely replacing the existing forces. The RMA Visionaries would argue that IW would be truly revolutionary only if it provides an entirely new means of intervention and paradigm of warfare at the military and grand strategic level. Crucially, they believe that it promises to do just that.

Information Warfare at the Strategic Level

One of the senses in which the term 'information warfare' tends to be coined is extremely broad and should, perhaps, be avoided for that reason. It is sometimes used to refer to all of the workings of government and the armed forces that deal with public information and the media and even, in some cases, to lobbying or public relations activities.[6]

In an era when Western states mainly face 'wars of choice' rather than struggles for national survival, it is clearly important and also potentially difficult for the government to maintain the support of public opinion for any commitment of forces. In the coalition operations that are now the norm, wider considerations of allied and world opinion need also to be taken into account. The task of managing the media is made all the more difficult by the increased technological sophistication and transnational character of modern news gathering. Nevertheless, the term 'information warfare' should not be used for such activities. Doing so risks obscuring more than it reveals, eroding the utility of the term by including many disparate elements that bear more relation to day-to-day government communications than to military operations. It is evidently tempting to use the language of warfare here, as in many areas of politics and business, but this is metaphor rather than reality. The activities concerned do affect military operations and have to be closely co-ordinated with military activities but they do not amount in themselves to a form of warfare. They are perhaps better seen as part of the broader context for military affairs rather than being directly linked to an RMA. Several of the phenomena identified are of considerable importance, but they can better be categorised as 'information policy', 'media/public relations' or even 'communications strategy'. The term 'information warfare' is better preserved for other things.

The claims about IW that most deserve the label and that can plausibly be described as 'revolutionary' lie at the higher levels of strategy. That is, they do not merely promise an additional element that would be bolted on to existing armed forces but rather hold out the prospect of an entirely new means of achieving national objectives: 'If information warfare means something new, it is the use of information as a substitute for traditional ways of fighting, rather than as an adjunct to them.'[7]

The Grand Strategic Level

Some thinkers see the US information advantage as decisive in fighting wars, but also as much more than that. Joseph Nye (a leading American academic and formerly a senior Pentagon official) and William Owens (referred to in the previous chapter), for example, suggest that what they call the US 'information umbrella' will provide similar leverage to that once provided by nuclear deterrence. It will help to engage Russia and China, preventing them from becoming hostile; it will prevent hostile states such as Iran and Iraq from becoming powerful; and it will help solve regional conflicts and bolster new democracies.[8] Arquilla and Ronfeldt refer to this sort of approach as 'netwar', which they understand as 'societal-level ideational conflicts waged in part through internetted modes of communication', or 'information-related conflict at a grand level between nations or societies'. Such conflict could be waged by states but also by non-state actors, and would comprise a wide variety of activities:

> It may involve public diplomacy measures, propaganda and psychological campaigns, political and cultural subversion, deception of or interference with local media, infiltration of computer networks and databases, and efforts to promote dissident or opposition movements across computer networks.[9]

This view of IW would locate it on the grand strategic level, that is, as a broad tool of national policy alongside military, economic and other means, as a source of power and influence in its own right, and as an alternative to the use of force. Conceptions of this sort can be identified in references to 'enlarging democracy', or hopes that the spread of liberal values will help to shape the world in ways favourable to US or Western interests.

On the one hand, such an idea appears to offer a sensible way to use Western strengths – exploiting what the International Relations literature refers to as 'soft' rather than 'hard' power – and to provide a bloodless alternative to combat. On the other hand, it could be highly dangerous. Such a campaign could be interpreted as an act of war and be met with an appropriate, perhaps asymmetric or escalatory response. Its systematic use by the United States could be seen as embracing the 'clash of civilisations' thesis and turning it into active policy.[10]

Many people in the Islamic world already fear 'cultural contamination' and the calculated use of information warfare on a grand strategic level could well appear to them as an attempt to turn this into an offensive weapon, confirming their worst fears regarding a new Western 'crusade' against their religion. Anyone who sees this argument as far-fetched should re-read the quotation from Arquilla and Ronfeldt cited above but this time assuming that the information campaign is being waged by Iran or Saudi Arabia (or even China) against the United States: how would American public and political opinion react? Liberal and democratic ideas are generally recognised as an important element in the collapse of the Soviet system and the victory of the West in the Cold War; some predict that the same forces will help quietly to undermine the Chinese regime and other authoritarian states. Yet the deliberate use of these ideas as a weapon (for that is how it would appear to its targets, whose reactions its advocates rarely consider) would be difficult in practice and would not necessarily be conducive to a more peaceful and stable world. At worst, this vision could be seen as introducing a new and insidious form of conflict to international politics.

The Military-Strategic Level

Most of the literature concentrates on the use of IW within conflicts and thus functions at the military strategic rather than the grand strategic level. This view would conceive of IW as a means of national power that could defeat an opponent on its own, either without any commitment of combat forces or, alternatively, as the principal means used with only a small deployment of troops. Either way, for many writers, IW would become a new form of warfare. Thus, James Adams writes:

> The real revolutionaries believe that for countries like the United States, information warfare offers the possibility of fighting and winning wars without the commitment of troops on the ground....The revolutionaries argue that even the very definition of 'ground' is changing as the world migrates from earth to cyberspace.[11]

(This last sentence is an egregious example of RMA hyperbole: the world is no more 'migrating' from earth to cyberspace as a result of the information revolution than it migrated to the skies following the advent of flight.) Arquilla and Ronfeldt argue that just as industrialisation led to attrition warfare and mechanisation led to manoeuvre warfare, so the information revolution is giving rise to cyberwar ('knowledge-related conflict at the military level'), in which information rather than mass or mobility will be decisive. They suggest that although blitzkrieg represented a development of attrition warfare, it still required the defeat of the enemy armed forces. Cyberwar, on the other hand, could allow the achievement of campaign objectives without attrition of the enemy armed forces, by 'striking at the strategic heart of an opponent's cyber structures, his systems of knowledge, information, and communications.' It therefore offers the prospect of a less destructive form of warfare.[12] Martin Libicki, one of the leading American RMA thinkers, predicts that US use of cyberspace (which he defines as 'the sum of the globe's communications links and computational nodes') will provide new means of intervention. The US would be able to demonstrate its capabilities with a limited number of initial strikes and then demand the disabling of remaining enemy forces rather than destroying them; it could disarm the enemy's heavy forces sufficiently to allow local allies to prevail; or it could selectively share intelligence and targeting information, either to assist allies without actual US involvement in combat, or to guarantee a peace settlement (for example on the Golan Heights).[13] If these predictions were borne out in practice it would be difficult to deny that the result would be revolutionary and that, as Nye and Owens put it, 'Knowledge, more than ever before, is power'.[14]

This elevation of information into a source of power in its own right has attracted some criticism. Lawrence Freedman argues that, 'The importance of the information revolution lies not in the accumulation of knowledge for its own sake, but in its impact on established forms of economic and military strength.'[15] Colin Gray writes: 'Nye and Owens are wrong: knowledge is not power, at least it is not military power, and information power is a strikingly perilous concept.' It requires combination with various forms of 'hard' power to become effective in practice:

> Cyberwarriors will ply their trade by and large for the purpose of rendering ever more lethal the geographically specific forces which operate by land, sea, in the air and in space. Information itself does not coerce or kill; it has to act on and through weapons systems of all kinds.[16]

This dispute can be compared with the theoretical debate in International Relations over 'economic power'. Although undoubtedly a useful concept, refining understanding of the sources of state influence beyond just military power, many accounts of it are inadequate. There is a tendency simply to assume that it is a form of power comparable to military power, with insufficient recognition of the differences: it is more indirect, more fragile, less tangible, more diffuse, less coercive and harder to apply outside its specific realm. It is of undoubted significance but cannot be precisely equated with military power. Similarly, information is not a form of power in its own right and is better seen as an enabler for other, harder power resources than as an alternative to them. Having a piece of information is of little use unless you can act upon it – the aphorism that the pen is mightier than the sword does not apply at the tactical level of warfare.

Claims that information warfare can be a strategic weapon come in two varieties. The first, less ambitious version would suggest that the US – most theories of IW refer to and are written by Americans – could avoid having to commit its own troops to a conflict but still secure its objectives by using information warfare to lend a decisive weight to a particular local faction. This information intervention would involve sharing intelligence with them or, if they were technologically compatible, 'plugging them in' to the American information system, and perhaps also conducting some offensive information attacks against the local group that the US opposed. This approach would offer the benefit of allowing the US to achieve its aims without putting troops on the ground, where they would be at risk, as well as avoiding the need for large-scale and time-consuming deployment of forces, creation of local logistical support structures and so forth.

Several recent interventions have taken the form of US air power co-operating with ground forces, mainly provided by local participants but also including some Western special forces. In Operation Deliberate Force in Bosnia, NATO air strikes were conducted in co-ordination with the British and French Rapid Reaction Force (notably its artillery) and, less explicitly, with a Croatian army offensive.[17] A similar strategy was applied in Kosovo, where NATO air strikes and operations on the ground by the Kosovo Liberation Army were mutually complementary, and in post-9/11 operations in Afghanistan, where US air power and special forces, with some allied contributions, worked in concert with the local United Front/Northern Alliance. In each case, technology was used as a substitute for large-scale commitment of US troops on the ground. The idea of some information warriors is that a similar model could be repeated in the future but using information instead of air power: rather than lend the support of air superiority and air strikes, the US would provide 'dominant battlespace awareness' and offensive information operations. It is worth noting that there is a near precedent in the Iran-Iraq War, when the US pursued its aim of preventing an Iranian victory by sharing satellite intelligence with Iraq, thereby greatly assisting its preparations to counter mass Iranian offensives.

A proposal of this sort is plausible and, moreover, would not demand any great technological leap forward. If it were conducted with the technology of today, it would not necessarily result in a 'revolutionary' development, but could still be a useful tool, providing options when there was not sufficient interest at stake for a full commitment of ground forces. Alternatively, it could in the future utilise some of the more ambitious technologies, capabilities and concepts proposed by IW enthusiasts, in which case it might be hailed even by the 'Visionary' school as revolutionary – though the fact that it still relied on using someone's ground forces (even if not our own) might weigh against this conclusion. The limitations of any such approach must be recognised, however, and largely stem from the implications of using proxies as an alternative to one's own forces. First, it can only be attempted if there is a local faction with some significant degree of military potential. Such a potential ally existed in

Afghanistan in 2001 but did not in Iraq in 2002-03, where the anti-Saddam opposition was weak and divided. Second, even if a potential ally does exist, its aims might not always overlap completely with one's own. The low-commitment option inevitably entails less say in the outcome than would be the case when ground forces are deployed. At best, this might involve only a partial achievement of the intervening state's own objectives; at worst it might tie it in to a group beyond its control, with potentially uncomfortable results. There might also be a risk that association with the US could cost the group concerned vital support within the state or the region. To turn to the case of Afghanistan once again, the US was not able to dictate when the United Front would begin its offensive, nor exactly where it would do so, nor delay its entry into Kabul, nor impose a particular government afterwards. The US administration was also embarrassed by allegations of human rights violations and war crimes committed by its allies. Finally, the age old problems of inadequate information, poor analysis and errors in practice would still apply here – even assuming that the local proxy possessed the level of technology needed to benefit from the information assistance the US was offering. The idea of using IW capabilities as a decisive 'force multiplier' for a favoured belligerent in a particular conflict therefore could have some utility, but its potential should not be exaggerated. If the means one is prepared to use are limited, then sometimes one must scale back one's aims accordingly.

A more ambitious version of information warfare at the military strategic level would not require the assistance of any local ally. Such ideas, which have also been referred to as 'cyber-war' or 'neocortical war',[18] have two main strands. The first is the use of offensive computer warfare, which envisages the use of government IW specialists (in effect, officially sanctioned hackers) to target key computer systems running critical infrastructure at the heart of the enemy, bringing to a halt his government, power generation and telecommunications systems, as well as industrial, financial and commercial networks (such as banking systems, chemical plants or air traffic control) and all kinds of military systems. This cyber-war would involve some or all of computer viruses and previously planted physical devices that would affect hardware and software, exotic weapons using electromagnetic pulses, microwaves or high energy radio frequencies, anti-satellite weapons, and, finally, conventional weapons directed against key targets. (Some analysts envisage a mixture of 'soft' weapons and more traditional ones, whereas others see such operations as being solely conducted using non-lethal means.) A successful attack of this sort would make any co-ordinated resistance impossible and would produce the results dreamed of by the most ambitious proponents of strategic bombing, but instantaneously and without any casualties among air crew or the civilian population of the opposing state. Moreover, once the enemy complied, his vital systems could be simply 'switched on' again, eliminating the need for costly and slow post-conflict reconstruction.

An additional strand of an Information War would involve waging a positive information campaign both against the opposing government, preventing it from putting over its views, and also against its population, manipulating what they see and hear. Some of the more ambitious thinkers even foresee the possibility of electronically taking over a rogue state's television and radio frequencies, and broadcasting fake messages purporting to come from national leaders but in fact crafted by experts in the intervening forces. The latter might be seen as a development of current practices of psychological warfare but raised by new technology to a far higher level. These two forms of IW could be used separately or together, and offer the tantalising prospect of rapid, low cost and clean victory. This would be a truly revolutionary development, claiming as it does to offer an alternative means of intervention that would not require the physical deployment of military forces.

However, there are a number of reasons to question whether this vision will ever quite be fulfilled. These doubts, of the sort that would be raised by the Sceptic school, apply regardless of technological improvements, as they are beyond the ability of technology to solve. First, information is not a physical, tangible resource such as fuel or ammunition that can be attacked directly; any targeting of information involves influencing the perceptions and judgements of a thinking opponent, and hence has an inherently indirect, psychological and subjective element (perhaps more comparable to targeting enemy morale than, for example, his oil industry – though even the latter can prove challenging). Such operations would require a very accurate and comprehensive understanding of the enemy. This in-depth familiarity would have to encompass all aspects of his politics, society, economy and military structures, from broad issues such as the cultural, historical and psychological background, the perceptions, aims, concerns and reaction to possible set backs of the government and also of various elements of the population (who could well start from a position of considerable suspicion or even hostility to the intervening powers, and who will also be swayed by competing messages), to very specific matters such as what systems and installations are critical to the adversary's economy or military. If the level of intelligence about the intended target fell below this very exacting requirement, which is far broader and deeper than might be assumed, there would be a risk of the attempted intervention either not having the intended effect or even of backfiring spectacularly. The pitfalls mentioned so far assume that the opponent was a state: it could, of course, be a non- or sub-state actor, in which case the intelligence required is likely to be all the harder to come by. Recent experience casts doubt on the achievability of the level of understanding of an opponent that would be called for. It could also be the case, of course, that the enemy would not be sufficiently sophisticated for computer attack to work: it has been suggested that this applied to the rump Yugoslavia at the time of the Kosovo campaign,[19] which is all the more striking given that many potential opponents would be still less advanced.

Second, such theories pay little attention to the possible reaction of the target. This could range from the collapse of the state concerned to retaliation in kind or escalation (discussed more below). This latter possibility is very real, given that unlike other more technologically and financially demanding elements of the RMA, many states (not least China) are putting considerable effort into developing capabilities for offensive computer warfare.[20] Another option for an opponent that was the target of such an attack would be to escalate the conflict – in this sense, a genuinely asymmetric response – either to conventional warfare against the perpetrating state, its allies or interests in the region, or even to a wider attack using weapons of mass destruction. Russia, for example, has stated quite explicitly that it might decline to treat a strategic information attack as a 'limited war' and would respond accordingly.

Third, and perhaps of even greater significance, proposals for strategic information warfare tend largely to neglect the political, ethical and legal context for such operations.[21] Considerations of this sort could at the very least impose significant constraints on such attacks or, at most, could rule them out. It might be thought unacceptable to use some techniques against a democratic government, for example, or to mislead one's own media, even if this only took the form of them picking up stories planted in the foreign press. Where physical destruction is used alongside electronic attacks, attacking civilian media outlets might be seen as unacceptable (for example, recall the criticism that NATO bombing of a Serb state television station attracted). It might not be deemed acceptable to attack 'dual use' systems that affect civilians as well as the government and armed forces of the target state. Similar criticisms have already been made about the 1991 attacks on power stations in Iraq (the same plants that powered the defence ministry also served hospitals and water purification systems). Moreover, attacking civilian targets in this way might be thought to set an undesirable precedent, not least in casting doubt on the definition of 'limited' war. There is some evidence that political considerations of this sort have already hindered the use of IW. *The Times* printed an article entitled 'Pentagon gets ready to wage a cyber-war': in fact, this title was a misleading choice by the sub-editor, because the piece stated that during the Kosovo campaign, the US 'considered an all-out cyber attack on Serb military targets and civilian services' but did not carry it out, on the advice of government lawyers who feared the legal and ethical implications.[22] The political problems would be all the more troubling if the government initiating a strategic information attack had to take into account the opinions and sensibilities of allied, friendly or regional states.

Finally, of course, the other side will itself be seeking to wage some sort of broad 'information warfare'. The experience of recent conflicts suggests that, to say the least, the Western states involved have not always enjoyed the best of the battle to influence opinion in the theatre, at home and in the international community more broadly. The very fact that Western intervention took place in Bosnia,

Kosovo or Afghanistan could be seen, at least in part, as 'information warfare' victories for the local factions who had sought external involvement. Within conflicts, Western governments have often had a torrid time with their media strategy. In large part these problems have been due to the relative openness of the states concerned, the fact that they are expected to provide a greater amount of more accurate information than undemocratic regimes, and also the higher ethical expectations that they have to meet. Whatever the cause of these difficulties, however, their frequency and effect suggest that the likely success of future IW campaigns will also be reduced. There could even be a dilemma in that the very military success of intervening forces, with or without the benefits of an RMA, could itself be 'spun' in such a way that it becomes another stick with which to beat the states concerned. Thus, the striking military successes in Iraq in 1991, Afghanistan in 2001 and in the initial military phase of Iraq in 2003, have all been portrayed by anti-Western elements as humiliations of Muslim states inflicted by aggressive neo-crusaders. It is not only the West that can wage information campaigns.

IW at the Tactical and Operational Levels

There are, then, many reasons to doubt that strategic information warfare will have the results that some of its proponents predict. Other analyses of the impact of information warfare are largely couched at the tactical and operational levels of strategy. The definition of IW in this sense would be actions taken to improve one's own information and to deny, degrade, disrupt and deceive that of the enemy, in the context of supporting broader military operations. Much of this area of the debate concerns areas that are beyond the scope of this book due to the technical detail involved or because of the classification of sources.

At first glance, the concept of 'information operations' appears to be more limited and plausible than the often rather sprawling 'Information Warfare' concept. In fact, however, it still covers a wide variety of activity, blending old and new, and is itself used inconsistently. The 1997 USAF definition of 'information operations' as 'actions taken to gain, exploit, defend or attack information and information systems' is notably broad and does not offer a very illuminating guide to what would actually be included or, even more, excluded by this definition.[23] Information operations can include military intelligence, psychological operations, command and control warfare, operational security, deception, electronic warfare, physical attack and computer network attack and defence. Some concepts falling into this category have long been recognised as important. It might be suspected that calling some of these activities 'information warfare' represents either imprecise useage of the term, or an attempt to lend them greater importance by attaching a fashionable label. Some writers seem to have overlooked the fact that gaining information and influencing the enemy's perception have a history as long as warfare; for others, use of the term 'IW' in this way is quite deliberate and is intended to emphasise precisely that this concept should include old familiar activities as well as more technologically glamorous ones. Many writers who include long-existing activities under the title of IW do so for a legitimate reason: while the task or role might have existed for hundreds of years, they would argue, the ability to perform it has recently undergone a vast improvement due to developments in technology. Thus, a series of related advances in information technology, sensors and weapons has created a truly new situation in, first, the technologically-driven leap forward in the ability to gather, process, distribute and use information; second, in the disparity that can be created between the belligerents' respective knowledge of the battlespace; and, third, in the concrete benefits that can be gained from this disparity. What is new, then, is not simply that information superiority is important but rather in the ability to gain this superiority, its extent and what can be done with it. The aims of information warfare are not new but the ability of modern forces armed with the appropriate technology to achieve these aims has been dramatically enhanced.

The 1990-91 Gulf War has propagated the concept of information warfare, just as it helped to popularise the broader notion of the RMA. Some of the discussion of so-called 'IW' in this conflict comes under the very broad category rejected above. Much, however, was of a more substantive character and does provide some evidence for those who see an important role for IW at the tactical and operational levels.[24] The disparity in the level of battlefield knowledge enjoyed by the two sides, and the practical effect of this gap when matched with an appropriate strategy, were clear. The strategy of the Coalition in the Gulf evidently attached great importance to gaining information superiority, including as priority targets for attack the Iraqi information gathering systems. Once the air campaign began, the Iraqi regime effectively became blind and deaf; the effect of this shortfall was magnified by Coalition deception efforts and psychological warfare. Conversely, the Coalition deployed a vast range of assets to gather information, ranging from the familiar (such as special forces, reconnaissance aircraft and various satellite-based intelligence gathering systems) to the more novel (notably the first widespread use by Western forces of unmanned aerial vehicles and also the JSTARS battlefield surveillance aircraft). The data gathered by these systems were assessed and distributed upwards to home governments and downwards to military units by a communications and computer network of unprecedented size and complexity, which had largely been improvised during the build-up phase.[25] The disparity in information allowed an operational approach (in the form of the wide sweep around the Iraq right flank) that relied on good information about Iraqi defences and also a significant degree of surprise, as well as allowing rapid and effective responses to such events as the Iraqi thrust towards Al-Khafji before the start of the ground campaign. As Chapter Three argued, the

Gulf War was exceptional in many ways and perhaps serves as a poor guide to the future. Yet, at the very least, it does demonstrate the possible impact of a significant information asymmetry in a conventional conflict.

Lest any reader be carried away by a heady impression of perfect information, it should be emphasised that there were many significant gaps or limitations in the 'battlespace awareness' enjoyed by the Coalition. First, the fact that the initial Iraqi invasion of Kuwait took the world by surprise offers a timely reminder that much remains opaque even in this so-called 'information age', not least the strategic intentions of potential enemies. A similarly cautionary tale is offered by Iraqi actions that caught the Coalition by surprise, including the attack on Al-Khafji and the scale and speed of the Iraqi withdrawal in the face of the ground offensive. Second, the air campaign suffered – as have all previous air campaigns – from inadequate information about the enemy war-making potential, industries, armed forces and, perhaps most of all, weapons of mass destruction programmes (which would presumably have been major target for Coalition intelligence efforts).[26] There were also numerous cases of faulty intelligence in the air campaign, notably the attack on the Al Firdos bunker: technical intelligence revealed that it was a communications centre but could not show that a large number of civilians were sheltering there. This was no minor incident and had significant effects at the strategic level, prompting the early ending of air attacks against the regime's administrative structures. More specifically, the whole of the aerial campaign against the Iraqi Scud missile launchers demonstrated the ability of a resourceful and mobile opponent to operate a key weapons system so as to elude detection even in the face of the Coalition's information superiority.[27] Third, the broader picture of military operations and engagements that emerges from memoirs and eye-witness accounts is not the smooth one that is suggested in some initial accounts in the news media and is very far away from complete knowledge of the battlespace. Those who emphasise the continuing importance, even with modern technology, of friction and 'fog of war' can find much evidence in the confusion and uncertainty that often prevailed, and resulted in several instances of 'friendly fire', as well as the misunderstanding between allied commanders and political leaders about whether 'the door was closed' when a halt was called to ground operations. Some other failures of information can be identified in the weeks and months after the end of Desert Storm, notably the belief that the Shias in the south and the Kurds in the north of the country had a good chance of toppling the regime, or indeed the prolonged difficulties encountered in unravelling the Iraqi WMD programmes, even with UN monitors on the ground. Finally, it should not be assumed that the advantages of the Gulf will be repeated in future: it is well known that the Coalition was heavily reliant on satellites for communication, intelligence and navigation. It could well be that the Gulf War was the last major conflict in which US use of satellites is totally unchallenged. As with sea power and air power, an opponent need not aim to eliminate all American satellites or seize control of space for itself but would rather seek to disrupt and degrade US use of its own satellites.

Some would react to these shortcomings by predicting that advancing technology will present solutions. An alternative, perhaps more healthy response would be to accept that such friction is likely to be an ever-present reality of warfare. Yet in spite of this, the Gulf War represented a striking operational success for the Coalition. A wider question, however, is the extent to which the Gulf conflict is a reliable model for the future. To assess this, other recent conflicts must also be considered. If 'information warfare' is to be accepted as a truly revolutionary development, then it cannot only be applicable to a single type of conflict. Indeed, its proponents claim that it is valuable right across the spectrum of operations. Yet in other recent interventions, the picture is much less encouraging than even the Gulf War for proponents of IW. Experiences in Bosnia, Somalia, Rwanda, Kosovo, Afghanistan and Iraq in 2003 draw attention to the fact that the Gulf conflict was unusual precisely because it was such a familiar and simple scenario, a conventional inter-state war. The enemy was known, easily identified and took the form of a state with the full range of potential vulnerabilities and weaknesses that this implies, including regular armed forces pursuing a conventional strategy. This contrasted strongly with the situation in the other conflicts, which were mainly intra-state, in which the enemy was often ambiguous and changing, while enemy forces tended to be irregular or militias and offered none of the easily targetable weaknesses presented by the Iraqi armed forces. When these detailed problems were combined with wider disagreements in the international community about desired end-states and the objectives of interventions, the result was a conflict in which IW could not prove a decisive force multiplier. Even complete 'information dominance' could not have fully compensated for the disadvantages and difficulties stemming from the fundamental lack of political consensus in the international community and the inherent complexity of the strategic situation.

In each of these conflicts there were important areas of uncertainty and insufficient information, both broadly about the region and the conflict and also more narrowly at the tactical level. Many high-technology systems were deployed, not least the well publicised and extensive use of unmanned aerial vehicles. Yet there were still conspicuous failures of information. In Somalia, for example, the problem emerged of insufficient specialists on the country – which was understandable given that neither Somalia nor the wider region had ever been priorities for intelligence or analysis. This gap in comprehension of local cultural factors and perceptions made it terribly difficult to devise appropriate information policies or psychological operations, and had serious consequences with the now notorious 'Black Hawk down' raid, which was apparently launched on the rash assumption that local people in the targeted neighbourhood would not oppose the US operation.[28] In Bosnia there was often uncertainty about how local factions would behave from day-to-day (this would often be what the intelligence community refers to as a mystery rather than a secret, because the factions themselves might not know how they were going to be behaving a few days hence); 'consent' could be present one day and absent the next. Many attacks were carried out on civilians without it being clear who had conducted them. It was also difficult to gather information on local forces since they tended to be light and mobile. These were all cases were analysis – turning information into intelligence or knowledge – proved difficult. There were also cases where the information itself was hard to come by: in spite of the much vaunted American 'information umbrella', the US failed to locate Aideed in Somalia or Bin Laden in Afghanistan, and even in the 1991 Gulf War, Saddam Hussein's location could not be pinned down sufficiently closely for an attack; he proved equally elusive in the 2003 Iraq campaign and for some time afterwards. In the case of Kosovo, initial NATO claims to have destroyed 200 Serb tanks were swiftly reduced to no more than a dozen in the aftermath of the conflict – and major platforms such as tanks are precisely what information warriors would be most confident about locating. There was also the celebrated incident of the bombing of the Chinese Embassy, which was a truly stunning intelligence failure. It was hard for some – not least the Chinese government – to believe that such an incident could happen by mistake when the US had at its disposal such a wide and high-tech array of intelligence assets. For those of a more cynical turn of mind, who tend to suspect blunders rather than conspiracy, it rather demonstrated the continuing shortfalls in information gathering and the eternal problem of human error. Much the same could be said about other examples of air strikes hitting trains or trucks that were carrying refugees and not, as believed, enemy troops. These were information failures that had significant political implications but there was a broader, and far more significant information error in the Kosovo campaign: the assumption that Milosevic and Serbia would back down after a few days of bombing. The perceptions and intentions of the Serbian leadership were more factors in the category of mystery rather than secret and it is hard to see how any information system could have revealed them. What was far less understandable was basing an entire strategy on a single assumption, apparently without any 'Plan B' in case it should prove unfounded. Information superiority is of little use unless combined with an appropriate policy and strategy.

Weaknesses and problems

There are numerous weaknesses in accounts of IW, not least a tendency to overlook the continuing likelihood of imperfect information and the related danger of exaggerating expectations about the level of information that can realistically be provided. This could create a risk of personnel in a confusing situation putting off decisions while waiting for the reliable information they have been trained to expect. Recent operational experience suggests that there are still many factors that can erode certainty and chip away at the aspiration to achieve complete battlespace awareness. The hope of IW enthusiasts is that shortcomings can be eliminated by technology or organisation but such a view seems to be excessively ambitious.

Mechanical failure and human error will never be entirely eliminated. Moreover, the defining characteristic of strategy is that it involves a thinking, reacting opponent who will be actively seeking to disrupt, deceive and confuse your information systems while trying to uncover the information that he needs. As Thomas puts it, 'even without information superiority, a thinking opponent can take actions that must be countered'.[29] The 1990s saw both Iraq and Serbia, though technologically far inferior, make extremely effective use of decoys, camouflage and deception in ways that caused serious difficulties for intervening Western forces. They were also able to work around Western attempts to cut off their communications, using civilian systems and mobile telephones. It can be assumed that the other side will be actively seeking to mislead you and to take advantage of the omnipresent media: the icon on your screen could be a military unit that is close to a hospital, orphanage or mosque, or could even be the building itself if the opponent is more technologically gifted. Even if the icon does accurately represent the enemy unit it purports to, some areas of doubt and uncertainty will remain, including the extent to which that old tank has been up-graded with sensors, fire control and passive defence systems that might be better than yours, let alone the state of training and morale of those manning it, or the intentions of its commanders. The known Western dependence on satellites would make them a tempting target; although anti-satellite weapons systems would be technologically demanding, it would be complacent to assume invulnerability. Besides, more technologically accessible approaches such as jamming are already available. As with previous experiences of warfare at sea and in the air, the opponent would not be seeking to gain control for himself but rather to deny the Western states the unhindered use of the medium that their strategy demands.

Enemy action could extend considerably further. The more effective our information system, the greater potential harm could be caused by any successful attempt to hack into it and either steal information or implant misleading data. As Harknett and his co-writers argue, the information net must be widely accessible to be useful but it then presents numerous vulnerable points: 'Each access point into the system of systems will be a potential Achilles heel in need of protection.' They also note that any measures taken to prevent access or reduce its impact should it occur will diminish the promised benefits of the system.[30] Further, any individual who assisted the enemy against his own side – and historically there have been plenty of people prepared to do so, for reasons of ideology, revenge or financial gain – could, by facilitating access to the system, do far greater harm than has previously been possible. The effects of any such penetration could be extremely serious, since the opponent would gain knowledge of the location of all of your units as well as being able to introduce false information. A single example of an information network having presented misleading or 'spoofed' information that led to a major case of collateral damage or 'friendly fire' incident could have a debilitating subsequent effect, since no data could be trusted and a shadow of doubt would hang over any information provided by the system thereafter. The very features of the system that make it useful would also greatly speed up the transmission of accidentally false or deliberately deceptive information, as well as greatly increasing the harm caused should a hostile party gain access to the system.

The consequences of failures of information are greater than ever before, given both the accuracy and destructive power of modern weapons: a Second World War tank firing on a friendly tank had a far lower chance of inflicting casualties than its modern counter-part. The point is illustrated by the comment from a USAF officer, cited by Campen, saying, 'A lethality system appears to exist that can provide continuous, instant almost 100% probability of kill for anything that moves.'[31] This begs the question of whether the moving object is really something that you want to 'kill', or rather an airliner, a lorry full of refugees or a car carrying journalists or doctors. Moreover, the high level of expectations surrounding the effectiveness of modern weapons means that any failure threatens to have all the more political impact.

A further risk is that even a successful IW campaign risks falling prey to the law of unintended consequences. Destroying or isolating an opponent's command and control systems will not necessarily prevent his forces from resisting; rather, it could lead to them fighting on, though in a less commanded and controlled way. This might make them combat ineffective but, alternatively, it could make them a tougher opponent. An enemy having asymmetry thrust upon him in this way would not necessarily be wholly to our advantage.

The other problem, more often recognised in the literature, is that of information overload. Signals intelligence gathering systems already hoover up far more information than can be analysed and assessed, and it is reasonable to suspect that a similar problem could apply to battlefield information in the future. A mass of data is not the same thing as practical and usable knowledge; merely entering a library does not make anyone educated. Another appropriate parallel lies on the internet which contains a great deal of useful information that is so swamped in trivia and junk that an inordinate amount of time is needed to find what you are looking for – and even more if you do not know precisely what you are seeking. The difficulty of filtering information and its implications are major problems that are often overlooked. One exception is a British Army officer who notes that it could produce an excess of information that leads to command paralysis, reducing initiative and risk-taking as commanders become too reliant on the flow of data or await 'full' information.[32] He concludes that overall the improvement of situation awareness will have a positive effect, yet his recognition of the possible pitfalls is encouraging. Some accounts seem to assume that gathering information is enough, overlooking the other crucial links in the chain, which include interpretation, assessment, understanding and, most important of all, reaching an appropriate decision on what action to take. Two examples suffice to make the point. First, the massing of Iraqi troops on the Kuwaiti border in July 1990 was spotted by US surveillance systems but this information did not lead to the conclusion that invasion was imminent, even though the US government consulted regional allies who were, presumably, better informed than it was. Second, the 1998 Indian nuclear test came as a surprise to the US government, even though such an event was an enormous undertaking and an issue that would, presumably, be a high priority for Western intelligence services. These cases are not cited as criticisms of intelligence agencies but as counter-examples to the view that information, let alone knowledge, will ever be perfect. Precision strike allows US forces (and to a lesser extent those of some of its allies) to hit any target: but knowing which targets to hit, what effect it could have militarily and, even more so, politically are far more difficult matters. A safe prediction might be that in future conflicts, Western commanders will not complain of having insufficient information. Rather they will suffer from having too much information in general and, simultaneously, not enough of the right information. New information technology might simply have the effect of making us aware far more rapidly than in any previous conflict of just how much we do not know.

A further problem would be senior commanders or political leaders believing that they have better information or knowledge about the situation of subordinate units than is actually the case, and hence meddling in what is the proper area of individuals lower down the chain of command. There have already been indications of US theatre and unit commanders chafing at 'interference' from superiors believing themselves to have better information than they actually possessed.[33] This tendency is all the more problematic since, it is generally accepted, the RMA requires more flexibility, initiative and responsibility being delegated to junior commanders. Their military and political superiors might well be required to display considerable self discipline, not least because of their own consciousness of the relentless media spotlight upon them. Disputes between the solider on the ground and those higher up and further back are another age-old feature of warfare that the RMA threatens to exacerbate.

The literature features an additional weakness in a tendency to overlook the potential use of modern information systems by the other side. Modern military technology (and even more, technology with a dual military and civilian use) is proliferating at an increasing rate and is well beyond the control of any single state or even any group of states. The availability to any state or non-state actor with a relatively modest budget of UAVs, commercial satellite imagery or even its own satellites, various sophisticated C4ISR or electronic warfare systems, GPS receivers, cellular telephones, the internet, as well as the international media (which is probably a more accurate and faster source of information than most of the world's intelligence services) could act as something of a leveller. Dunlap suggests that in a future conflict the situation could be one of 'information equality' rather than 'information dominance.'[34] Denying an opponent such sources of information in time of conflict would be fraught with practical, legal and political difficulties. It could well be that weaker powers will be able to achieve their own tolerably effective information capability rather more easily than hitherto. Further, it should not be assumed that all opponents will require the same level of information as high-technology Western forces: guerrilla or irregular forces have often proved capable of tailoring information gathering to their needs.

Perfect information is unattainable for a host of reasons, including complex and constantly changing situations, the time-lag between the collection of data and the delivery of a usable product to those who need it (which can be reduced but not eliminated), mechanical and human failings, and the simple fact that some issues are matters of interpretation not discernible by intelligence gathering systems. As an analogy, if someone is intending to place a bet on a football match or a horse race, whether data about recent performances and current conditions are sought from the most visually dazzling and up-to-date internet source or a crumpled newspaper, there is still a need to use intuition and judgement in assessing the information to formulate a conclusion regarding which participant to back. Crucially, information gathering systems cannot read minds and can at best provide nothing more than clues to intentions, perceptions and motivations. Moreover, it will not always be clear which information is unreliable and which is definitely true.[35] There is a danger that personnel could come to assume that icons on an electronic display are reality rather than partial representations of what is believed about reality, which may or may not be accurate. Some writers explicitly state that current and emerging technology will eliminate the fog of war and friction. Followers of Clausewitz would insist that his approach still applies; you will never eliminate uncertainty, so you must rather train officers to expect it and to have the mental agility to cope with it better than their adversaries. Proponents of IW will dismiss these objections, insisting that they are aware of the unattainability of perfect knowledge and that they are simply predicting an increasingly decisive disparity. Yet the claims made by many Information Warriors do seem to require that uncertainty will all but disappear. Should it survive, a great deal of the conceptual edifice they have constructed will prove to have distinctly shaky foundations. The shortcomings described above are much more than just a matter of detail. They suggest that information as an independent means of warfare is likely to be an enabler for other forms of power, not a replacement. One feature of Information Warfare applies at all levels of strategy: information alone is impotent without understanding, judgement and the right policy decisions.

IW as a Threat to the West

So far this chapter has examined information warfare as a potential tool that the West can utilise, though also recognising that an opponent could both frustrate Western IW and put together an information system for his own use in any conflict. The 'Pessimist' school would warn that IW could equally provide an appealing asymmetric response to Western conventional military superiority, either at the operational or the strategic level, by providing a new means of direct attack against governmental, public utility, economic or commercial targets on which advanced industrial states depend. In such a case, it might not always be obvious that an attack had occurred – problems might simply be attributed to bad luck or gremlins in the system – let alone who had perpetrated it. The Pessimists would further emphasise that the developments in IT that give rise to new means of attack have also created faster ways of disseminating new technology; a host of programmes to assist hackers is freely available on the internet, while advanced computer programming and software industries exist in many non-Western states. There is therefore a fear that IW capabilities and concepts could rapidly spread to hostile actors who might be less constrained by ethical concerns about their use and who might see them as particularly attractive against a West that is both peculiarly vulnerable to such an attack and also effectively invincible in conventional warfare.

Such attacks on the West could be perpetrated either by individuals or by hostile states. Modern IT increases the ability of individuals to be mischievous, a costly nuisance, or even a menace – some computer viruses have inflicted very significant financial costs on companies and governments – but it is not clear that they represent a genuine military threat or that the term 'information warfare' is properly applied to them. The sporadic activities of such individual hackers might plausibly be seen as vandalism similar to graffiti or as theft, possibly as commercial or political espionage, or even as a domestic security problem rather than as a military attack. As such, the appropriate responses would be mainly by individual companies, local government, the police and security services rather than the armed forces.

More worrying would be the activities of individuals or organisations that actively sought to attack the institutions of a state or society in a more systematic way or with a more purposeful political or military objective. There is clearly potential, for example, for significant costs being imposed by attacks on companies or government databases, or significant harm or disruption being caused by interference with air traffic control systems or power plants. Such attacks could be carried out as one-off strikes comparable to terrorist attacks, or as one asymmetric element of a broader onslaught that occurred in the context of a regional crisis or conflict in which the West was involved.[36] The vulnerability of Western states to computer hacking is sometimes over-stated. The computer systems of a modern developed economy tend to be decentralised and have multiple redundancy, and there is no shortage of IT security experts pointing out weaknesses and making a good living in doing so (the reaction to the 'Y2K' problem being a case in point, although the process of examining potential vulnerabilities might have been valuable in itself). Many separate systems would have to be attacked to bring to a halt an entire sector of the economy. Whilst there may well be vulnerable nodes that would have broad effects if brought down, it might be more difficult than is sometimes suggested to inflict by computer attack truly devastating strategic damage on a state, as opposed to mere disruption or nuisance. However, it is reasonable to suggest that a concerted effort to attack a number of key systems simultaneously could well bring about significant results, especially if it was directed against a combination of military and non-military systems.

It could be objected that a widespread and serious attack has not yet occurred, so the proclaimed 'threat' must be exaggerated. This conclusion might be a little complacent. If a hostile state were planning such an assault, it might be expected not to launch it unless and until there was some strategic purpose in doing so, notably in the context of a regional conflict, such as distracting the US or hindering its response to a regional crisis. In recent years, US military specialists playing the 'red team' in exercises have broken into important computer systems and even disrupted the activities of major US military commands. There have also been innumerable reported cases of hackers successfully breaking into US government computers, including some at the Pentagon, several of which have been traced to foreign government agencies. The fact that fewer stories about similar penetrations of UK government systems have appeared in the press might be because British institutions are a less attractive target than those of the US and hence less frequently targeted, because British targets are better protected or, more likely, simply because the UK government tends to be more reticent about informing the press when it happens. Various commissions on protection of critical infrastructure have been set up in the United States, to identify and mitigate potential vulnerabilities, though doing so is complicated by the fact that many key systems are outside the control of federal or state governments. There have not been similarly well publicised moves in the UK, though, again, whether this is because they do not exist or rather simply because they have not been publicised is hard to judge.

One interesting possibility is that computer hacking could introduce a new form of low intensity conflict that changes the familiar calculation of power among states, given the ease with which it can be conducted by individuals or non-state actors operating either genuinely alone or as a modern-day form of privateer, or state organisations acting under the cover of 'plausible deniability'. There have already been several cases of international tension or crises (such as between India and Pakistan, China and Taiwan, or Israel and the Palestinians) being accompanied by computer hacking.[37] Clearly there is a danger of escalation to conventional conflict if serious damage is inflicted, whether by accident or design, or if mutual retaliation spirals out of control. What if, for instance, a state should interpret glitches in intelligence gathering or military communications systems as a deliberate precursor to a pre-emptive attack? In a crisis, the knowledge or even strong suspicion that a neighbouring state has offensive computer warfare capabilities might well result in over-reaction to the activities of patriotic hackers operating on their own initiative. As such, hacking could become a cause of old-fashioned warfare as well as a new covert means of waging war. For the same reasons, computer network attack might also prove more dangerous and escalatory than some of its proponents hope, due to the uncertainty of the effects of any campaign and the unpredictability of the victim's reaction.[38]

The suggestion that computer warfare would amount to a cleaner, more surgical form of warfare is open to question. Once again, a parallel with air power theories seems relevant: Douhet believed that air power would lead to a more humane form of war, since any state that conceded command of the air would inevitably and immediately surrender, thus making extensive bombing of his cities unnecessary.[39] Subsequent events, of course, proved him rather too optimistic. For the Pessimist, another prophetic writer offers a more useful parallel for the potential impact of computer warfare. H.G. Wells wrote an account of air warfare that predicted that since it would be impossible entirely to eliminate an enemy's air force, war would become endemic and society would collapse.[40]

Both the academic literature and the more popular media tend to feature far more pieces worrying about an 'electronic Pearl Harbor' than articles downplaying or dismissing the potential danger. While this fact might suggest that there is little danger of complacency, the threat of computer network attack is a difficult one to meet because it demands attention from so many organisations, both inside and outside government. Perhaps counter-terrorism provides a better parallel than conventional military operations, since military institutions have a relatively small role in countering the threat. The question remains of whether this form of IW is an additional, possibly serious, impediment that will be added to the existing complications that bedevil foreign and defence policy, or whether it represents an entirely new form of warfare. While some of the rather breathless suggestions about the possible implications of this development seem somewhat far-fetched, there have been enough publicly reported examples of individuals creating computer viruses that bring much of the internet to a temporary standstill, or hacking into sensitive computer systems, to suggest that there is some substance here. Yet whilst this development certainly promises to make life more difficult for a number of organisations, whether it amounts to a genuine RMA in its own right is highly doubtful.

The Air Power Parallel Re-visited

This chapter has drawn several comparisons between interpretations of the impact of air power and views on the possible implications of information warfare. Another parallel that might be even more apt than air power as a comparison for IW, is electronic warfare. This is an area of activity that permeates modern armed forces and warfare at all levels and in all types of conflict. A significant superiority is difficult to achieve – electronic warfare is a continuous process of fix and counter-fix – but carries enormous advantages, even if only temporary, and can dramatically improve effectiveness while reducing losses. Its impact is perhaps enough for it to be considered a new dimension of warfare, which is fundamentally integrated into all types of military units, but it is mainly an enabler, a force multiplier and a basic element of a modern unit or platform, and only to a limited extent a separate or self-contained form of warfare in its own right. Hence, while there are some national assets and also many units and platforms in each of the armed services that are dedicated solely to electronic warfare, all units must pay attention to it since it is so fundamental a part of the environment within which they operate. The eventual impact of information warfare could well prove to be comparable.

There are other, more detailed lessons from the debate about and experience of the introduction of air power that might hold some relevance for discussions about IW. First, proponents were tempted to make bold and exaggerated claims, either to overcome scepticism or to spur cumbersome bureaucracies into action. Second, those who questioned the more dramatic claims tended to be dismissed as hidebound conservatives and thoughtless reactionaries (when there were often respectable reasons for doubting some of the extreme predictions) or as vested interests (when there were institutional, professional and financial interests on both sides). Third, the full use of air power was very much a tool of total war: in practice, and in many of the conflicts faced since 1945, there have been significant political, legal and ethical constraints on what air power has been permitted to do, which has reduced its theoretical impact. Fourth, in both total and limited wars, the fragility of civilian targets (people, governments, industries and vital services) was much exaggerated. In practice they have been more resilient than was expected, and promised effects were slower to emerge. Finally, air power among other factors did help to restrict the number of states that could be classed as first-rank military powers but it also led to some useful capabilities for weaker states, which have at times resulted in the ability to deny their opponents complete freedom to use the air or at least raised the threshold of intervention against them in terms of scale of effort and potential cost. Whether air power represented rapid evolution, one contributing element of a wider RMA, or an RMA in its own right depends fundamentally on the definitions used.

Conclusion

While there is some value in the Information Warfare debate, there is perhaps somewhat less to it than at first meets the eye. Much of what is written is exaggerated and misleading. Some of the substance lies in references to activities that armed forces and governments have been performing for generations. Here, the debate is useful in drawing attention to some of the requirements for successful operations but is misleading if it is understood to mean that what is called IW is either completely new or a single phenomenon. In these cases, the label would be useful if it facilitated thorough consideration of the whole breadth of tasks that might be referred to as 'information warfare', alongside the other elements of planning military operations.

The term 'information warfare' is sometimes used less to advocate new technology than to suggest a broader and more thoughtful approach to strategy, which devotes systematic attention to how an opponent might be influenced.[41] Such a way of thinking – if it allowed the use of force to be made more effective, brought it into closer harmony with other policy means and set it in the broad political context – would represent a considerable advance even if no great leap in technology was involved.

There can be no doubt that gathering, assessing and exploiting information are extremely important in any conflict. Equally, there can be no doubt that a significant disparity in the information possessed by opposing forces could well have a decisive effect on the outcome of a conflict. These evident facts, however, are hardly new. It is true that the means of performing these tasks have improved, but the friction, uncertainty and fog of war that characterise warfare, whether conventional or 'non-warfighting operations' are still significant impediments. There is a danger that the term 'information warfare' as many analysts use it risks over-estimating the quality of information that will be enjoyed in a conflict and the advantages that it will confer.

Thus it is said that one who knows the enemy and knows himself will not be endangered in a hundred engagements. One who does not know the enemy but knows himself will sometimes be victorious, sometimes meet with defeat. One who knows neither the enemy nor himself will invariably be defeated in every engagement.[42]

Many intelligence reports in war are contradictory; even more are false, and most are uncertain. What one can reasonably ask of an officer is that he should possess a standard of judgement, which he can gain only from knowledge of men and affairs and from common sense. He should be guided by the laws of probability. These are difficult enough to apply when plans are drafted in an office, far from the sphere of action; the task becomes infinitely harder in the thick of fighting itself, with reports streaming in.[43]

Enthusiasts for information warfare frequently cite Sun Tzu, not least the first passage quoted above. There is a great deal in Sun Tzu that is worth reading and contemplating but there is a tendency to over-idealise it and to treat it as a source of arcane wisdom that might reveal an easy, bloodless answer to the problems of warfare. The writer or writers of *The Art of War* were well aware of the importance of gaining information, of deceiving the enemy and of using knowledge of the battlefield to frustrate his plans. Yet the book's eager embrace of such activities at times approaches an implication that actual violence can be thus avoided or, at least, minimised (though this element was more aspiration than reality in ancient China). It is understandable that many contemporary analysts are seduced by the possibility of a cleaner, low cost means of assuring victory, which they believe they have found in information warfare. They could find reasons for caution in the words of Clausewitz, cited in the second quotation above. He was well aware of the practical limitations and shortcomings of information in war time and would have been very sceptical of claims that perfect information is achievable or that 'dominant battlespace awareness' can confer the advantages that its proponents expect: 'The good general must know friction in order to overcome it wherever possible, and in order not to expect a standard of achievement in his operations which this very friction makes impossible.'[44] He also doubted that violence could be eliminated from warfare. Reacting against an earlier generation of strategists who had sought to remove combat from theories of warfare, Clausewitz argued that while deterrent deployments, effective marches and manoeuvre were important, battle itself still had a fundamental place in warfare. He likened its role to that of cash settlement in business, where there might be credit and bartering but at the end of the day, there had to be a tangible sum of money involved. War, he believed, was a social and political activity, but was distinguished from other such activities by combat and violence.[45] Clausewitz also gave a central place in his theory to friction, chance and the human factor. He appreciated that warfare always involves many elements that are inherently non-linear and chaotic, which defy full comprehension, let alone predictability or control.

This chapter has looked at the possibilities of information warfare at various levels of strategy. At all levels, proponents of IW tend to exaggerate the quality of information that will be available, as well as neglecting the distinctions between data, information, knowledge, analysis and understanding, let alone wisdom and judgement in determining an appropriate and effective course of action. RMA devotees tend to emphasise the ability to see the battlefield but, as Sherlock Holmes often explained to Dr Watson, seeing alone is not enough:

'I can see nothing,' said I, handing it back to my friend.

'On the contrary, Watson, you can see everything. You fail, however, to reason from what you see.'[46]

Truly strategic versions of information warfare – that is, suggestions that it could be an alternative to physical deployment of armed forces – are not convincing, precisely because the various shortcomings discussed above add up to a significant gap between aspiration and reality. This is not to argue that attempts to influence the perceptions and opinions of others are unimportant but simply to deny that they will ever replace the use of harder forms of power. IW does not appear to be creating an RMA as the 'Visionary' school would define it.

Conceptions of IW at the operational and tactical levels are more convincing, although here too, the continuing impact of friction and the fog of war is likely to disappoint many IW enthusiasts. As the previous chapter argued, significant improvements in the ability of armed forces to use information are, together with other developments, having a transforming effect on military capabilities and on warfare more broadly. Yet using the term 'information warfare' for this phenomenon may be misleading. Many of the activities that are covered by the term are becoming increasingly important, including some recent developments such as attempts to attack and defend computer networks. Nevertheless, they are being added to existing forces and practices, merging with them and forcing them to evolve, not threatening to replace them. Information warfare looks no more likely to create by itself an entirely new paradigm of warfare than air power did.

Chapter 6
The RMA and the Spectrum of Conflict

How well does the Revolution in Military Affairs 'fit' the various forms of conflict that are likely to be faced in the near future? Do the various predicted capabilities and concepts apply equally, if at all, across various types of conflict? If not, do the developments truly amount to a 'revolution'? The main reason for posing these questions is that many analysts concentrate on military capabilities more than, or in some cases to the exclusion of, the international strategic context for their use. To use an analogy from economics, such approaches stress the 'supply' side of changing technology, military doctrine and organisation rather than the 'demand' side relating to the nature of contemporary conflicts. Both sides of the equation must be understood if we are to derive an accurate understanding of the utility of emerging military capabilities.

Assessing the alleged RMA would have been challenging even if the Cold War had continued. As it is, however, the debate must take place against the complicated background of a rapidly changing strategic context. Threats and problems have diversified, and new and more challenging forms of conflict have either emerged or, where they have been around for some time, have become more prominent. A great deal of the literature about the RMA appears at times to be seeking higher-tech means of defeating a Soviet armoured push across Western Europe or, in the case of the slightly more progressive writers, more efficient ways of winning Desert Storm. This form of conflict, however, will not be the only one that the Western states have to face and is unlikely even to be the most common. Many accounts either ignore other types of conflict or too easily assume that emerging technologies will apply to them to the same extent and in the same ways as they will to conventional warfare. These are assumptions that need challenging and exploring.

The Spectrum of Conflict

It is generally accepted that there is a broad spectrum of military operations from the highest intensity combat operations at one end to routine presence at the other. Yet many analysts of the RMA do not fully take account of the implications of this observation. There is a marked tendency in the literature to concentrate on the top end of the spectrum, emphasising high-intensity, high-tempo warfighting. Most accounts of RMA capabilities and their effect on warfare make no systematic attempt to examine underlying assumptions about the varieties of conflict that the new forces will face. They tend, usually implicitly but often explicitly, to be directed against a late twentieth century regular army conducting conventional operations. Other forms of warfare are overlooked, which is a serious omission, not least because of the neglect of recent operational experience that it involves.

The tendency to lean towards high-end operations is understandable. First, many of the technologies and ideas that form the heart of the current debate had their origins during the Cold War period. They were directed against what was then, quite naturally, the main preoccupation: mass Soviet heavy armour, air power and the vast support and supply network behind it. Second, the 1990-91 Gulf conflict occurred at a formative time for the RMA debate and provided an ideal showcase for many of the technological capabilities that were then emerging and for ideas about how to use them. It ensured that high intensity operations remained at centre stage for defence planners, particularly in the United States. Finally, high-intensity warfighting is the most demanding and generally the most important task that a state's armed forces face, so it naturally tends to be their principal focus. It also happens to be the just the sort of operation for which the capabilities of the purported RMA are most relevant.

However, concentrating too much attention on this form of warfare, to the exclusion of all others, would be a mistake. Even during the Cold War, let alone the period before 1939, the main Western militaries faced a great number of lower intensity conflicts and had to develop a competence for them.[1] Any analysis of warfare that omits them thus represents a misunderstanding of recent history as well as of the present; the fact that they are now more prevalent and more obvious does not mean that they are a new phenomenon, as in fact the majority of conflicts have long been within rather than between states. In the post-Cold War era, the likelihood of high-intensity warfare is less than before, though such conflicts are still likely to occur. They are certainly not the only form of conflict that will be faced, however, nor even the most likely. There is therefore a potential risk of a mis-match between the types of operation that will need to be conducted and the military capabilities that are emerging.

This argument should not be misunderstood as suggesting either that high-intensity conflict will not happen or that it is not an important eventuality to prepare for. Some authors do believe that 'traditional' state-against-state warfare is declining, and with it much of the Clausewitzian paradigm that has been dominant for the last few centuries.[2] Their argument is that intra-state conflict is the pattern of the future, with wars between nation-states (an entity that some of these thinkers believe is itself on the way out) fading away. This argument is not wholly convincing. It is true that intra-state conflicts have become relatively more prevalent than inter-state warfare, both in that more are occurring and also that more attention is devoted to them due to the demise of the Cold War. It does not follow, however, that they are replacing inter-state conflict. There have been many conflicts between states in recent years and there is no reason to predict that this will change in the near future. The truth is probably quite the reverse. Many regions of the world contain a host of actual or potential disputes over issues that have traditionally caused conflicts between states, notably clashes over resources (water being a prime example for the future, in addition to more traditional raw materials), territory, sea communications, religion, ethno-nationalism and ideology, as well as classical motivations such as a desire to dominate or fear of an increasingly powerful neighbour.[3] The list of possible triggers for conflict has lengthened with the addition of humanitarian issues and concern over weapons of mass destruction. These potential causes of conflict exist against a background of many states simultaneously becoming more nationalist and more insistent on defending their interests, and also becoming wealthier, turning much of this wealth towards armaments – which international arms markets are happy to provide. The combination of an increasing number of states with a growing ability to pursue what they define as their interests, with a large and varied set of issues that could cause conflict, suggests that obituaries of state-against-state warfare are sadly premature. It is true that intra-state conflict and non-state threats have become more prominent, for the major Western powers at least,[4] but they have been added to inter-state conflicts rather than replacing them. Those who argue the contrary are guilty of extrapolating the experience of North America and Western Europe to other parts of the world to which it simply does not apply. The NATO states now generally face what have been called 'wars of choice' as opposed to 'wars of survival'. Yet just because they are in the happy situation of no longer facing major, direct threats to their territory from other states does not mean that this is also the case everywhere else in the world. The list of unpredicted wars that have broken out between states over the past 20 or 30 years demonstrates the foolishness of assuming that such conflicts will not continue to be a feature of what is generally recognised as an unstable and dynamic international system. Those who dismiss out of hand the prospect of state-against-state conflict are just as guilty of failing to recognise the breadth and diversity of contemporary conflict as those who focus their attention solely on conventional inter-state warfare.

Even if the major Western powers face a much diminished direct threat to their territory from other states, it does not follow that they can afford to ignore high-intensity conventional warfare. First, experience of peaceful periods in the past, such as the late nineteenth century, or the 1920s and the early 1930s in Europe, suggests that the current absence of a clear state-based threat cannot be assumed to last. In both cases, complacency about continuing peace proved damaging when the international system abruptly took a turn for the worse – and it is worth noting that in both periods, there was no shortage of thinkers proclaiming that major conflict between the great powers was a thing of the past.[5] Allowing the ability to fight wars to wither would be difficult if not impossible to reverse quickly and would represent an enormous gamble, not least at a time of considerable change and instability in the international system. Further, even if no such conflict occurs over the next decade or so, it would not follow that investment in capabilities for it had been wasted, since some level of insurance is prudent and deterring such conflicts is preferable to fighting them.

Second, the idea that the West need pay no attention to wars in locations that are not contiguous to its own territory seems curiously old-fashioned in a time of 'globalisation'. It is generally recognised that these states have vital security interests, as well as humanitarian concerns, in various parts of the world that might well see inter-state warfare. Indeed, the term 'overseas' is itself rather misleading since such conflicts cannot be excluded in Europe itself, as well as in adjacent areas in North Africa and the eastern Mediterranean. Some of these conflicts, and others further afield, could plausibly spawn problems with security implications for Western states, or for their economic interests and nationals abroad. They could even lead to direct threats to home territories, albeit on a far smaller scale than the potential threat represented by the USSR. In the absence of a seismic shift in how the Western states define their security, they will need to retain the ability to conduct high intensity operations in regional conflicts in various parts of the world.

Third, it would be deeply misleading to suggest that 'intra-state' and 'low intensity' are synonymous, or that 'low intensity' and 'non-combat' operations are the same. An intra-state conflict could well include belligerents with considerable conventional forces and even an operation that is broadly characterised as 'low intensity' will often have higher intensity episodes.[6] Any intervention in such a conflict could therefore require warfighting capabilities, as was demonstrated in the various conflicts in the former Yugoslavia, where peacekeeping operations, let alone peace enforcement, required assets such as heavy armour and sophisticated combat air power. The suggestion that Britain could abandon warfighting capabilities to concentrate solely on peacekeeping was considered and roundly rejected during the 1997-98 Strategic Defence Review. This conclusion rested largely on the realisation that preparations for the most demanding operations make possible the conduct of non-warfighting operations (albeit that the latter also require specific, additional skills), while the converse is untrue.[7] The issue of similarities and differences between warfighting and other operations is considered at greater length below.

Any taxonomy of different types of conflict that seeks to establish an order of intensity will inevitably be contentious for what it includes, the order in which they are placed and what it omits. Classifying conflicts into different types is something of a terminological minefield, as there can be some blurring at the edges of the categories, individual conflicts might fit into different categories during different stages, and some operations would be difficult to fit into it at all. Nevertheless, a rough scale would place a major nuclear exchange at the highest intensity end. The highest intensity conflict after that would be general war with a major power; after that would come major and minor regional conflicts respectively. Moving towards the lower-intensity end of the scale (though bearing in mind the provisos made above) would be peace enforcement, one-off air or missile strikes, peacekeeping, non-combatant evacuations, humanitarian assistance, routine presence and constabulary tasks. The details of what is included and where it is placed is less significant than the broader point that future military operations will be varied, forming a broad spectrum of conflict types and intensities, involving many different sorts of opponent.

Accepting that there is this sort of breadth of conflict types is important but is only a first step since the strategic environment of the post-Cold War world is in some ways even more complex than this suggests. State-against-state warfare is possible, and could well involve Western intervention, even if this is elective rather than strictly necessary for survival. There is a higher probability of intervention in serious intra-state conflicts, as well as one-off strikes and counter-terrorist operations, which will require sophisticated combat capabilities. Other types of operations likely to be faced will include various types of peace support operation (both peace keeping, peace enforcement and, still more challenging, operations that combine the two) as well as sanctions enforcement, humanitarian assistance, disaster relief and evacuations of non-combatants from crisis zones. Opponents could include peer or 'near' competitors, regional powers, 'rogue states' and various types of sub-state or non-state actors, including secessionists, ethno-nationalist groups, terrorists or international criminal organisations. Many situations, such as a failed state or a complex emergency (where an internal conflict wrecks the institutions of the state, adding a humanitarian crisis to civil war) could well involve multiple parties, with shifting alliances among them, whose disposition towards intervening forces ranges from friendly to actively hostile, possibly changing from day to day. The conflicts themselves as well as their consequences can easily spill across borders. It is likely that many conflicts will involve more than one type of opponent at the same time and possibly different conflict intensities in adjacent areas.[8] Future foes could use either conventional or non-conventional means, or a combination of the two. The techniques and means usable by all types of opponents have broadened to include threats ranging from weapons of mass destruction to computer hacking, and there could be further unpleasant developments in the future.[9]

Having established that there is a broad spectrum of conflict, the next stage of the argument is to suggest that the various newly developed and emerging capabilities might apply unevenly across it. Again, it must be made clear that this is not to argue that RMA-type capabilities have no relevance to 'operations other than war', but rather to suggest that their utility in such cases cannot be assumed to be either exactly the same or quite as great as in warfighting operations, and also to suggest that this issue does not receive the attention it merits in the literature. Such high-end capabilities are undeniably important but other forms of conflict also demand consideration. The rest of the chapter will consider the implications of this spectrum of conflict for the applicability and utility of the RMA. The analysis will make use of a broad distinction sometimes made in the literature between 'warfighting' and 'other' operations. Doing so risks being misunderstood as suggesting, first, that operations fall into just two categories and, second, that a hard and fast line can be drawn between warfighting and non-warfighting operations. Hopefully these points have been refuted sufficiently clearly to avoid giving such a misleading impression. This basic two-fold division is used merely as a convenient tool to investigate the arguments of various schools of thought about the RMA.

Warfighting Operations

Warfighting operations receive the lion's share of attention in the RMA literature, which is no coincidence since they represent the form of conflict best suited to the capabilities cherished by its enthusiasts. This sort of operation involves conventional warfare of the type seen during the Cold War period in Korea, Suez and the Falklands, as well as various other post-1945 regional conflicts, such as those in the Middle East or between India and Pakistan. The kind of opponent involved is a peer or near competitor, a hostile regional power, a well armed sub-state actor, or any combination of these. The defining characteristic of an opponent in this sort of conflict is the possession of conventional forces of a significant size, which could apply to a belligerent in an intra-state conflict. The military tasks involved vary but are largely of a 'force-on-force' character, where combat with the opposing forces is a crucial element and the immediate objectives sought are largely military. As was mentioned above, however, even conflicts within a state could confront intervening Western forces with opponents that possess significant regular forces; the category of warfighting operations is rather broader than might be assumed.

This form of warfare was the focus of attention for the major powers during the Cold War period, due largely to their concentration on the European theatre, and dominated their research, development, procurement and conceptual efforts. The inevitably long lead-times of complex research and development meant that many of the weapons programmes initiated during the late 1970s and the 1980s were not fielded until after the end of the Cold War.

Indeed, had it ended a decade earlier, many of them might well never have seen the light of day. The United States therefore ended the 1980s with several strikingly advanced weapons systems just coming on line, at a time when the superpower opponent against which they had been conceived had thrown in the towel strategically. As Chapter Three argued, the conflict in the Gulf occurred at a crucial time, and provided a striking showcase for many of the new systems and ideas against an opponent who appeared to do his best to flatter American advantages and preferences. Clearly, the various systems and concepts used in the Gulf War were at an early stage and had moved on significantly by the time of later conflicts in the former Yugoslavia, Afghanistan and (once again) Iraq.

For proponents of the RMA, its essence, as either (depending on their point of view) demonstrated or foreshadowed in the Gulf, was that new capabilities in gathering, processing, distributing and using information may be combined with computerised command and control systems and increasingly accurate, long-range precision strike capabilities to form a system of systems, the whole of which would be far greater than the sum of its parts. It would permit 'dominant battlespace awareness', a situation in which one side enjoys near perfect knowledge, in real time, while its opponents are denied accurate information. The effect of this, when combined with increasingly accurate firepower, is expected to be devastating. The enemy's forces will be instantly identified and targeted for rapid destruction with long-range, highly accurate and highly lethal weapons, while a vast array of strategic targets will be struck simultaneously and accurately on the outbreak of war. His information and command and control systems at all levels will be crippled, thus blinding him and multiplying the shock and dislocation effects of the rapid physical destruction of his armed forces and their supporting facilities. The effect will be that his forces are rendered incapable of resistance in an unprecedentedly brief and decisive campaign. The focus of such ideas on warfighting operations is evident.

RMA perspectives and warfighting operations

How do the various schools of thought on the RMA that were identified in Chapter Four believe that it will affect high-intensity conventional operations? The Radical school would expect these operations to be performed by ground forces that are lighter and more mobile than those of the current Western armies (much of their bulk would be eliminated by reliance on non-organic firepower and more efficient logistical systems). These forces will continue to include armoured vehicles and attack helicopters, whose basic functions of mobility, firepower and protection are still required, although they might look very different from those now in service as various innovations, such as active protection or electromagnetic main guns for tanks, help them to evolve. Large manned platforms will operate as part of the new, broader and more closely integrated 'system of systems' and will have the support of unmanned platforms, sensor networks, long range fire support, information warfare capabilities and so on. They will operate in a more dispersed manner but will be far better interlinked with each other, as well as with sensors and strike systems, by information technology. They will operate jointly with other arms as the distinction between the services becomes increasingly blurred. Air power will still include manned aircraft but will make increasing use of UAVs, both for surveillance and targeting, and also for some strike missions. Naval forces will be more optimised for participation in land battles, with various land attack and strike systems contributing to the support of ground forces, supplementing their own longer-range firepower. Information operations will be a more important aspect of warfare, to gain and exploit 'information superiority' over any opponent. The battlefield will become less linear, more fluid and deeper, with less distinction between the close, deep and rear battles and between the tactical, operational and strategic levels of warfare. Military personnel will be better prepared for all of the eventualities they are likely to face, in any sort of terrain or type of operation, due to the improved training made possible by increased use of simulation for individuals and for units of all sizes.

Although this picture of future conventional war might seem to be a great step forward, it is still too conservative for the Visionary school. Although they would concur with some aspects of it, they would dispute the continued dependence on ground forces, large platforms and manned aircraft.[10] They believe both that these elements will be too vulnerable on the future, post-RMA battlefield to have a viable role, and that far more effective alternatives will be available in the form of unmanned systems, many of which will be robotic. They also tend to be more optimistic in their expectations about the level of awareness of the future battlefield, suggesting that the 'fog of war' will be dispelled. They also view the Radicals' conception of information warfare as stunted and backward: rather than being added to current forces, it will in many cases replace them, making deployment of combat forces (even the higher-tech future ones) unnecessary by directly affecting the will and ability of any opponent to resist. Hostile combat forces might not even need to be targeted as strategic effects could be achieved without their physical destruction. Warfare would therefore come to look completely different from the current pattern, as information warfare offered a more usable, less costly option for policy makers, which would allow them to intervene in a conflict decisively and successfully without committing troops on the ground. Without costly and time-consuming logistical preparations, such operations could be launched far more swiftly than an expeditionary force can be deployed today.

These first two schools accept the idea of an RMA fostering a transformation in warfare, differing only in their judgements of just how fundamental its effects will be. Others are more doubtful about whether an RMA is underway or even imminent. The Moderate school is happy to embrace any technological enhancements that emerge from IT and other novel technology. Steps forward in battlefield surveillance, situational awareness, new types of precision guided weapons and other benefits from digitisation are seen as offering very useful enhancements to the armed forces concerned, for military operations generally but particularly in conventional operations against traditional foes (as will be explained below, the arguments of this school fare better than the two previous schools in their applicability to other forms of conflict). Such developments will have many benefits in improving the effectiveness of properly equipped armed forces but these represent incremental steps rather than the complete transformation anticipated by RMA enthusiasts. This school would therefore predict that forces will indeed change but that many aspects of the current model will continue, albeit evolving as they go.

The Moderate perspective comes closest to the apparent view of the British government, which took a number of important lessons from the Gulf War and other conflicts in the 1990s. Several new programmes were launched as a result of this experience, including the more widespread use of GPS in armoured vehicles, far more aircraft being fitted to use PGMs and several new, more advanced stand-off weapon programmes being initiated (such as Storm Shadow, used for the first time in Iraq in 2003, and Brimstone), Tomahawk cruise missiles being acquired and fitted to nuclear submarines, Apache Longbow attack helicopters being ordered for the army, various UAVs being procured and the ASTOR (Airborne Stand-Off Radar) aircraft being initiated. Overall, the experience of the 1990s led to greater British attention being devoted to C4ISTAR capabilities rather than to platforms, particularly in the form of the Joint Battlespace Digitisation programme, which 'is fundamental to our future defence capability' and 'aims to improve operational effectiveness by integrating weapons platforms, sensors and command, control, intelligence and information systems'.[11] Each of these is a useful development and together they will significantly enhance the capabilities of the UK armed forces. It is open to doubt, however, that these additions, even together with numerous other programmes in the pipeline, amount to a revolution. The overall picture of future force structure demonstrates an assumption of evolutionary change; there is a continuing emphasis on armoured vehicles, large surface warships and manned combat aircraft, all of which are still seen as fundamentally important, even if they are planned to change considerably and to operate with the admixture of other means.[12]

The Moderate school is basically optimistic, albeit more cautious than the Radical or Visionary schools. The Sceptics raise more doubts and also some grim possibilities. At one level, they dispute the likelihood of conventional warfighting operations, questioning whether RMA enthusiasts are looking in the right direction. Indeed, the very implausibility of the emergence of a true peer competitor to the United States, which would be required before much of the RMA was fully embraced and fully funded, makes the realisation of the dreams of RMA enthusiasts less likely. Second, they suggest that proponents of the RMA are far too ambitious in their claims, neglecting such ever-present factors as friction, the fog of war and chance, and raising expectations that their technologies will simply be unable to meet. It is true that many claims made by RMA enthusiasts are fanciful and quite implausible in the near future; this tendency to exaggerate in the interest of securing support for pet projects, familiar from previous technological innovations, may well be quite counter-productive due to its effect of fostering scepticism and opposition. An additional problem lies in a failure to take fully into account various political, legal and moral factors that might prevent the US from using some of its planned capabilities in a conflict, ranging from fear of escalation if an opponent views information warfare as a strategic attack, to the undesirable precedent set by attacking infrastructure with civilian as well as military uses. A final difficulty that could arise but receives little attention in the literature is the implications of the RMA for coalition operations if, as seems possible, the US pushes so far ahead of potential partners that interoperability is jeopardised or even rendered impossible. A United States in such a position could become either less willing to involve itself in messy regional problems, or more unilateralist, or perhaps even oscillate between the two.

A third sceptical argument would be that RMA fans tend to under-estimate the reactions of possible opponents. One element of this, the problems caused by asymmetrical responses, is the subject of the next chapter but some comments should be included here. Even in conventional warfighting operations, the opponent might take some action that could at least pose problems for intervening Western forces; and given that the latter are likely to be involved in a war of choice rather than one of survival, their relatively limited commitment will make it possible and attractive to target their will to intervene (or to continue the intervention) even if their battlefield defeat is highly unlikely. Those fearing this tendency would emphasise that new military capabilities are now more widely, and more quickly, available than hitherto to anyone who can pay for them. Only a peer competitor, the least likely future scenario, could aspire to imitate the whole array of technologies planned by the United States. Other less equal competitors could still make use of niche technologies to assist them. Satellite imagery is already available from commercial sources; UAVs and stand-off weapons can be bought on international markets. The existence of even a basic strike system capable of delivering weapons of mass destruction might well deter local states from offering host nation support or deter Western forces from committing their forces, especially where vital national interests are not clearly involved.

Further, the emerging US system of systems depends heavily on use of the electromagnetic spectrum; there has not yet been a conflict in which control of this spectrum (or, indeed, of space) has been seriously contested and even if an opponent does not wrest superiority from US forces that rely on it, merely degrading their ability to use it could have significant effects, especially if combined with other imaginative steps.

As will be argued below, Sceptics suggest that still greater problems lie in the applicability of the so-called RMA to non-warfighting operations. However, even in the type of conflict that should be the best for RMA capabilities, they suggest that significant shortcomings and potential pitfalls exist. Indeed, the most pressing problem could be less that there is a gap between proponents' plans for high-end and for other operations, but rather that there is a more fundamental weakness in the gap between hopes and reality in all types of operation.

The Sceptics stress problems in wars of intervention. The Pessimists, as the label suggests, go considerably further. They agree with the Sceptics that RMA proponents place too much reliance on opponents 'playing the game' and accommodating Western political and military preferences and restrictions. It is naïve, they would argue, to assume that a regional power or hostile non-state actor involved in a future conventional, force-on-force clash with Western forces would not go further in its use of asymmetric responses, particularly when several new technologies increase the menu of what might be available. Such opponents might be less scrupulous in what they use or whom they target, either rejecting Western moral convictions or asserting that they are fighting back with the only means available to them. Actions by rogue states might include terrorist attacks against home countries, possibly conducted by deniable third parties, or use of computer warfare or weapons of mass destruction, or various steps to make the use of force against themselves more difficult, such as placing willing or coerced human shields near strategic targets. This subject will be considered in more depth later. For now, it is sufficient to note that even conventional military operations could be drastically affected by asymmetric responses or other ingenious uses of novel technology.

This section has so far considered conventional warfighting operations that, for all but the Visionary school, involve the deployment of forces into the region in which the campaign is to take place. Two further possibilities arise that may reduce the need to conduct such large-scale deployments. First, if an effective, capable and proven force exists that possesses some of the capabilities predicted, and is backed by the appropriate political will to intervene, it could have a significant deterrent effect on potential regional challengers. An RMA force could make routine presence more robust and effective as a deterrent, or even mean that forces did not need to be deployed forward to act as a deterrent. It could have a similar effect on crisis management and attempts to prevent a dispute from escalating. The lighter, more quickly deployable forces envisaged by the Radical or even the Moderate school could make crisis prevention (through deterrence) and conflict management easier and more effective, as well as allowing speedier deployment or reinforcement in the event of deterrence failing. Their future force would be far more capable of conducting rapid and decisive warfighting operations and hence less likely to have to do so.

Second, the Visionary school (joined by some in the Radical camp) presents an alternative to deploying forces in the form of what might, for want of a better term, be called 'off-shore strikes'. This option would build on the existing US preference for relying on air power rather than accepting the risks of putting troops on the ground, but would enhance it with vastly improved strike systems as well as strategic information warfare. All the various sceptical arguments outlined above would be equally relevant here. An additional problem is that if plans for effective long-range strike systems are vindicated in practice, they could foster a tendency to become involved more often and to lower the threshold of the use of force – which might well, among other effects, nudge potential opponents more swiftly towards asymmetric responses. Such plans exacerbate a tendency to believe that technology can solve the problem of limited will and commitment. Several recent conflicts (as well as innumerable proposals for interventions that were mercifully never put into practice) have suggested that air power offers an easy way to achieve US objectives without risking American lives.[13] The results achieved have suggested that air strikes can offer a useful policy tool but that they are no substitute for presence on the ground and cannot accomplish the same objectives. More likely is a reduction in the ambition of the political objectives sought in order to match the limited military commitment that decision makers are prepared to accept. This applies to warfighting operations and even more to the other categories, to which this chapter will now turn.

'Other Operations'

The very fact that this class of operations is defined negatively, in terms of not being the previous type hints at the terminological difficulties involved. Essentially, 'other operations' (or 'non-warfighting', 'non-combat' or 'unconventional' operations, 'small-scale contingencies' or 'diplomatic military operations'[14]) is a broad category that includes most military activities other than conventional, force-on-force warfighting. There are enormous differences between the varieties of non-warfighting operations: as stressed above, there is a spectrum of conflict, not simply two types. This term is used here to refer to a considerable part of that spectrum, not only to a single form of operation. One distinction sometimes offered is that warfighting operations use primarily military means in pursuit of primarily military objectives, whereas other operations involve a greater use of non-military means and will often have non-military objectives as their immediate aims. This distinction is potentially useful but should not be drawn too starkly; it is a matter of degree rather than being absolute.

The aim in 'other operations' will not be the defeat of enemy forces but rather some objective that does not necessarily require the use of force against an opponent. The missions concerned might be to monitor a border or a ceasefire, to separate participants in a conflict, to provide security and other support for a peace settlement, to protect refugees or humanitarian aid, to evacuate non-combatants from a crisis zone, or to act against international criminal or terrorist targets. The opponents in 'other operations' might include regular, irregular, paramilitary or guerrilla forces, or even criminals and rioters. However, there might not even be clear 'opponents' or, if there are, their identity might change from day to day. It will often be difficult to identify just who is an opponent, both in the sense that the same people could be co-operative one day and shooting at the intervening forces the next, and also that even in the latter cases, it might not be clear whether this represents an isolated instance of indiscipline on the part of a small group or rather a change of policy by the whole of the faction that they represent. They are likely to have less obvious and less identifiable chains of command and also to have much less in the way of strategic assets, command and control or logistical infrastructure that can be held at risk to incline them towards compliance or attacked if co-operation breaks down. The opponents are therefore likely to be quite different from those faced in conventional operations; 'potential opponents' might even be a better term. Non-warfighting operations could take place in the same locations as warfighting operations but are more likely than the latter to be conducted in urban settings, which present a more difficult environment than open terrain. This sort of operation is likely to involve a coalition of participants with widely varying degrees of competence. The restrictions imposed in terms of rules of engagement as well as broader political considerations are likely to be more challenging. Moreover, a greater sensitivity to casualties, among one's own forces and among locals, is likely to apply, and will be all the more problematic in an operational context that could be confusing and rapidly changing. Self-restraint and obvious proportionality are all the more important in such situations, especially with the near omnipresence of the international news media.

As with many concepts, it is easier to provide examples of 'other operations' than a completely satisfactory definition. Recent cases would include UNPROFOR and then IFOR/SFOR in Bosnia, US and UN intervention in Somalia, the operation to assist the Kurds in northern Iraq, the no-fly zones over northern and southern Iraq, and the interventions in Sierra Leone and East Timor. Some stages of the interventions in Afghanistan from 2001 and in

Iraq from 2003 would also count. A detailed examination of these conflicts is beyond the scope of this chapter but even general awareness of a selection of them should be enough to establish two points. First, although this sort of operation does not primarily involve combat operations, it may well include quite serious episodes of combat. Second, these cases present many difficulties for intervening forces. Furthermore, the experience of the first ten years of the post-Cold War era suggests that there is likely to be a great number of this sort of conflict. While major regional clashes cannot be ruled out, it does seem plausible that this alternative variety of conflict will continue to be more common.

If, as is sometimes suggested, an era had begun when only non-warfighting operations are to be expected, this would truly amount to a revolution in military affairs with enormous implications for force structures and defence planning. It would also be an easier world than the one that actually exists, in which the major Western powers must plan and prepare for both warfighting and other operations. This gives rise to the question of how far the requirements for the two sorts of operation differ. Recent experience seems to suggest that there are more similarities between them than might initially be apparent. First, it is not the case, as might be assumed, that 'other operations' are less important than warfighting operations. In an era when the West is unlikely to face wars of survival, even conventional warfighting operations are largely matters of choice. The interests involved in the two forms of conflict might be similar and they might take place in the same geographical areas of concern. Either could have significant impact on vital Western interests and have serious implications for Western security. Setting aside any doubts over the wisdom of the policy response to any of the specific recent conflicts mentioned above, none of them was trivial or of marginal significance.

Second, as has been stated above, it cannot be assumed that non-warfighting operations do not involve combat or that they do not require sophisticated military capabilities. Although the tasks involved may sometimes bear closer resemblance to policing than to conventional operations, combat potential is often a necessary attribute for participants in non-warfighting operations. (The converse is also true: warfighting operations frequently involve non-combat tasks at some stages.) As was argued above, the terms 'non-combat' or 'other than war' refer to the overall character of the conflict and must not be allowed to obscure the reality that they can involve intense fighting and significant casualties.[15]

Third, they can be highly demanding. It was noted above that the 1998 Strategic Defence Review rejected the idea that preparing solely for non-warfighting operations was a plausible option for a state such as the United Kingdom. It is sometimes suggested that, on the contrary, preparation for the high end of the spectrum of conflict automatically confers a capability for the lower end; competence in the former brings with it competence in the latter like a free gift in a breakfast cereal.[16] While less potentially damaging than the first view, in that it is far easier to step down than it is to step up, this proposition is also flawed. A true ability to conduct non-warfighting operations requires many of the same military capabilities as warfighting but it also involves additional and quite different tasks and skills, which require dedicated doctrine and training; this statement seems to gain support from the fact that the armour-heavy US forces that advanced at such an impressive speed across Iraq in 2003 proved to be ill-suited for the subsequent stabilisation and reconstruction phase. The peculiar challenges presented by lower intensity conflicts have been demonstrated by the difficulties often encountered in peace support operations by some NATO armies that are generally considered to be well trained. They require very different skills than warfighting operations – often in addition to rather than instead of those required in the latter.

Finally, non-warfighting operations are not necessarily 'small-scale contingencies', which was one misleading and somewhat dismissive term used for a while by the Pentagon, as they can often involve the commitment of substantial forces for a considerable time. As well as being inaccurate, the impression that warfighting and other operations are completely different, with the latter being less demanding, could also lead to dangerous policies. It could foster a national doctrine that either dismisses them as not worthy of attention, or that takes the opposite route and seeks to optimise forces for non-warfighting operations, leaving them ill-suited to anything but the least demanding cases. Furthermore, taking on a non-combat mission without understanding the full implications could lead to a force being deployed without the complete range of assets it requires. This very shortcoming could encourage disgruntled local factions to escalate the violence above what those frustrating them can handle and hence increase the risk of casualties and of failing in the mission. A force shorn of sophisticated combat capabilities would therefore risk being incapable of performing even many 'non-combat' operations.

There are several ways in which 'other operations' bear comparison to warfighting operations. The principal differences between the two classes of mission lie in the uncertain and inconstant nature of the opponent in non-warfighting operations, the different nature of the aims and the lower levels of force generally used. These very differences often make non-combat operations more challenging than warfighting and also potentially more frustrating for decision-makers and public opinion (which is particularly significant in an era of wars of choice) as well as for the forces committed to them. They also mean that some of the capabilities beloved by RMA enthusiasts would have considerably less impact in these operations than they would in warfighting.

RMA *perspectives and 'other operations'*

Although there tends to be little explicit mention of this sort of operation in the work of the Visionaries, if pressed they would insist that their favoured techniques would have considerable utility in all types of conflict. They look to technology to provide near perfect awareness of any battlefield, so that urban or jungle environments will become as transparent as the desert. Long-range, precision strike capabilities, one of their big themes, would seem to have less relevance in this sort of conflict. However, this school would also place a great deal of faith in information warfare – not merely as a useful adjunct to help troops on the ground in such a conflict but rather as an alternative means that could eliminate the need to deploy them at all. Nye and Owens, for example, argue that information power will be valuable in peacekeeping operations and against other threats such as terrorism and WMD proliferation.[17] Arquilla and Ronfeldt concur, stating: 'We expect that both cyberwar and netwar may be uniquely suited to fighting non-state actors' and other unconventional adversaries.[18] At times this approach includes the assumption that the US would not itself become involved beyond lending decisive information assistance to willing collaborators who actually put people on the ground.[19] On the whole, however, the view of the Visionaries towards non-warfighting operations is one of neglect; their analysis of the fit of the RMA for such operations is difficult to fault because there is so little there to examine.

The Radicals share to some degree the approach of the Visionaries, in that they tend to underplay non-warfighting operations. Yet it would be unfair to suggest that they ignore these cases completely. They were not considered important in the 1993 US 'Bottom Up Review' that referred to them rather dismissively as 'lesser included cases'.[20] The more recent *Joint Vision 2020* document, however, pays them more attention than might be expected. The central objective envisaged in that paper is 'full spectrum dominance', which is defined as: 'the ability of US forces, operating unilaterally or in combination with multinational and interagency partners, to defeat any adversary and control any situation across the full range of military operations.' The breadth of the range of operations envisaged is also set out:

> The full range of operations includes maintaining a posture of strategic deterrence. It includes theater engagement and presence activities. It includes conflict involving employment of strategic forces and weapons of mass destruction, major theater wars, regional conflicts, and smaller-scale contingencies. It also includes those ambiguous situations residing between peace and war, such as peacekeeping and peace enforcement operations, as well as noncombat humanitarian relief operations and support to domestic authorities.

Full spectrum dominance is to be achieved by dominant manoeuvre ('the ability of joint forces to gain positional advantage with decisive speed and overwhelming operational tempo in the achievement of assigned military tasks'), precision engagement, focused logistics and full-dimensional protection. The paper states that each of these will be applicable to conflict and to 'other situations'. Thus, in non-combat operations, dominant manoeuvre 'allows the force to occupy key positions to shape the course of events and minimize hostilities or react decisively if hostilities erupt'; the presence of a decisive force in a peacekeeping mission 'may provide motivation for good-faith negotiations or prevent the instigation of civil disturbances'. Precision engagement is explicitly defined as including 'nonlethal actions' in non-combat situations: 'These actions will be capable of defusing volatile situations, overcoming misinformation campaigns, or directing a flow of refugees to relief stations, for example.' Focused logistics and full-dimensional protection would both have clear relevance for all types of operation.[21] One striking point that emerges from the US Joint Vision documents is the view that the same force will be able (and will need to be able) to conduct both warfighting and other operations. Some analysts doubt this, suggesting an increasing divergence in what is required at the different ends of the spectrum of conflict.[22]

The Moderates generally have some doubts that there is an RMA at all; their doubts apply even more to non-warfighting operations. They would recognise, however, that even if the conduct of non-combat operations is not going to be 'revolutionised' by emerging technology, many of the individual capabilities and concepts that are bundled together by RMA enthusiasts could have very useful applications. The types of opponent and the environment in which non-warfighting operations are conducted are more challenging than open-environment, conventional warfare, but even unspectacular advances in the field of sensors that do not quite fulfil the '100% transparency' hopes of the Visionaries could offer useful assistance, especially if they can be used in urban or jungle operations. Any improvements in the ability to collect, analyse and disseminate intelligence will be gratefully received by troops conducting non-combat operations. However, in this type of conflict satellite imagery and electronic warfare, though useful, are often less important than human intelligence, gathered by people on the ground, as well as broader regional expertise including culture and languages, which has not always been a strong point of the more technologically blessed intelligence agencies. The 'Black Hawk down' operation in Somalia, for example, would have been facilitated by the deployed forces enjoying better situational awareness. Yet this would not have ameliorated the basic misunderstandings of the perception and likely actions of the local population which were so important in the problems that were encountered. Non-warfighting operations will often involve small infantry units, operating in a dispersed manner, so there will be great value in any advances in communications and connectivity that improve their links to each other, to their commanders, to surveillance and intelligence systems, and to fire and logistical support. Operations that can be classed overall as non-warfighting may well on occasion involve the threat or the use of sophisticated combat power. Precision strike capabilities would be valuable in such high-intensity episodes, as well as for intra-conflict deterrence. Other useful RMA assets would include improving UAVs, mine clearance and counter-sniper systems and protection against artillery and mortar shells,[23] all the way to broader improvements in training, through increased use of simulation, and in more timely and efficient logistics, which would offer benefits in all types of operation.

Some analysts pay considerable attention to 'non-lethal weapons', which are 'designed to achieve the same…ends as lethal weapons but not intended to kill personnel or inflict catastrophic damage to equipment.'[24] They would have many applications in non-warfighting operations, particularly in crowd control and policing situations. They are not inherently an element of the IT-driven changes in modern armed forces (indeed the attention devoted to them indicates once again how a great number of unconnected innovations tend to be gathered under the fashionable umbrella terms of RMA and information warfare). Nonetheless, some non-lethal weapons have been fielded (for example, by US Marines in Somalia) and others are under development. They could provide more appropriate means than long-range strike systems for some forms of operation, though they could also foster unrealistic expectations about the likely costs and risks of operations. Above all, they are likely to be used in conjunction with rather than instead of traditional sorts of weapons.[25]

It would be quite wrong to suggest that RMA capabilities have little or no relevance for operations other than conventional warfighting. (To make yet another comparison with air power, a further similarity between it and RMA capabilities would be that both are best suited to conventional, force-on-force warfare, yet both still have substantial, albeit less, utility in other sorts of operations.) The most challenging case would probably be a combination of irregular fighters interspersed with a variably discontented population, without the developed infrastructure of a state, fighting in an urban environment. Even in this case, the various roles required of intervening forces would be greatly assisted by capabilities that offer greater mobility, more reliable communications (including with coalition partners), better situational awareness, improved intelligence gathering systems (such as unmanned aerial and ground vehicles available as far down the chain of command as squads or even individuals), improved personal protection, more accurate and more discriminate precision strike capability against a variety of targets, a range of non-lethal weapons, better vision at night and in low light, and more efficient logistical and medical support. As long as the expectations for each of these remains realistic, all are achievable advances and none requires a great leap forward in technology.

When non-warfighting missions are broken down into the specific tasks that must be carried out by intervening forces, it becomes clear that many are similar to those required in higher intensity operations; hence many RMA capabilities will be useful, albeit not promising a transformation in the ability to conduct these operations due to the relatively smaller role of combat in them.

The view of the Moderates, then, is that a number of the technological assets envisaged by RMA proponents would have widespread utility in non-combat as well as in warfighting operations. In this they might seem to be similar to the Radical school. The difference between the two viewpoints is that the Radicals believe that the whole is very much more than the sum of the parts and that all of the incremental changes together add up to a revolution. Whilst the Moderates would concede that it is conceptually possible for many incremental advances to combine to form a revolution, they do not believe that this is the case at the present.

The Sceptics tend to be even more doubtful of the value of the so-called RMA in non-combat operations. They would emphasise that a force prepared and trained for warfighting might well have an inappropriate mindset for lower intensity operations, in which there is rarely a real 'battlefield' or 'enemy force' to dominate. The temptation for such a force, they warn, would be to use its high-technology weapons even in cases for which they were not at all appropriate, in the hope that technology and firepower could solve complicated political problems. To those who raise doubts that this could happen in practice, they would respond with a single word: 'Vietnam'. Indeed, some of the American actions in the former Yugoslavia or Somalia have seemed to bear out the suspicion that parts of the US military sometimes fail to grasp the nuances of difference between warfighting and non-combat operations: the emphasis on force protection and the means used to assure it have often proved counter-productive in non-warfighting operations. Some of the concepts envisaged in the RMA community would be quite inappropriate to non-combat operations, such as pre-emptive dislocation of C4I capabilities or strategic strikes against support systems. An additional weakness would be that RMA enthusiasts tend to envisage smaller forces that will avoid close contact with the enemy; indeed, reductions in the number of personnel and major platforms are essential to pay for the desired modernisation. Yet this aim seems at variance with the requirements of non-combat operations, which require a certain size of presence on the ground – numbers do matter in such cases – and a certain degree of direct contact between the intervening forces and the local population.[26] RMA advocates look to technology and stand-off systems to dominate ground but this sort of operation requires human presence in the territory concerned rather than destroying 'enemy' platforms. There is some irony in the fact that while

RMA enthusiasts eschew major platforms for their own forces, they seem to focus on destroying those of the opposing force; this capability might be unhelpful if the problem faced is paramilitary forces or a disgruntled civilian population. Some Sceptics would rest on a more fundamental point, namely that the US lacks the will to become involved in conflicts that are not amenable to solution by technology and firepower. The inappropriateness of RMA capabilities for other operations is not, on this view, a serious problem in practice since the US has little intention of becoming involved in such scenarios anyway.

The Pessimists would go a little further in suggesting that pursuit of RMA capabilities is likely to blind the US to the sorts of problems it needs to confront. The US seems to be optimising its force structures increasingly for high-tempo, force-on-force operations, which is leading them further away from many types of operation that they are likely to need to conduct. It largely neglects considerations of interoperability with partners, even though the vast majority of 'other operations' in recent years have been conducted by coalitions. This school of thought would also add many of the concerns about asymmetrical responses that were referred to in the previous section, stressing that many emerging technologies or carefully selected elements of the RMA could be used in singularly nasty ways by unscrupulous opponents: the 'army after next' would be of limited use against a fanatic covertly bringing a nuclear weapon into the country. A further concern would be that the warfighting and non-warfighting operations of the future might require quite different force structures, suggesting that a genuine RMA force might be inappropriate for the interventions that will actually be required. This school of thought also tends to be pessimistic on the strategic level, fearing that current factors are leading to greater fragmentation in the international system. Thus not only will the US face greater dangers from unconventional conflicts but these will become more prevalent. The Pessimists would therefore see the RMA as at best irrelevant to the conduct of non-warfighting operations and at worst as positively harmful.

Conclusion

This chapter has argued that the future strategic environment is likely to feature a broad spectrum of types of conflict. It will include inter-state warfare, despite optimistic predictions to the contrary, as well as intra-state conflict, which will be far more common. The major Western powers that perceive a need to act militarily on the world stage will therefore require the ability to undertake both warfighting and non-warfighting operations. It is difficult to draw a clear line between the two categories, since the distinction is often blurred and there are more similarities between them than might be thought. Non-warfighting operations tend to present particularly complicated situations to those who would intervene and are often more challenging than warfighting for conventional forces. The RMA literature does not fully reflect either the additional difficulties presented by 'operations other than war' or their relative frequency compared to more straightforward operations.

RMA capabilities are best suited to warfighting against a conventional, symmetrical, regular force. Against such an opponent, in the right circumstances, the effect of the RMA will indeed amount to a huge leap forward. If it is not quite as 'revolutionary' as its most enthusiastic advocates hope, it could still represent a transformation along the lines predicted by the Radical perspective. Even some within that school of thought might in the end be somewhat disappointed, however, as the potential impact they expect will in practice be chipped away by the reactions of opponents, self-imposed restrictions (of a political, moral and legal nature) and the inability of the planned programmes to deliver all that has been claimed, for practical reasons and also due to resource constraints. As explained above, those who insist on a stricter definition of RMA (the group this book has labelled the 'Visionaries') could quite coherently argue that the emerging model represents at most a 'minor RMA', due to the continued elements from the previous paradigm of warfare, notably the continuing centrality of major platforms. They will take what is offered while awaiting the true RMA.

For non-warfighting operations, the RMA is likely to create not a transformation but rather a number of useful steps forward. Capabilities ideally suited to combat against a regular opponent fighting a conventional strategy are less decisive in operations where combat has a limited role. These operations present considerable challenges that will leave much of the RMA either irrelevant, unusable or less than fully effective, due to the nature of the opponents, the political and military objectives and also the various restrictions that will hamper the use of force. Many useful incremental benefits will be provided for such operations but the idea that new systems will provide an easy, low-cost solution to complicated conflicts is too ambitious, while claims that the RMA will render unnecessary the physical deployment of ground forces are likely to prove fanciful. This is not to argue that the utility of the various advances lumped together under the RMA brand is confined to one sort of conflict with none in others; rather, they are more useful in some types of conflicts and less so in others, and the latter are more common. The greatest restraint on the RMA in lower-intensity conflicts is likely to be more indirect; that is, limited willingness to become involved in what are very often confusing and deeply unpleasant conflicts will hinder military intervention regardless of the impact of any RMA.

It could be argued that if contemporary developments do not confer equal benefits across all types of operation, then they cannot be considered a true RMA. Whilst this objection is plausible, it does involve setting the bar for qualification very high; so high, indeed, that it would exclude several candidates that are generally acknowledged to be RMAs. As explained in Chapter Two, the armies that were the product of the French Revolutionary/Napoleonic RMA enjoyed success against other states using a familiar strategy but encountered problems against dissimilar approaches to warfare, such as British maritime power or Peninsular guerrillas. The same point could be made in relation to the Industrialisation and Interwar RMAs, both of which gave rise to forces that enjoyed much success against symmetric opponents, but suffered reverses in lower intensity conflict. It would be quite coherent to deny that these amounted to RMAs, along with contemporary developments. The alternative would be to acknowledge that there are limitations to the impact of an RMA and that even a genuine example does not necessarily solve all strategic problems.

Perhaps firmer grounds on which to question the existence of a current RMA lie in extending the argument presented above, that a transformation is underway in warfighting but only incremental changes in other sorts of operations. It was argued that the latter type of conflict is more probable in the contemporary security environment. It is possible to go rather further and suggest that the very extent of the transformation in warfighting capabilities, which will vastly increase an already significant Western advantage, will itself make such conflicts less frequent as future challengers are pushed ever more firmly towards asymmetric strategies. This prospect does not mean that there is no value in pursuing the RMA: first, as was argued above, RMA capabilities will considerably improve, if not 'revolutionise', capabilities for non-warfighting operations; second, greatly reducing the likelihood of major conventional warfare would in itself be no mean achievement. The impact of the RMA would be significantly blunted, however, if it had the effect of increasing the prevalence of asymmetric warfare, which is the subject of the next chapter.

Chapter 7
Asymmetric Warfare and the RMA

There are only two kinds of charge in battle, the unorthodox surprise attack and the orthodox direct attack, but variations of the unorthodox and the orthodox are endless. The unorthodox and the orthodox give rise to each other, like a beginningless circle – who could exhaust them?[1]

Asymmetric warfare has recently become very prominent in the concerns of policy makers. Throughout the 1990s, a number of analysts had suggested that asymmetric warfare was a greater problem than was often realised. After the attacks on New York and Washington of 11 September 2001, such warnings were no longer necessary. References to asymmetric warfare have now become ubiquitous but as with many concepts that suddenly become fashionable, mere frequency of use does not always indicate a deep understanding; for example, it tends to be treated as being synonymous with terrorism which is, in fact, only one element of a far broader phenomenon. Asymmetry is often treated inaccurately as something that is totally new, or as something quite distinct from and unrelated to 'regular' strategy, or as some sort of irresistible magic weapon against the West. It sometimes appears that the concept of asymmetry has gone directly from neglect to mythology without the usual intervening stage of comprehension.

Asymmetric warfare has a wider importance, quite independent of any effect on the Revolution in Military Affairs; the most convinced RMA sceptic would have to concede the importance of understanding it. Asymmetry is particularly important for the present study, however, due to its implications for how the RMA might play out in practice. Whether one believes that a true revolution is underway that will result in a great leap forward, or rather concludes that the whole notion is mere delusion and that the future is likely to be one of continued incremental change, asymmetric warfare is a hugely significant issue.

This chapter will explain what asymmetric warfare is and why it might prove attractive, explore some of the forms that it might take, suggest some of the elements that might form the basis of a response to it and examine the challenge that it poses to strategies and capabilities based on the RMA.

What is 'Asymmetric Warfare'?

The attacks of 11 September were a startling instance of asymmetric warfare,[2] but the phenomenon itself is far from new. The term simply means fighting an opponent by using forces, tactics or strategies that are dissimilar to his. Sometimes in warfare it is appropriate to meet like with like but it is often preferable to pit like against unlike, whether to exploit a particular advantage of one's own or a weakness of the enemy, or to avoid or minimise a strength of the opponent. Alternatively, asymmetric warfare could be conducted by an actor that is quite unlike its adversary, and which hence lacks the option of an orthodox approach.

There are several different elements or dimensions of asymmetry. First, the fundamental nature of the opponent would be inherently asymmetric from the point of view of the major Western powers if it were a sub-state or non-state actor. Such an opponent would have characteristics, capabilities, advantages and vulnerabilities quite different from those of a state. Second, asymmetry could lie in the strategy of an opponent. A hostile state might not be an asymmetric actor but could still embrace a strategy that involved asymmetry in terms of political and military objectives, definition of victory and defeat, or delimitation of the battlefield. Such a strategy could accompany more conventional approaches, and could either be a counter to a Western intervention or be initiated by the state concerned. The third, related dimension of asymmetric warfare lies at the tactical level, including specific actions, selection of targets, choice of weapons and capabilities used. Again, asymmetric action at the tactical level could fall within a broader strategy that was otherwise largely symmetric. Fourth, there could be a significant asymmetry in values, with legal and ethical considerations differing between participants in a conflict or being applied unevenly, or the scruples of one side being exploited by the other. Fifth (fitting in with the 'Pessimist' perspective identified in Chapter Four), an asymmetry of vulnerability would exist if Western states presented more tempting targets than their likely opponents due to the openness of their societies, their sensitivity to casualties or their dependence on complex social and economic infrastructure. Finally, many conflicts involve an asymmetry of commitment, when, as in Vietnam, the issue simply matters more to a local actor than to a more powerful yet more distant intervening state. This factor is particularly significant in an era when the West mainly faces what have been termed 'wars of choice', that is, conflicts in which neither national survival nor fundamental interests are seriously threatened and involvement is therefore elective. In such conflicts a challenger does not need to aspire to the battlefield defeat of the Western states, but rather would aim to persuade them that intervention was not worth the likely costs.

A number of implications follow from this analysis. First, symmetry and asymmetry are not synonymous with, respectively, state and non-state actors. A state could employ asymmetric strategies or tactics, or exploit asymmetries in values or commitment. Equally, some non-state actors (especially sub-state actors, with control of significant territory) could well have regular armed forces or infrastructure that permit symmetric approaches. Further, symmetry and asymmetry are by no means mutually exclusive, and the Western powers are likely to be confronted by a combination of the two. Thus, a state with a predominantly symmetric strategy could supplement it with certain asymmetric elements. Alternatively, in a regional conflict against a state, the West could simultaneously be targeted by a non-state actor, either formally or informally aligned with the opposing state, or even unconnected but acting out of sympathy or even convenience.

Second, asymmetric warfare is not new. It is an age-old feature of conflict of which many of the Western powers have a great deal of operational experience both before and during the Cold War. Moreover, it is by no means distinct from 'regular' strategy but is rather one form of it, an application of such basic strategic and tactical principles as avoiding strength and attacking weakness. It has long been a fundamental element of conventional warfare at all levels. In the Napoleonic era, for example, light infantry were useful for harassing and wearing down heavy infantry, but were vulnerable to enemy cavalry that heavy infantry could hold off. The tactical benefits of pitting elements of your order of battle against dissimilar enemy forces (as in the school playground game of scissors-paper-rock) gave rise to the combination of the various combat arms. The success of blitzkrieg owed much to its blending of armour, motorised infantry, artillery and tactical air power, each of which offered advantages that could be pitted against particular enemy vulnerabilities, as well as helping to compensate for weaknesses in the other elements of the force that might have proved crippling had they operated alone. At the broader levels of operational and military strategy, asymmetry has an equally long history. Napoleon repeatedly crushed opponents who sought to fight him symmetrically but met his downfall mainly because he could not adapt to those who played by different rules, notably British sea power, the combination of guerrilla and regular warfare in the Iberian Peninsula and Russia's refusal to concede strategic defeat after losing on the battlefield.[3] Guerrilla warfare, which itself has much in common with light infantry tactics or operations by special forces, has a history stretching back for thousands of years. It has long been a response of the weak against the strong, either as a strategy in its own right or as one element of a strategy. A succession of great powers has found it far more difficult to counter than a regular opponent fighting in familiar ways. One good example of an asymmetric approach from the World Wars is Germany's use of submarines against British merchant shipping, as an alternative to the symmetrical strategy of building up a battlefleet capable of challenging its British counterpart. Indeed, it is difficult to think of a truly symmetric opponent that Britain has fought since the wars against the Dutch in the seventeenth century. A more recent case can be found in the arguments of RMA proponents, who envisage a decisive favourable asymmetry in their forces' ability to gather and exploit information, thus reducing the need for symmetrical, force-on-force clashes. The use of asymmetry in strategy, therefore, has a long history in conventional forces.

This argument should not be misconstrued as broadening asymmetry to the point where the term loses all meaning, but rather seeks to establish that it has long been a fundamental element of warfare from the tactical to the strategic levels. It also implies that there is a spectrum of asymmetry; one opponent could be more asymmetric than another, as recent experience shows. From the British point of view, the 1990-91 Gulf War was largely though not entirely symmetric. The former Yugoslavia, as a much less militarily powerful state than 1990s Iraq, was a less symmetric or more asymmetric opponent. Further along the line to less symmetry and greater asymmetry would be the Bosnian Serbs, since they had some but not all of the attributes of a state, and hence in both character and methods they were further away from the standard Western model. A terrorist group would be still more asymmetric, in both basic characteristics and methods. Even within the category of terrorist organisations, different degrees of asymmetry can be discerned. The Provisional IRA, for example, has tended to observe more self-limitation on the targets it attacks than al Qaeda, which has sought to inflict a level of casualties far greater than most Western European terrorist groups. 'Asymmetric' actors are therefore a highly heterogeneous group and it would be a mistake to assume that they are all the same.

Asymmetry does not exist in isolation but is rather a relationship.[4] Two guerrilla armies fighting each other, or opposing communities conducting terrorist attacks against each other would not be examples of asymmetric warfare. The term is generally used to suggest a contrast to the modern Western style of warfare encompassing state-based, regular armed forces, using conventional strategy and tactics. 'Asymmetric' actors or methods therefore differ from these. This shorthand should not be permitted to obscure the other side of the coin: if they are asymmetric in relation to us, then the converse is also the case. An actor that has opted for an asymmetric approach has done so precisely because its opponent enjoys a significant advantage in another field, and this gap can be exploited.

'Asymmetry' in contemporary warfare could therefore apply either to the broad character of an opponent, or to his overall strategy, or to specific elements of his forces, or to particular tactics or actions, or to some combination of these. An 'asymmetric opponent' might be a non-state actor such as a terrorist group or even a disaffected individual. An 'asymmetric strategy' might involve a rogue state that seeks to avoid conventional war but pursues its objectives via other means. 'Asymmetric forces' might include terrorists, guerrillas, irregular militias, special forces or even computer hackers acting either individually or as agents of a state or an organisation. 'Asymmetric tactics' or 'asymmetric actions' could be utilised by states or by non-state groups, using conventional or unconventional forces, and could take place either in the context or a regional conflict or quite separately. Before the possibilities of contemporary asymmetric warfare are considered in greater detail, one recent case where it was extensively involved will be examined.

Asymmetry and the 1990-91 Gulf War

Several forms of asymmetric warfare can be identified in the 1990-91 Gulf conflict. This might at first seem a strange assertion, since that war is generally seen as the most prominent recent example, possibly even the epitome, of a conventional and symmetric conflict. Nevertheless, asymmetry was important and an explanation of how it featured helps to shed light both on what asymmetric warfare is and also on its implications for the RMA.

The Coalition's broad strategy and operational approach were both designed to take advantage of its own asymmetric advantages in air and maritime power, manoeuvre warfare, intelligence and communications, and logistics. Its strategy was carefully devised to avoid Iraqi strengths, exploit their weaknesses and to use technology to minimise casualties. As Chapter Three explained, the conflict also demonstrated an enormous asymmetry in the two side's ability to gather, process and exploit information. It was this latter asymmetry that has been seized upon with such eagerness by many RMA proponents, who hope to enhance the ability of the United States and others to benefit from favourable asymmetries.

There were also numerous actions or potential actions by the opponent, whether successful or not, that could be classed as asymmetric. Saddam Hussein initially used Western citizens trapped in Iraq at the beginning of the crisis as hostages and later hinted at using captured pilots as 'human shields' at likely targets for air attack. Although he subsequently relented when the international reaction was critical and the policy did not bring any gains, it was the first of several attempts to exploit asymmetries of values. Saddam sought to sway public opinion in the region, attacking the presence of non-Muslim troops in Saudi Arabia and proclaiming that he was fighting for the Palestinians. He did the same internationally, allowing former or would-be Western statesmen to visit him in Baghdad for discussions and photo opportunities in an attempt to influence anti-war sentiment, targeting the political cohesion of the coalition forming against him. Iraq's operational approach was based on the assumption that the Western states, and the US in particular, would not accept high casualties; it therefore sought to exploit this asymmetry in outlook by constructing elaborate defences to inflict high losses on attacking Coalition troops. After the beginning of the Coalition air campaign, Iraq fired Scud missiles at Israel in an attempt to provoke its entry into the war, hoping thereby to fracture the Coalition and, at best, even bring other Arab states into the war on Iraq's side. Scud missiles were also used against Saudi Arabia and Bahrain in an attempt to inflict casualties on Coalition troops in rear areas. Iraq resorted to what some have referred to as 'environmental warfare' or 'environmental terrorism', pumping oil into the Gulf and setting fire to Kuwaiti oil wells. Throughout the crisis, Iraq sought to exploit the international media, allowing journalists controlled access to areas where there had been civilian casualties, or manufacturing incidents to embarrass the Coalition (such as the bombed 'baby milk factory', as a hand-written, English-language sign propped up against a wall proclaimed it to be). Iraq was reported to have placed military facilities and high-value weapons close to hospitals, religious sites and schools, so that they would either be protected by the scruples of the Coalition planners or would provide useful propaganda if they were attacked (despite the fact that international law would place the responsibility for any ensuing civilian casualties on those who had placed them at risk by stationing military targets in civilian areas).

The actions listed were all performed or attempted by Iraq during the conflict. It is important to note, of course, that the mere fact that an action is asymmetric is no guarantee that it will be successful. Some Iraqi actions proved quite counter-productive, notably the taking of hostages, the harassment of French diplomats and the parading of mistreated pilots on television. Far from unleashing a wave of demands to stay out of the war, these actions firmed up public and political resolve in the states concerned. Other activities had little effect or caused nuisance and annoyance but without compensating for broader strategic weaknesses and failures. Asymmetric warfare is often cited in almost reverential terms, with the implication that it is certain to defeat or frustrate the West. The example of Iraq in 1991 is a useful reminder that this is not always the case.

A more alarming category lies in things that Iraq did not do but might have attempted. It could have conducted terrorist attacks on Coalition troops during the build-up phase, when they were highly vulnerable. As previously noted, General Schwarzkopf revealed that he greatly feared an attack on recently arrived troops in high-rise hotels along the lines of the 1983 car bomb attack on the US Marine barracks in Lebanon.[5] Similarly, during the conflict there were fears of terrorist attacks in Western countries, conducted either by Iraqi agents or by groups that were nominally or genuinely independent but sympathetic to its cause. Perhaps the greatest concern of Coalition commanders was that Iraq would use chemical weapons to inflict mass casualties on advancing allied troops or on their support infrastructure in rear areas. Use of chemical weapons against Israel would have guaranteed Israeli entry into the conflict, quite possibly in the form of nuclear retaliation, and at the very least significantly complicated Coalition strategy. Finally, the comment is widely quoted (usually attributed to 'an Indian general') that 'lesson number one' of the Gulf War was not to confront the US without possessing nuclear weapons. One can imagine the effect on Coalition strategy if the Iraqi invasion of Kuwait had been preceded by a successful nuclear test.

The aim of these actual or potential actions was, or would have been, to complicate the diplomacy and military strategy of the Coalition, making the most of the fact that there were sections of opinion among and within the Western countries and their regional allies that opposed the use of force against Iraq. One final set of asymmetric responses can be found in Iraq's actions after the end of the conflict. Saddam's regime refused to concede defeat and insisted that in fact it had won (indeed, given the survival of the regime and the successful and brutal suppression of risings in the south of the country, there were some grounds for this boast). It then continued to defy the West and the United Nations, maintaining its programmes for ballistic missiles and weapons of mass destruction, skillfully fomenting and exploiting political divisions and commercial ambitions in the international community. Gradually, many in the West came to the view that maybe Desert Storm had not been quite the stunning success it had initially seemed. On the tenth anniversary of the invasion of Kuwait, Saddam Hussein was still in power and it took another military intervention – which created still more bitter divisions in the United Nations – finally to bring about his downfall.

The US and its allies have devoted a great deal of attention to learning lessons from the Gulf War. It can safely be assumed that other states and non-state actors, particularly ones that might be hostile to the West, are equally keen to learn from it. In the scale of his battlefield defeat, in some of the things he did but might have done more effectively, and in the things he did not attempt but might have done, the Iraqi leader provided ample food for thought for those who would challenge the West.

Contemporary Forms of Asymmetric Warfare

Asymmetric warfare has become relatively more prominent since the end of the Cold War. First, by definition, the demise of the only plausible 'peer competitor' to the US, or the West generally, means that there is no truly symmetric potential opponent. Increasingly powerful regional actors might wish to challenge the West but their clear inferiority in conventional military power would make asymmetric strategies and tactics all the more tempting; the 1991 Gulf conflict demonstrated with brutal clarity the folly of confronting the US and its major allies with their ideal form of warfare. Some regional powers also exhibit asymmetries of outlook, objectives and values in comparison to the West, which therefore labels them 'rogue states'. They too could find asymmetric approaches appealing.

Second, a great variety of non-state actors has gradually become more significant and influential in international affairs over the past few decades. Some recent Western military interventions in intra-state conflicts have been opposed by well-armed and determined internal factions. Besides these, disaffected groups within certain states have grievances or aims with an increasingly international dimension together with a growing ability to take them onto the world stage. Both of these types of non-state groups either lack conventional military power or are vastly inferior to their foes, and will out of necessity look to asymmetric responses. Various trends in international politics have increased the potential impact of asymmetric actors, including the effects of globalisation, modern communications, the ease of travel in the modern world, the ubiquitous coverage of international news media that are beyond the control of any single state and the development and proliferation of weapons technology (especially but not only WMD). Moreover, some features of Western states make them particularly vulnerable, including the openness of their societies, the freedom of movement enjoyed by their residents and their concern for law and civil liberties. It is probably true that the major Western societies feel more vulnerable than they really are but this sentiment still influences policy.

Future opponents that might embrace asymmetric warfare can be divided into two broad groups. First, a symmetric state opponent could use conventional forces in an unconventional way or against an unexpected target, or could add some asymmetric means to an otherwise orthodox strategy. One plausible example might be China, which is widely reported to be devoting considerable resources to the development of offensive information warfare capabilities as a complement to its improving conventional forces. A future state opponent might threaten to use weapons of mass destruction or attempt to disrupt key systems upon which the US relies, such as satellites or the electromagnetic spectrum. Both of these are areas in which the US has enjoyed effectively unhindered dominance in recent conflicts: determined pursuit of niche RMA capabilities could allow an enemy to deny free use of space or the electromagnetic spectrum to the US even if it could not dominate either itself. An opponent might seek to deny the US its favoured form of warfare by exploiting techniques and environments that have proved challenging to US military forces in recent operations, such as urban warfare, or guerrilla or terrorist strategies. Alternatively, such a state might resort to an entirely asymmetrical strategy. The 2000-01 outbreak of foot-and-mouth disease in the UK seems to have had natural causes and there is no evidence that the 2001 anthrax attacks in the US were initiated by another country, but either might have been a hostile act, with the additional advantage of plausible deniability.

Second, the opponent could be a non-state actor, such as a terrorist organisation, a local warlord, an organised criminal group or even a disaffected individual. These actors might use traditional means such as bombs and bullets, or newer possibilities such as computer attack or weapons of mass destruction. Some developments can be identified in the mode of operation of international terrorists that increase the fear they cause and hence the impact of their activities, notably an apparent intention to inflict large numbers of casualties compared to their predecessors. They have also become more technologically sophisticated, not least in exploiting advanced and often encrypted computer and communications systems. The aspiration to acquire weapons of mass destruction is clearly widespread, and their use by terrorists has long been predicted and has already occurred in Japan, with a religious cult making several unsuccessful uses of anthrax and one moderately successful use of sarin gas in Tokyo. Clearly, the possible use WMD raises the potential impact of terrorists to a still higher level, though it should be noted that the 11 September attacks were technologically simple if well organised. Many current terrorist groups are structured in ways that make them hard to penetrate and counter, with flexible and diffuse networks of planners, funders and sympathisers in addition to the expendable activists who carry out the attacks. As noted above, various features of the contemporary international system have benefitted terrorists: there is some irony in the fact that al Qaeda is motivated in large part by bitter hatred of the results of globalisation, yet is fundamentally parasitic upon it. International terrorism uses the characteristics of open societies against them, taking advantage of freedom of movement to operate and of freedom of speech to spread its message, whilst exploiting the presence in them of active or passive sympathisers in migrant communities and benefiting from the constraints imposed by the political cultures and legal systems of the target states. At the same time, the nature of the groups undertaking these actions makes them elusive targets for any conventional military response, which in any case is opposed by some elements of opinion within Western societies. If the target's response is perceived as hasty, disproportionate or ill-conceived it can lead to propaganda success for the terrorist, who is not held to the same standards of conduct.

Of course, the two types of opponents identified above may not be so distinct in practice. The dividing line between a 'rogue state' and a terrorist group might in fact be blurred, as it was in the case of al Qaeda and the Taleban regime in Afghanistan. It is quite possible that a state could use a non-state group as a proxy, either in a conflict or separately, or that a terrorist or organised criminal organisation could come to hold significant influence inside a weak state. Terrorist groups could have varying degrees of support from within a number of states, whether in terms of hosting them, providing money, information or technology, or in simply following common goals. It is quite conceivable that an agency of a government could act in a way unauthorized by its nominal political superiors, thus providing some of a state's resources to terrorists. There is therefore a range of asymmetric actors, and their menu of possible options is enormous and potentially terrifying, as several authors have suggested.[6]

The concern has been expressed that the West is increasingly facing opponents whose basic cultural outlook on warfare is utterly different to its own, and that this disparity will greatly complicate military interventions against such 'warrior' groups.[7] Some interpretations of the RMA seem to widen this already significant cultural gap between the West and many of its likely opponents, not least in encouraging the aspiration towards effective intervention without troops on the ground. This argument does not suggest that RMA capabilities will be useless against such opponents. Rather it is another helpful reminder of the need to take into account the broader factors of culture and strategy, which provide the context within which military capabilities and technology are used.

Hostile actors are likely either to reject Western moral convictions or to assert that they are fighting back in the only ways they can (there have already been references in the media to terrorism as 'the poor man's air power', thus beginning to provide it with a more respectable gloss).[8] Hostile regimes will make propaganda use of any civilian casualties, which they could promote by using willing or coerced human shields. The manufacturing or infliction of casualties on their own people cannot be ruled out, since the media and sympathetic international opinion would be reluctant to believe that such cynical actions had occurred.[9] Placing key facilities close to religious buildings, schools, hospitals or sites used by international organisations or the international media could cause additional difficulties. The likely mismatch in values could also lead to prisoners being mistreated and exploited for the international media, or to the use of 'environmental warfare', rape or the deliberate creation of refugees as tactics. It is distinctly likely that hostile states and non-state actors alike will increasingly reject the 'laws of war' and international law more broadly as a Western construct that acts in its own advantage; such criticisms will not, of course, prevent such actors from claiming the protection of these systems of law when it suits them. An opponent could seek to escalate a conflict horizontally, to other regions or states (especially against those in the region providing diplomatic or host nation support, or against the homeland of those intervening) or vertically, to other categories of weapons. At the worst end of the scale of possibilities it could lead to a use of WMD, either against deployed troops, support areas and bases (either in the immediate area of conflict or elsewhere in the region) or even the homeland of the intervening states. Weapons of mass destruction, comprising chemical, biological, nuclear or radiological (that is, a 'dirty' conventional bomb, laced with radioactive material), could be used without responsibility being acknowledged; in the case of biological weapons it might not even be obvious that an attack had taken place. Even attacks against the homeland that used only conventional weapons could take advantage of another perceived asymmetry: vulnerability. Whether correctly or not, a future opponent could conclude that Western states and societies were particularly soft targets, or that their public opinion was weak and easily swayed.

It would be a serious mistake to assume that 'asymmetric warfare' is necessarily low-technology. Modern technology has increased the capacity of rogue states or non-state actors, be they terrorist groups or disaffected individuals, to do harm. Whether it takes the form of computer hacking or biological attack, the scale of potential harm has grown enormously and the response to it has become complicated by the difficulty of identifying the perpetrator and distinguishing between the domestic and foreign, opportunistic or calculated, sociopathic or political. Again, it must be emphasised that the objective of the opponent would not necessarily be the military defeat of the intervening states but would rather be to deter them from becoming involved in the first place or, failing that, to deny them their favoured operational approaches, to complicate and frustrate their strategy, to foment and exploit political divisions (internally, among coalition allies, within the region and in world opinion more generally) and to persuade them that the interests involved in the operation were simply not worth the risk and costs. As argued above, there is no guarantee that asymmetric actions will succeed; they could, in fact, fail or even prove to be quite counter-productive if they harden public and political opinion in the target country or create the will to intervene, at considerable cost if need be, in a conflict not previously seen as a vital interest. Such was the result of the 9/11 al Qaeda attacks on New York City and Washington DC: neither the US government nor American public opinion was subsequently inclined to treat the war on terrorism and intervention in Afghanistan as a mere 'war of choice'.

Asymmetric Warfare: Elements of a Response

The principal challenge posed by asymmetric warfare is that by its very nature it targets and takes advantage of the West's vulnerabilities in ways that also seek to avoid or sideline its strengths. The difficulty of countering asymmetric warfare is precisely that it is a response to Western advantages and hence is inherently dynamic. As one vulnerability is shielded, the opponent will seek out a new one: the defending actor is always reacting and there is a danger that as one stable door is bolted, a horse will slip out of another. The outlines of a solution can be found by applying the traditional principles of strategy, which are the same methods used by asymmetric opponents: identify, minimise and protect our vulnerabilities; identify, exploit and target the weaknesses and vulnerabilities of the opponent, and direct our strengths against them. Clearly, setting out such broad principles is only a first step in devising an approach to counter asymmetric warfare but it is at least a start and suggests some promising directions to pursue.

The main strengths of the major Western states include conventional military power (especially its reach and precision) and the ability to gain and exploit information. They also benefit from attributes that are peculiar to states – and which are particularly useful against non-state actors, which have no choice but to play on an international stage defined and dominated by states – including human, financial and physical resources far in excess of what any non-state group could muster and, critically, the ability to win the support of other powerful states.[10] Careful diplomacy and the acceptance that some non-state groups pose a threat to many countries could multiply Western assets by adding to them those of other states. Such international co-operation, whether it leads to military, economic, intelligence, policing or diplomatic action, provides a very valuable weapon against all forms of asymmetric warfare.

What are the weaknesses of the West? Perhaps the most significant is the sheer size and extent of its interests, which present a vast array of targets for opponents and a consequent difficulty of defending all of them. As with anti-submarine warfare in the two battles of the Atlantic, the attacker holds the initiative and the defender requires far more resources. The US Secretary of Defense, responding to criticisms of the intelligence services for not having provided advance warning of the September 11 attacks, warned: 'A terrorist can attack at any time at any place using any technique. It is impossible to defend at every time in every place against every technique.'[11] A second feature (which is simultaneously in some ways a disadvantage and in some ways an advantage) is the very nature of liberal-democratic societies. Their openness allows their enemies to move about with considerable ease and even to use their territory for indoctrination, funding and spreading their message, while legal and ethical scruples can inhibit the response by states. Public opinion can often be fickle, resisting expenditure on intelligence or security precautions, yet reacting furiously when attacks occur. Some of the specific vulnerabilities of the West can be defended, albeit never absolutely, by devoting more attention to civil defence and home security,[12] though here too it would be an error to characterise either the threat or the response as primarily military: many agencies of the state need to be involved alongside, and often ahead of, the armed forces. Wise action in this area can improve public confidence, and hence the feeling of security (which is inherently subjective). Nevertheless, some of the weaknesses of an open society simply have to be accepted and public opinion educated to understand the true level of risk, which is generally less than is perceived.[13]

What are the weaknesses of potential asymmetric opponents? A hostile state can be isolated economically and diplomatically from the international community and will, to varying degrees, have high-value targets that can be attacked. By definition, rogue states are unlikely to be democracies so economic sanctions or military attacks directed against 'public opinion' or the 'public support' of an enemy regime are unlikely to be appropriate. Nevertheless, the ruling political and military elite will have interests, whether material or simply personal survival, that can be held at risk to deter or to punish either symmetric or asymmetric hostile action. Two problems arise here. First, if the context is a regional conflict, deterrence might go both ways: that is, if the opponents were known to have capabilities such as WMD, it would either be dangerous to take them on in the first place, or it might prevent the West from using some capabilities against them. Second, it might not be immediately obvious who the aggressor was if, for example, certain actions were taken without any claim of responsibility. The response then becomes more like that which is appropriate to the non-state threat.

If the opponent is not a state, it is likely to lack valuable infrastructure that can be attacked or economic vulnerabilities that can be exploited. Modern terrorist groups present a particular problem, because their structure tends to be dispersed and cellular, and (in particular, by definition, that of a successful organisation) will be extremely difficult to identify, let alone attack. Nevertheless, even terrorist groups can still have vital assets that are analogous to those of states. These might include physical facilities such as offices, weapons stores or training sites located within a state, often with the co-operation or at least acquiescence of the government concerned. In this case, they could be attacked directly or the state where they are located could be put under pressure to expel them or prevent them operating. Alternatively, even a more nebulous opponent will still have an organisation of some sort, notably key individuals and financial systems, which can be targeted by patient international intelligence and police efforts or even by carefully targeted military operations. The smaller the group, the harder it would be to pin down, and a lone disaffected individual would be the most difficult, but even though modern technology potentially allows such an individual to wreak considerable destruction, a larger organisation would be needed for widespread and ambitious campaigns with strategic aims. The US-led intervention in Afghanistan suggests both that it is possible to devise a military response against a non-state actor and also that conventional forces have considerable utility in such operations. It also showed that the West can act asymmetrically too: the opponents seem to have assumed that they would not be identified, or that they would not be located, or that the US would not have the will to act against them in what had previously been safe havens.

It was suggested earlier that much discussion of asymmetric warfare contains an element of 're-inventing the wheel'. In fact, the major Western states have a great deal of past experience of dealing with asymmetry, even if its exact nature evolves over time. There is a paradigm that has considerable value for the 'war against terrorism' and might also have some relevance for combatting asymmetric warfare more broadly. The British approach to counter-insurgency was developed during the Cold War but drew on a great deal of previous imperial experience. It conceived insurgency as a predominantly political problem, with a military dimension. It therefore emphasised the close co-ordination of all agencies and all means (political, diplomatic, financial, legal and military), the importance of good intelligence and the principle of minimum force, with military power being used in a carefully targeted way and in support of the civil power. Central to the strategy was winning the 'hearts and minds' of the population being targeted by the insurgents; this did not represent either bribery or 'giving in to terrorism', but rather a pragmatic recognition that separating the insurgents from their broader support in the target population was essential in its own right, as well as to improve the effectiveness of other means such as force. Where military means are used they would often be a blend of conventional and unconventional operations: the combination of the two is crucial, as each can compel the opponent to adopt deployments that can make him more vulnerable to the other. Above all, this approach stressed the need for patience and a recognition that success will not necessarily be swiftly or cheaply achieved.

One danger in the immediate aftermath of the attacks of 11 September was that defence planners would leap from underestimating asymmetric warfare to over-estimating it. There might have been a temptation to assume that such dramatic terrorist attacks were now the major or even the only threat that was faced. Such a response would have been deeply misguided: terrorism, like asymmetric warfare more generally, amounts to an additional problem, not an alternative one.[14] Moreover, as the campaign in Afghanistan demonstrated, many of the capabilities procured for 'conventional' operations were equally relevant to the war on terrorism. Balanced forces are crucial. If the future held only warfighting or only non-combat operations, or if future opponents and their strategies were only either symmetric or asymmetric, then policy decisions would be much easier. In reality, however, the spectrum of operations is broad and the West will be confronted by both conventional and asymmetric opponents and strategies, sometimes in a single conflict. There is therefore a need for balanced forces – not least because the more specialised one's capability and the more precisely it is tailored for a narrow range of scenarios, the greater the opportunity presented for an enemy to act asymmetrically. More flexible and mobile forces optimised for expeditionary operations are needed for those conventional operations that will still be conducted and these same forces will also be able to turn their hand to other sorts of operations. The way to either deter or cope with asymmetry is to have a balanced capability, with well-trained, flexible and determined forces, able to operate across the whole spectrum of operations, and to demonstrate the ability and will to commit these forces in pursuit of strategies appropriate to the situation. Such characteristics, of course, will be immensely useful regardless of whether an RMA is under way, and regardless of just how far its effects prove to extend.

The Challenge of Asymmetric Warfare to the RMA

The general challenge of asymmetric warfare to the West and its way of warfare has already been explained. How, specifically, does the prospect of asymmetric warfare affect the Revolution in Military Affairs?

First, it is a challenge to some of the arguments of the more enthusiastic RMA proponents. It was suggested above that the attraction for those who embrace asymmetric warfare is precisely that it offers a viable option in a world in which the United States enjoys a massive superiority in conventional military power. Even if there is no substance in the RMA debate, even if no improvements at all emerge from the RMA, the West would still face a growing threat from asymmetric warfare. However, any advances that do result from the RMA, whether they are minor and incremental or a truly transformational leap forward, will further increase the attraction of an asymmetric response. The aim of such approaches would be to reduce the impact of the RMA and the advantages its proponents hope it might confer; they therefore have the potential to blunt the pay-off that might otherwise be expected. Indeed, it could be argued that the effect of the capabilities promoted by RMA enthusiasts will be so reduced and marginalised in practice that doubt is cast on the claim that there is a Revolution in Military Affairs. This argument might carry scepticism too far but it is fair to say that at the very least, the impact of any RMA that does occur will be limited in practice by a combination of symmetric and asymmetric reactions by potential opponents. Some RMA enthusiasts believe that it promises to deter and prevent the emergence of any peer competitor.[15] Yet if potential causes of tension or conflict remain, if powerful states do not share the world view of the United States, a successful RMA could have the effect of deterring only a symmetric response – such a challenger would not become a peer competitor but would rather look to other, asymmetric means of confronting the single superpower. The result could be that the RMA would have the effect of channelling hostility into directions that the West would be hard pressed to counter, thus negating an existing advantage rather than magnifying it and having a counter-productive effect. It could also be the case, of course, that the RMA could itself offer ways of overcoming the US, which leads to the second point.

Some niche capabilities thrown up by the RMA could provide new options for asymmetric use by terror groups, rogue states or other potential opponents. The RMA could help a regional power by giving it an edge over a neighbouring state, or by giving it the ability (or the belief that it has the ability) to deter or frustrate Western intervention. Computer network attack, ballistic missiles, selective use of satellites, biological weapons or any of a number of other unpleasant possibilities (for example, using precision guided weapons against airliners or public buildings) could be used by state or non-state opponents to target specific weaknesses in the overall Western military or civilian structures. That is to say, for pessimists, the RMA will make it easier for enemies to attack the West or its overseas interests and allies. Moreover, the RMA promises to increase still further the existing conventional military advantages enjoyed by the Western states; this trend, particularly if it leads to ill-conceived interventions, could swell the sense of powerlessness and rage felt by some peoples in the world, increasing still further their determination to challenge the status quo, and thus have the undesirable consequence of multiplying hostile non-state actors, with all the more motivation to use the newly available capabilities to strike against the West.

Third, it could be argued that the armed forces must seize the opportunities presented by modern technology (regardless of whether this is seen as an RMA), while also insisting that they can and must prepare to act against asymmetric threats; but it could then be objected that the same forces cannot do both. That is, it could be argued that the combined effect of contemporary technological innovation and the present growth of asymmetric threats is forcing a split in armed forces: the high-end units needed for force-on-force operations will increasingly diverge from the less high-tech units needed for non-combat operations and for many operations against asymmetric opponents. For some states, it could be argued, this process will lead to a perilous gulf between two categories of forces; others will be forced to choose whether to prepare for one or the other – and leaving out either will open the state concerned to unpleasant risks including, of course, asymmetric attack from the direction of whichever element is abandoned.

The possibility of asymmetric responses does not mean that the RMA should be spurned. The current gap in conventional military capabilities is such that they will occur anyway. At worst, the RMA will increase this trend. Some promised or proposed RMA capabilities could, of course be of great use against asymmetric opponents in the same way as they might be valuable in non-combat operations. Benefits might flow from specific capabilities such as surveillance or precision-attack systems or, more broadly, in providing better ways to gather and make use of information, or in offering means of intervention that are less risky for those conducting it, more accurate and more discriminating in terms of avoiding unintended damage. Another possible benefit would be a reduced dependence on bases within the region where an intervention was taking place, which might be subject to attack, with a resulting risk of casualties or complications for political relationships with local allies. Some advocates of the RMA hold out the prospect of lighter, more easily deployable forces whose 'reduced logistical footprint' would have just that effect. The fact that much of the RMA literature overlooks asymmetric warfare and, more widely, forms of conflict other than conventional warfare, does not mean that the RMA is irrelevant to them but rather implies that more thought needs to be devoted to the issues of how and to what extent emerging capabilities might be applied against asymmetric responses. Military planners, regardless of whether they accept the existence of a contemporary RMA, must accept that potential opponents will seek to blunt and disrupt their strategy and key capabilities, and must systematically consider how this might be done and what might be done to prevent it.

Conclusion

This chapter has stressed that asymmetric warfare is by no means a novel phenomenon, that it is solidly rooted in broader military history and strategy, and that terrorism is only one aspect of it. Asymmetric warfare can take the form of actions by a state or a non-state actor, can be conducted by conventional or unconventional forces, and can take place either in the context of a regional conflict or quite separate from it. Asymmetric warfare requires armed forces that are intellectually as well as physically agile, and calls for balance and flexibility to face a range of types of operation across a broad spectrum of conflict intensity. However, a response cannot be confined to ministries of defence. Broader adaptation is needed in many other government agencies to improve their own capability to counter those elements of asymmetry that they might face and to enhance international co-operation with their counterparts in other states. Asymmetric warfare is not a minor additional factor but demands a great deal of intellectual effort and serious attention in training and in planning operations.

Understanding asymmetric warfare, what it is and how it can be countered, is important independently of the Revolution in Military Affairs; it should concern even those who entirely reject either the RMA concept or the claim that one is currently underway. Asymmetric warfare and the RMA are relevant to each other, however, since any widening of the Western advantage in conventional military power will provide all the more incentive for would-be challengers to embrace asymmetric responses, and these actions could diminish the impact of otherwise revolutionary change. This does not imply, however, that asymmetry will wipe away all of the potential benefits of the RMA; rather, it forms an element of the background political and strategic conditions that are so crucial to understanding how it will play out in practice. To use once again, the schools of thought identified in Chapter Four, Visionaries and even some Radicals hope that the RMA will provide a leap forward in military (and, indeed, in non-military coercive means) that is every bit as relevant for asymmetric warfare as for any other type of military operations. This seems unlikely. Asymmetric responses will blunt the advantages that accrue to the leading powers from the RMA but will not eliminate them. The previous chapter concluded that RMA capabilities will have considerable utility in lower-intensity operations, albeit not quite as great and not exactly the same impact as some of its proponents predict it will have on conventional military operations. A similar argument might be applied to the relevance of the RMA to asymmetric warfare; it will offer some benefits, though no easy answer and only in the context of a wise overall strategy. From the Pessimist perspective, of course, a misplaced faith in the RMA could combine with a failure to understand the idiosyncrasies of asymmetric warfare to create utterly inappropriate force structures, doctrine and even military ethos at the widest level.

This chapter has sought to de-mythologise asymmetric warfare and to suggest that it has more in common with 'regular' strategy than is usually recognised. It must be seen as an inherent part of strategy and warfare rather than as a phenomenon somehow detached from them. Clausewitz sought to explain that war was one form of political and social interaction, rather than something distinct from it, writing: 'Its grammar, indeed, may be its own, but not its logic.'[16] The same might be said of the relationship between asymmetric warfare and warfare more broadly. The quotation from Sun Tzu with which the chapter opened suggests the logical and reciprocal relationship between the symmetrical and the asymmetrical in warfare, and it is within this context that the RMA must be understood.

Chapter 8
The RMA: Alliance Implications

The alliance implications of the 'Revolution in Military Affairs' is a difficult topic to address since it brings together issues ranging from the narrowest technical matters to concerns at the broadest political level. Evolving alliance politics depend on a vast number of issues, which are by no means confined to defence matters alone. It is therefore a complex and changing subject that inevitably involves a large degree of speculation.

Nevertheless, it is important to consider, as the RMA could potentially have significant effects on alliances. The converse could also be true, since how individual states respond to the cluster of developments that some describe as an RMA will depend in part on the political and military choices made by other states, including current or future potential coalition partners. This chapter will explore the possible impact of the RMA on the two major alliances within the Western world, that is, on the relationship between the US and Europe, and on relations within Europe. In both cases, it will attempt to take account of the evolving nature of the underlying political relationships by considering two alternative future scenarios: the first, a continuation of the recent pattern and the second, a major discontinuity. The analysis of these two alliances has some broader relevance, as many of the points made apply to other states too, both to non-European states that are allies of the US and also to the many states that are more comparable to European states than to the US in terms of the challenges and possible benefits presented by the RMA.

Some light can be shed on this issue by applying the different perspectives on the RMA outlined in Chapter Four. This approach will identify a number of problems that the RMA could pose for alliances, and vice versa, as well as some potential solutions and some ways in which the RMA might actually help relationships.

The Atlantic Alliance

Whilst it was argued in Chapter Four that the US does not enjoy sole control over the RMA, there is no doubt that it is very much leading the way and is largely setting the agenda, to the extent that some analysts even refer to 'the American RMA'. For the European allies of the United States, the RMA presents as many dilemmas as it does opportunities. It also has significant implications for the trans-Atlantic relationship which, according to the perspective from which it is viewed, could be either positive or negative.

The existence or otherwise of a crisis in relations between the US and its European allies is a perennial subject in the media, with a considerable range of suggested causes of an actual or potential breach. The most obvious factor is the negative one of the demise of the common Cold War threat that did so much to bind the two pillars of the Atlantic Alliance in the post-1945 period. Without the strong diplomatic glue that this threat provided, it is argued, a plethora of contentious issues now has free rein to fracture the alliance. The RMA is only one of many defence questions to affect trans-Atlantic relations. Other military issues also have an impact, notably unease in some West European capitals over US plans for missile defence, or the aspiration to forge an autonomous Western European defence identity. Broader security concerns enter the picture, including disagreements over policies towards Russia, China and 'rogue states' such as North Korea, Iraq and Iran. Other, non-security matters are also important, including the environment, trade questions such as additives in food and subsidies to airlines, or even the use of the death penalty in the US. A feeling that there is an increasing divergence in the basic American and European approaches to politics only became more widespread with the inauguration of the George W. Bush administration.[1] Clearly, if there were to be a deep and lasting breach between the US and Western Europe, although it would be a quite distinct issue from the RMA and with largely unrelated causes, it would have major implications for how the RMA played out in practice. Indeed, it could even be seen as revolutionary in its own right in political and strategic terms.

There is clearly some anti-American sentiment in Europe, exacerbated by current concerns over globalisation and the lack of a strategic counter-balance to the US. Equally there are some voices in the US that would urge their government to press home the post-Cold War opportunity that they perceive, in a way that might fairly be described as 'unilateralist'. The ugly American or the reckless gun-toting cowboy and, on the other side of the Atlantic, the sandal-wearing European pacifist or the 'cheese-eating surrender monkey',[2] are all mere caricatures that belong to comedy routines rather than serious analysis. Yet they do point to real disquiet and potentially serious tensions. Some policy-makers in Europe genuinely feel that Washington does not pay sufficient attention to the international institutions and international legal framework that it did so much to create in the aftermath of the Second World War. Equally, there has long been a strand of opinion within the United States that feels suspicious of and unappreciated by Europeans who accept American protection with remarkably bad grace while contributing in return shamefully little to the defence of Europe, let alone Western interests further afield.

There are, however, many reasons to suggest that a catastrophic breach in relations across the Atlantic is neither inevitable nor imminent. There is a tendency to exaggerate vastly the disagreements across the Atlantic, concentrating upon and playing up every fleeting dispute while allowing the deeper and longer-term areas of consensus and shared interests to go unremarked. The long Cold War history of co-operation has created ingrained habits of consultation and compromise that militate against a sudden break. Moreover, there is still a considerable body of shared values and shared interests, which would form a strong reason to avoid any major and lasting split. The occasional disputes within the Western Alliance should not be over-stated and should not be allowed to conceal the deeper links that remain resilient and strong. The common interests of the US and Europe are hardly trivial, given the extent of trade between them, their ideological, cultural, institutional and historical ties, let alone the record of co-operation in security issues.

In any case, it is too easily forgotten that there was a litany of disagreements between the US and Western European countries even during the Cold War, over numerous trade questions, Latin America, the gas pipeline from the USSR and the Strategic Defence Initiative, without these ever holding the potential to fracture the Atlantic alliance. It is of course true that the Soviet threat presented a compelling reason for compromise during this period and that this unifying factor no longer exists. Yet that does not make a parting of the ways inevitable or even likely. When policy differences arose between the George W. Bush administration and some European capitals, there was a tendency on the part of some commentators to paint the Clinton years as the 'good old days' in allied relations but even in that supposed halcyon period there were many important disagreements, much stressed by the media at the time, over Bosnia, Kosovo, land mines, nuclear testing and a host of trade issues. None came close to derailing the NATO alliance.

In most cases, moreover, representing the disagreements as being between the US and 'Europe' is a grotesque over-simplification since the European states are themselves habitually divided. Moreover, of course, significant differences over foreign policy can be discerned among competing strands of political opinion within the US, as well as within individual European states. Thus, over missile defence, France and Germany opposed the plans of the George W. Bush administration, as did some American commentators, but the UK, Spain and Italy were supportive, as were other European members of NATO who were then outside the EU, including Turkey, Poland and Hungary.[3] The diplomatic fissure over the Iraq crisis of 2002-03 was frequently characterised as 'US versus Europe', yet this description was a travesty for a situation in which the US enjoyed the active support of the UK, Spain, Italy, Portugal and Denmark (and the less vocal support of several others) within the EU, as well as the backing of the former eastern-bloc states that were on the verge of joining the EU, notably Poland. Naturally, each individual state on either side also contained many voices that dissented from the policy of its government. It suits some West European commentators to depict disagreements within the Western alliance as 'US vs. Europe', creating with a stroke of the pen the united European bloc they would like to see in practice, but examples where this is true have been very much the exception rather than the rule.

There remains a web of pressing mutual interests binding the Atlantic alliance together. It is easy to lose sight of the magnitude of the achievements already secured of retaining and reorienting NATO for the post-Cold War world, taking on new tasks and new members and, far from least, in transforming its relationship with former adversaries. It could be argued that the full long-term effects of the demise of the single unifying threat that gave NATO a rationale during the Cold War have yet to become fully apparent. There might be an echo of the evolution versus revolution distinction that can be found in definitions of the RMA: NATO has evolved considerably and as it continues to do so, must it not reach a stage where in effect 'NATO', as traditionally understood, no longer exists? Hence, more likely than a sudden collapse is a gradual distancing over many years due to slow shifts in interest and a widening of the gap in approach to politics. Even this more evolutionary parting of the ways is by no means inevitable, however, as most European states and the United States are likely to continue to have many interests, objectives and even threats in common. The trans-Atlantic relationship seems to offer too many benefits to both sides for either of them to risk jeopardising it. Predictions are always dangerous but the most likely outcome seems to be some loosening of NATO as it expands, with military operations being conducted on a more ad hoc basis, but the organisation continuing to serve as a significant security umbrella that brings together the two sides of the North Atlantic. Such a change would not amount to a breakdown or a crisis.

Relations between the US and Europe could, then, either continue broadly as they did during the 1990s, with occasional differences between the two remaining less significant than disagreements among the European members, but neither causing lasting problems. Alternatively, a major breach could develop, either in a political 'big bang' or through more gradual distancing of world views and policies. In either case, it is issues at this broad political level that set the context for the RMA and not vice versa. The range of potential implications, positive or negative, that the RMA could have for the US-European alliance is vast, but the outcome is crucially dependent on the quality of the underlying political relationship between the two at the widest level. Bearing this point in mind, the views of the different RMA schools of thought identified in Chapter Four can be explored regarding the problems, and possible benefits, that might arise.

The Visionary perspective suggests that the US has the option of embracing a genuine Revolution in Military Affairs, which will have effects truly worthy of the name. According to this viewpoint, the US could (if it so chooses) in the near future find itself operating in an entirely new paradigm of military operations.

The Visionaries can be further divided into positive and negative strains. The negative tendency would predict an American jump ahead to a completely new model of warfare, which none of the European members of NATO will be able to follow without a level of investment in their armed forces that is entirely implausible. Even if a post-RMA US wished to co-operate with Europe, it might be simply unable to do so. Coalition operations could become so problematic that US allies would be more of a military encumbrance than an asset and the practical difficulties of their involvement would outweigh the political and diplomatic benefits. Such a development would not necessarily have undesirable effects: even complete incompatibility at the operational and tactical levels need not jeopardise effective co-ordination and co-operation at the broader levels of military strategy and foreign policy. However, the result of a total inability to operate together could have serious implications. Old debates about burden sharing and free-riding could return to the fore. If European states were in practice incapable of contributing forces to an operation, they would lose even the limited weight in planning that they currently possess, initially in specific operations but eventually more widely. Moreover, the prospect of having to act without support could lead the US to decline to undertake an operation that it saw as less vital than the European states. Alternatively, increasingly advanced US military capabilities might allow it to intervene more easily and at lower cost, due to its technological superiority over any opponent being even wider than it is today. Yet even this ability could lead to more frequent interventions that some allies would oppose. European resentment of US 'unilateralism' could swell, albeit due in part to Europe's inability to act as an effective partner. Any growing disagreements could be exacerbated if the new capabilities spawned ethical and legal disputes, especially between RMA 'haves' and 'have-nots'.

The more positive members of the Visionary school would agree that the RMA promises to raise the US to new military paradigm. However, they would expect developments in information technology to enable these forces when necessary to step down and share information with less technologically advanced allies, who could simply 'plug in' to the American information network. On this view, while RMA capabilities will increase the technological gap between the US and its allies, they also promise to make its practical impact less problematic. Furthermore, in facilitating the interaction of technologically disparate forces, the RMA would be not only preventing the emergence of future problems but also solving existing ones: operational experience in the 1980s and 1990s often demonstrated the difficulties experienced by the individual US services in joint operations as well as those they all encounter in acting together with foreign allies. Thus rather than create new troubles, the RMA might help to solve existing ones that have long bedevilled joint operations by the different US services as well as coalition operations.

Either the Radical or the Moderate view of the RMA would predict a similar range of potential implications for alliances to those anticipated by the Visionary school, except that the negative case would be seen as less likely, given the slower pace of change and the fact that the transformation of the armed forces is not expected to lead to a totally new paradigm. Indeed, given the less drastic nature of the change envisaged, with the US diverging from the current model to a lesser degree than is sometimes assumed by the most ambitious RMA exponents, they would predict few negative implications for alliance relations from the RMA (though there might be from the other, wider political issues referred to above). Indeed, it could have a positive impact on allied relations, in the sense of making US involvement in regional security around the world less controversial to American and local opinion and in facilitating various forms of co-operation with European allies.

On the other hand, even the more modest progress predicted by the Moderates could lead to major difficulties if it coincided with a severe downturn in broader trans-Atlantic relations. Without the accompaniment of wise diplomacy, US faith in RMA could lead to the adoption of policies that might harm relations between it and the Europeans. Problems for relations between the US and its European allies are, on this view too, more likely to result from broader political factors than technological divergence, though controversies arising from new technology could themselves cause difficulties.

A Moderate could strike a further downbeat note, pointing out that the current situation is hardly one of parity and seamless interoperability. In fact, the US is already far ahead of any of its allies – the 1991 Gulf War demonstrated this in the clearest fashion imaginable, while the increasing subsequent divergence in US and European spending on research, development and procurement suggests strongly that this gap will have grown significantly since then.[4] On this view, even without a paradigm shift along the lines foreseen by RMA fans, even if there is merely continuation of the current level of innovation without any dramatic acceleration, the gap that already exists will gradually yet inexorably widen. The US and Europe will find themselves increasingly out of step with each other and could eventually pass a threshold where co-operation becomes every bit as difficult as predicted by the pessimists among those who believe strongly in the RMA. It might be that more gradual evolution would be easier to manage than a sudden step change. On the other hand, the steadily growing gap between the US and its allies could in time still culminate in a disparity similar to that envisaged by those who believe in an RMA, and this disparity could be exacerbated by wider political issues.

The Sceptics do not believe that the RMA will provide the benefits promised. Their caution rests on doubts over whether the technology is feasible, whether it will be funded, whether it will survive bureaucratic turf wars in Washington and whether the effects will be as dramatic as is hoped instead of merely representing rapid evolution (if that). They would dismiss the concern that an American leap forward in technology might lead to fundamental technological incompatibility with its allies, though they might share the concern mentioned previously that a growing gap will appear anyway. Fears about the RMA leading to a rift in the alliance will prove unfounded simply because the results will in practice prove to be too modest. The Sceptic would, however, warn that misplaced and exaggerated US faith in the RMA might be followed either by disillusion about intervention generally or by a refusal to engage in any but the most straight-forward conflicts, thus exacerbating the existing problem of combat reluctance. That is, having created a military designed for a scenario that does not occur, planners could become reluctant to attempt anything different and more risky. On this view, an RMA that proves to be overblown could still have negative effects.

The Pessimists, like the other schools, could jump either way on the implications of RMA for alliances. On the one hand, they could argue that the more unstable and dangerous world it will create, along with the increasingly nasty options it provides for hostile actors, will perforce bring the two sides of the Atlantic closer together to co-operate in the face of common peril. On the other hand, the Pessimists could predict that the threats will apply unevenly to the US and to Europe, and could lead to each side becomingly increasingly reluctant to involve itself in and to risk being identified with the other's policies, thus bringing down on themselves the wrath of someone else's enemies. The RMA could therefore provoke a major disagreement over foreign policy at the widest level. Again, the outcome that this school would predict depends on broader political factors, not only or even mainly on issues of military technology. The beneficial (or at least neutral) effects of the RMA on alliances depends fundamentally on the overall political context remaining positive. Equally, whether emerging technology leads to revolutionary or more modest change, it could cause problems if accompanied by a falling out at the wider foreign policy level.

US strategy

Perhaps the critical determinant of whether the RMA has beneficial or harmful effects on American relations with her allies depends on the grand strategy that underpins it. Clearly the RMA could influence the way that the US perceives the rest of the world and its policy towards it, but it is only one factor.

Some critics of US policy perceive a worrying tendency on the part of the United States to act unilaterally. They feel that the sole remaining superpower – or even 'hyperpower', to some – is throwing its weight around with scant regard for the sensitivities of other states, whether they are allied or potentially hostile. If the RMA does deliver the technological leap forward that its proponents promise, this tendency could become even more marked. If military power becomes easier to use successfully, and at lower cost, it could lower the threshold for the use of force. Such a scenario could see the US increasingly going its own way. While an outcome of this sort would not be exclusively a result of the RMA, resting primarily on broader foreign policy considerations, the RMA could have the effect of hastening or increasing the trend. It would do so by providing the means by which those who favour such a policy could seek to put it into effect.

A distinct but related development might occur if the US became frustrated by disagreements with its allies and exasperated by the complete inability of many of them to co-operate at the tactical and operational levels. It could face a post-RMA world in which direct threats to the US homeland were an even more pressing concern than they are today and American personnel stationed overseas were increasingly vulnerable and attractive targets for attack. This scenario could lead to isolationism, with a prickly and suspicious United States adopting something of a bunker mentality and shrugging off entangling alliances with all the diplomatic and strategic compromises they require. Again, RMA developments would not be the principal cause of such a situation but could contribute to it by diversifying the threats posed to American territory as well as by giving the US government at least what appeared to be a military option that allowed it to respond without keeping forces overseas or having to pay heed to the concerns of its allies.

These possible implications of the RMA would be grave for Europe. There are some voices in Europe that would welcome greater European self-reliance or even an American withdrawal from the eastern side of the Atlantic. Any euphoria on their part would prove short lived, however, as the critics of the US would soon be brought up short by a realisation of the extent to which they would need to raise defence expenditure to replace what would have been lost. Even if they did not feel a need to replicate fully the current American military presence in Europe, some augmentation of forces would be needed to deal with instability in, and potential threats emanating from, adjacent regions. Ironically, this might provide the trigger required to compel continental European governments to undertake serious reform of their militaries and perhaps also to look to embracing more RMA capabilities. They would also come to regret the end of the US presence as instability spread in regions uncomfortably close to Europe, to say nothing of broader international volatility that could have serious economic effects for Europe. At best, Europe would find itself having to spend a great deal more on defence to achieve the same security in a more uncertain world. At worst, it would not be able to form a consensus to do so and would therefore have to learn to live with far greater insecurity.

The prospects of the US lapsing into either isolationism or complete unilateralism should not be exaggerated. Although hard-won lessons from history and experience do tend to fade over time, most US officials and politicians have learned from the twentieth century that they cannot ignore the world outside their hemisphere because it will not ignore them. Indeed, the nature of emerging threats could create even greater imperative for involvement in various unstable regions around the world; calls for isolationism in the post-Cold War world were further discredited by September 11. There are intense debates in the US over how to interact with the outside world, not over whether there is any need to do so. There was some initial concern that the George W. Bush administration would lapse into isolationism; it was often forgotten by critics that similar fears surrounded the coming to power of a Clinton team that in its election campaign had famously defined the principal issue as 'the economy, stupid', yet in office committed US forces to a number of overseas military interventions.

What is perhaps more likely – in the absence of the low-cost, high-success silver bullet that some American analysts expect from the RMA – is greater selectivity in, and a broader range of varieties of, US military intervention. The US is likely to carry out some punitive or preventive uses of force with which its allies are unhappy (or, at least, proclaim themselves in public to be unhappy). Once again, the novelty of this issue should not be overstated: there have been several previous examples of the US conducting 'out of area' operations in the face of vigorous opposition from some of its NATO allies without jeopardising the Western alliance. Operation El Dorado Canyon of 1986 is a case in point, when only the UK among Washington's European allies offered public support and access to air bases for retaliatory air strikes against Libya, and even the Thatcher government criticised the operation in private. If the RMA provides improved long-range strike capabilities then it could increase the likelihood of such operations (though whether European states supported or opposed such action would depend on the circumstances in which it took place and the internal politics of individual European countries). If the US were to remain engaged in regional affairs, then the effects for Europe of a true RMA would not be too detrimental, although if the US was bearing even more of the burden of intervention than it does now, the Europeans could find themselves frustrated at having less influence and being more dependent on the Americans. Conversely, Washington might become increasingly irritated at the lack of contribution to mutual security being provided by its European allies.

Another, related possibility is that the US might increasingly reject commitment of ground forces in certain operations, particularly those that are not directly related to vital US interests. In such cases, it might look to sympathetic states to conduct such operations with US assistance short of commitment of combat troops. This issue is considered further below. Some schools of thought on the RMA predict capabilities, particularly in information warfare, that could be used to lend decisive advantage to friendly forces in interventions that have American blessing.[5] Before this is dismissed as far-fetched it should be recalled that there have already been conflicts in which the US has taken this approach. In the Iran-Iraq War, for example, it provided the latter with significant quantities of intelligence from satellite imagery to assist it in preparing for and defending against Iranian offensives. Current developments in ISTAR suggest a far greater potential for assisting allies, or even less closely aligned states, than was possible in the mid-1980s. The development of a model for the use of force along these lines can be discerned in Operation Deliberate Force in Bosnia (when the Croatian advance and the NATO air campaign, which was accompanied by action on the ground by British and French forces, complemented each other), Kosovo (where the KLA operated on the ground, in de facto co-operation with NATO), Afghanistan (US air power, US and British special forces and the local Northern Alliance) and in the northern part of Iraq in 2003 (US air power, US and British special forces, again, this time operating with Australian and other allies, and with Kurdish fighters). The RMA could therefore result in a broadening of what 'participation' in an operation means, though a division of labour of this sort could run into political problems if it seemed that the US was providing the IT while its allies were risking the casualties. Equally, there tends to be a correlation between influence over policy and physical presence of forces on the ground. Any deviation from this principle towards some kind of 'limited commitment' option would require difficult compromises.

Intra-European Relations

The implications of a full RMA within Europe would mainly depend on political factors, notably the extent and nature of the future American role in European security and the extent to which the leading European states co-ordinate their approaches to the new technological possibilities. As with US-European relations, a range of possibilities can be suggested.

The Visionary school, in either its positive or negative sub-varieties, would offer less grim predictions for inter-European relations than it would for Europe's relations with the US. This is for the simple reason that however far and fast the US advances, all of the European countries will remain a long way behind it. An increasing gap between the US and Europe might lead to knock-on effects, good or bad, within Europe; in other aspects, though, there would be little difference in practice between the Visionary perspective and that of the Radicals.

For both schools of thought, negative consequences for Europe could emerge from a smaller-scale replication of the gap between the US and Europe. A considerable distance could develop between Britain – and any other European states that take on some elements of the new model – and their more technologically primitive neighbours. This could lead to serious problems in coalition operations if the two paradigms became utterly incompatible, a scenario that becomes all the more plausible in view of the fact that several European states are slashing defence spending while simultaneously shying away from much-needed reforms in the structure of their armed forces. An alternative outcome would be less a simple two-fold split within Europe but rather a broader spectrum of technological level and military capability, which would have a less damaging effect on co-operation. The process of transition would, on this view, be easier to manage.

The more optimistic Visionaries and Radicals, however, would assert that the RMA could provide the solution to existing and future problems of interoperability, assuming that states take the appropriate steps. Compelling political reasons, as well as the more restricted range of technical options available, make co-operation easier to achieve among the Europeans than between Europe and the more advanced United States. The RMA could, therefore, make European military co-operation more necessary while at the same time providing the technical means by which even very different European force structures could operate in an integrated manner. Thus, the RMA could both pose the problem and also provide the solution. Even if this proves accurate, however, there could be another factor working in the opposite direction: differences over doctrinal, legal and ethical issues could pose more of a problem for a multinational European force than they would for the US, which aside from being a unitary actor, would not have the same military need for allies and could set the terms under which a coalition it dominated would operate. Moreover, there is a fundamental difference between a single state assessing and incorporating the RMA and a large number of states seeking to do so in co-operation and by consensus.

Those taking what has been described as the Moderate point of view would have fewer worries about the RMA leading to problems and would be more inclined to the view that it could facilitate intra-European military integration. Further, the RMA and other current pressures could increase the attraction for European states of closer industrial integration, which could itself facilitate interoperability by establishing the standardisation that proved largely elusive throughout the Cold War. However, the Moderates, joined here by the Sceptics, might have some concern over the cumulative effect on European defence co-operation of a growing gap in defence spending between member states and a failure to grasp the nettle of military reform in some countries. This factor is a concern anyway and would be a problem exacerbated, not caused, by current technological improvements of any sort.

The Pessimist school might suggest that the European ability to benefit from RMA is far less than that of the US, but that European states are at least as likely as North America to face new and more dangerous threats from hostile states or non-state actors. Indeed, their lower military capability, their proximity to unstable regions including the Balkans and the Middle East, and the difficulty of reaching consensus among such a large group of states could make them even more vulnerable to asymmetric attack or counter-attack. If this were to occur, the implications could be serious for the foreign policy of the EU or its member states, driving a wedge between different capitals, forcing some or all of them to appease threats or to withdraw support for US military bases and polices, or at worst making a common or even co-operative foreign policy impossible as different European governments opted for different responses to problems. This school would dismiss the potentially beneficial effects of the RMA for intra-European military co-operation on the grounds that even if new capabilities are properly funded and military structures reformed, there will not be the consensus to agree structures for armed forces, let alone to deploy them in risky operations that might provoke retaliation against European states, perhaps not limited to those contributing forces to an intervention.

As was argued with regard to US-European relations, the various possible outcomes suggested above would depend less on the technological options that become possible and more on the political context in which the technologies will be developed and fed into doctrine and force structure. The effect of the RMA on intra-European relations depends above all, of course, on how far and in what direction political integration proceeds, and the extent to which it extends to defence policy. This issue is clearly the subject of intense debate and is well beyond the scope of this book, but a brief exploration of the possibilities might be useful. At the least novel end of the spectrum would be a continuation of the current pattern, resting principally on inter-state co-operation, with some limited integrative initiatives. The degree of supranational integration continues to vary in different policy areas, with foreign and defence policy being the most jealously guarded by national governments. The more radical possibility would be the option openly advocated by some in continental Europe of what would in effect be a single European army. This latter scenario is not very likely, given that one of the few areas of agreement between the principal European military powers, the UK and France, is a rejection of the idea that defence policy should be taken away from national control and made a matter of supranational decision-making in the European Union. It is no coincidence that the states that most favour majority decision-making in any European defence policy tend to be those that are the least militarily significant and have been the least willing to commit their forces in recent operations.

Britain and France are by some distance the leading European powers in terms of a force projection capability, that is, an ability to deploy and sustain military forces at a considerable distance from the home base (although France's military reforms have some way to go before they fully match up to British capabilities in this respect). Any European 'defence initiative' that does not involve both of them would be difficult to take seriously. However, there has long been a fundamental disagreement between London and Paris over the relationship of a European defence identity to the Atlantic alliance. The UK has consistently been a staunch supporter of close links with the United States, for many years having a 'special relationship' with Washington that is occasionally derided but nevertheless very real and significant, most of all in defence and intelligence matters. Britain's engagement in, and embrace of, a European defence identity since the 1998 Anglo-French summit at St Malo has been predicated on ensuring that any such identity is both compatible with and complementary to NATO. France, on the other hand, has habitually been the most sceptical European state about the Atlantic alliance, or even, at times, the most overtly anti-American (though never quite to the extent that the most extreme Gaullist rhetoric and posturing might suggest). France would be happy to have more integration in defence policy on the condition that it was on her terms. The dilemma for France is that many of her fellow-members of the EU that would be prepared to accept more integration in defence are solidly Atlanticist. There is little support for the view sometimes emanating from Paris that a European defence identity should act as a balance to or even a competitor with the US. There are good reasons to believe that any significant European defence co-operation (as opposed to routine photo-opportunity announcements) is likely to remain on an inter-state basis rather than leading to a genuine European army, and is likely to be compatible with the Atlantic alliance, even if some limited operations might be undertaken by the Europeans alone.

EU defence capabilities

Since the end of the Cold War, the European Union has taken some steps towards acquiring a defence and security identity. It agreed to establish a European Rapid Reaction Force (ERRF) that would be able to deploy up to 60,000 men, at two months notice, and to sustain them for up to a year. The fine print of this agreement demonstrates just how distant a European army remains. First, this initiative envisaged a menu of units that national governments agreed might be available, from which contributions could be requested for a specific operation. It was no standing army and each government retained the final say over whether its troops would be deployed on any particular occasion. Second, although the pledges of the various states involved were in some cases numerically impressive,[6] mere numbers are no guarantee of quality of training and equipment, nor of an actual ability to deploy to the region of concern, nor of whether the political will would exist to commit the forces concerned, nor of their availability when needed (rather than already being deployed on another operation). The great majority of the states involved were conspicuously lacking in some or all of these criteria. Third, the ambitions for this force as initially agreed were distinctly limited. The envisaged roles were restricted to the 'Petersberg tasks', non-warfighting operations up to mid-level peacekeeping (though not a full enforcement operation). Fourth, it was subject to serious practical limitations. Although it had its own planning cell, this was a small-scale body and nowhere near the size needed to act as an operational headquarters. For that sort of capability, and others such as strategic lift, intelligence and logistics, the force would rely on NATO assets or those of individual EU members. Thus NATO and the United States retained a de facto veto over major operations, if not a formal one.

The ERRF was therefore rather modest. Fears – or hopes, depending on one's perspective – that it could challenge NATO or emerge as a European Army assume that it will develop a great deal further. While that is possible, and the ambitions of some states suggest that they desire it to do so, there are serious impediments to such evolution. The first is that many of the states involved would not agree to further moves that would have such a result; combat deployment of armed forces seems to be the last area in which most major states would agree to forego their veto over decision-making. The second, perhaps more decisive, is that there is little sign that the states involved are willing to devote to defence the substantial additional resources that would be needed. To have a capability that was genuinely independent of NATO – for which read the United States – either Europe as a whole or individual states would have to acquire hugely expensive and technologically demanding assets in such areas as strategic intelligence, strategic lift (air and sea) and strategic air power, as well as undertaking costly and politically painful reform of the structure of their forces. These conditions are extremely unlikely to be met; therefore the most ambitious predictions about the effect of the ERRF will remain unfounded.

The existing European defence identity could potentially have a number of positive effects, however. First, it might make some modest increases in defence spending more palatable to finance ministries. Second, although the first point currently seems rather optimistic, the expressed goals might encourage existing defence budgets to be spent in a more useful way, enhancing capabilities that are plainly inadequate: the problem today is not simply that budgets are too small (though they are clearly far too modest to meet the stated aspirations) but that they get very poor value for money. More sensible spending of existing funds would be useful but political and bureaucratic obstacles to reform suggest that this hope might also be unfounded. Third, the ERRF could potentially allow the participation in military intervention of states that would otherwise find it difficult due to their history (notably Germany) or their former neutral status (such as Sweden, Finland, and Austria).[7] Finally, if the force does become a reality, even with its present modest purview, it could offer a useful capability for some small-scale operations when the United States opts not to get involved. It could therefore become a useful tool of burden sharing, which is an issue that will be returned to below.

There are also some risks associated with the ERRF, even if the more lurid predictions referred to above are discounted. First, if badly handled it could harm relations with key allies – notably the United States but also other NATO members such as Turkey and the East European countries that have not yet been admitted to the EU. Second, it could result in an illusory capability that looks impressive on paper but that either would be unavailable when called upon or, more seriously, might fail ignominiously if and when committed to an operation. Third, it could distract the attention of the continental states from a very real need to reform their out-dated defence structures.

This last is perhaps the most serious: it is rather premature to discuss a Revolution in Military Affairs in relation to states that cling to a distinctly nineteenth or early-twentieth century focus on conscript armies for territorial defence. With the exception of Britain and France, which for reasons of history have a less overwhelmingly continental mindset and are less averse to intervening overseas, there is a pressing need for European states to adopt a more up-to-date, expeditionary approach, so as to be able to deploy and sustain forces away from their borders. The continental members of both NATO and the EU (even, to some extent, France) need to undertake considerable reform to get to the position the UK was in the late-1990s, so talk of an RMA is rather putting the cart before the horse. The adoption of the plan for the ERRF might optimistically be interpreted as a sign that the need to make these changes might have been accepted but there are as yet few concrete indications that the nettle has been grasped. If the continental West European states were to embrace the need for change, commit the required resources and press ahead with fundamental reform, some might even label the result a European RMA. At the very least it would begin to reduce the often laughable gap between rhetoric and military capabilities. It is difficult not to sympathise with the sentiment that 'Europe is effectively out of the war business'.[8]

Since the members of the EU plan to be able to co-operate closely with each other, they will clearly need to establish common standards for interoperability, notably modernised, efficient and compatible communications, information technology and military doctrine. Given that this will be required in any case, it should be possible to ensure that these standards are compatible with the United States. The additional investment required to achieve this aim would secure useful dividends in terms of retaining an ability to operate with the US, whether this meant fighting side-by-side or, as suggested above, linking into certain American capabilities when Washington supported an operation but did not want to commit its own ground forces. The EU states are committed to creating forces that can operate with each other in expeditionary operations; these same changes are also what are needed to make the Europeans more efficient and useful allies for the US. From another point of view, it would be useful for Europe to have some degree of capability to conduct operations without always having to rely so heavily on the US. Reform of old-fashioned armed forces, together with the additional spending that this would make possible for particular military capabilities (including some elements of the RMA) would serve two ends: it would make individual European states more capable allies for the US and it would also provide them with some form of usable European intervention force.

Interoperability

Although the RMA touches upon many issues relating to alliances, it has most impact on interoperability. There are several forms of co-operation between allies, of which the most demanding is full integration. This form of co-operation can be seen in the presence of a British armoured division in a US armoured corps during Desert Storm in 1991. It is an exacting goal that requires a great deal of both compatibility and practical familiarity in communications, doctrine, training and language. It is noteworthy that not all NATO members currently have this level of interoperability with each other; it is important not to give the inaccurate impression that there is complete compatibility between today's NATO forces that the RMA could jeopardise. Still, this is what is required if states are to send their armed forces into battle side by side even under the current paradigm – though it is important to note that less demanding forms of commonality can still allow some degree of co-operation, and this has often been the situation in recent operations. In spite of the evident benefits of standardisation, especially during the Cold War confrontation with the Soviet bloc, moves in this direction within the Western alliance were limited. Nevertheless, there are fears that if the US does rush into the RMA, and if it delivers all that has been promised, substantial problems could be caused. America's allies already lag far behind it in many ways, not least in communications. The time could come when the US did not deem it worthwhile to invest in the capability to communicate with its lower-technology allies. Indeed, if the digitisation of its forces moves ahead as far as some hope it will, it might simply be impossible for them to work together.

However, the view that there will necessarily be a problem is a pessimistic one. It rests on certain political assumptions rather than technical feasibility. A more optimistic view would be that the problems of communicating and operating together could well be mitigated by advances in information technology. Different coalition partners could be privy to different levels of information or integrated with American systems to different degrees, in much the same way as is the case today. Just as present day distinctions are drawn on the basis of a number of factors, including political will, military competence and security considerations as well as the purely technical issues of compatibility, the same will continue to be the case in the future. Besides, the very fact that complete incompatibility is seen by both the US and its allies as something to be avoided gives some grounds for optimism. The US clearly has an interest in remaining interoperable with its allies. The allies' military contribution in the 1991 Gulf conflict, Afghanistan or Iraq in 2003 was not essential for strictly military reasons, as was also the case with the Pacific campaign in the Second World War or the Korean War, but was nevertheless useful militarily and, moreover, of considerable political importance. In some operations, the participation of allies is essential for domestic and international political reasons; in others it might be desirable if the US has sufficient interest to contribute to an operation but not enough to conduct it alone.

The technical obstacles to ensuring interoperability are difficult for someone without an extensive background in the technologies concerned to assess. Nevertheless, it seems reasonable to point out that it is no new problem: during the Cold War, the Gulf conflict, and the interventions in the former Yugoslavia, members of the respective coalitions were initially not all able to communicate with each other and measures had to be improvised to give them sufficient connectivity to conduct the operations. The coalitions in the Gulf and in the Balkans included states that were not members of NATO and even some that had shortly before been classed as potential opponents. Naturally some national contingents were better integrated than others, while the least technologically able could simply be co-ordinated rather than fully integrated. The lesson taken could be that it was possible to put together ad hoc solutions that worked or, less comforting, that in another situation either the delay involved or any limitations in the system might have had serious consequences. Clearly it would be preferable not to have to look to improvisation but the fact that it was necessary in several successive cases suggests that this issue has not yet been solved.

If the US does make the great leap forward that some propose, purely technical matters of interoperability are less likely to be a problem than a more basic disparity in force structure and concept of operations: it would be difficult to have a mechanised division from the Second World War operating in close harmony with a Napoleonic-era unit. Indeed, if the most dramatic predictions of the Visionary school come true, this comparison would under-state the differences between the future American and continental European models. The broadening range of capabilities promised by RMA proponents is also likely to give rise to contentious ethical, legal and political problems about when and how to use force, and to complicate rules of engagement. Again, coalitions have long been dogged by such issues, but the RMA could make them worse. Potential partners might, for example, disagree with the US about the desirability, legality and morality of strategic information operations against enemy computer systems, or might seek more exacting target confirmation rules for long-range strike. Heightened and then disappointed expectations in domestic, allied and world opinion about avoiding collateral damage and friendly casualties could well prove problematic. The response to this would be much the same as it is now: patient discussion between diplomats together with calculations of whether the political and military value of a possible contributing ally is worth the restrictions that its participation might impose.

Clearly, one vital need is for close contact and consultation between allies over emerging capabilities, in order to reach at a minimum a mutual understanding and at best common views on many issues such as rules of engagement, the role and desirability of information operations, and other questions that have legal and ethical as well as military dimensions. Such discussions are important in establishing a reasonably common outlook on the various issues, and have the additional benefit of being attractively cheap in comparison with the efforts required to achieve technical compatibility. There is really no excuse for failing to establish such exchanges, both within Europe and between Europe and the US.

The US attaches considerable importance to the question of interoperability. The 'Joint Vision 2020' document makes this clear, stating:

> Since our potential multinational partners will have varying levels of technology, a tailored approach to interoperability that accommodates a wide range of needs and capabilities is necessary. Our more technically advanced allies will have systems and equipment that are essentially compatible, enabling them to interface and share information in order to operate effectively with US forces at all levels. However, we must also be capable of operating with allies and coalition partners who may be technologically incompatible – especially at the tactical level.

It adds that multinational operations require not only technological compatibility but also 'a shared understanding of operational procedures and compatible organizations'.[9] One interesting point that arises from these statements is the recognition that different allies might enjoy different levels of compatibility with US forces. This view seems accurate. The UK, for example, neither needs nor aspires to the whole range of capabilities envisaged in the RMA but modern communications and digitisation of its forces are clearly one of the top priority areas. The British armed forces hope to embrace digitisation at least to the extent necessary to remain interoperable with the US. Greater problems could remain with other allies. The basic picture is likely to be the same as it is today, with different allies being able to co-operate with the United States to different degrees, yet the gaps between the various categories are likely to become more stretched out. As already argued, these technological considerations will be related to other factors that might impede co-operation, including willingness to commit forces (either at all, or in the specific area concerned; it is unlikely that many European states, for example, would contribute forces to an operation in Asia) and the political constraints imposed on forces by their national governments. As is the case with Britain, it is in the interests of America's allies to maintain the ability to co-operate closely with it. As Freedman puts it:

> The most important allies of the US will make an effort to stay abreast of these technologies and to adopt them where possible, if only for purposes of interoperability and to gain access to US policy-making in times of crisis and war. It will become the subscription to be taken seriously as an ally.[10]

Naturally, doing so might be prohibitively expensive for many US allies, who would find it difficult to remain a serious ally by Freedman's definition. One alternative might be for some smaller allies to divide their forces into two tiers. The upper tier would consist of relatively small, high-technology forces, that are trained, equipped and structured for expeditionary operations and are as closely interoperable as possible with the Americans and other like-minded allies. The remainder of their forces (if indeed there was a long-term case for them) would be less advanced, cheaper units that could be held back for less demanding operations or as reserves for territorial defence.[11] While such a move would create some difficulties it might nevertheless be useful for some continental European states that would value the ability to contribute forces to a multinational coalition but might be unwilling or unable to equip all of their forces to the required standard. This option might be particularly applicable for those countries that cling to national service, with intervention forces restricted to volunteers.

The other possibility would be for some more explicit form of role specialisation. The Cold War period saw various examples of this phenomenon in NATO – for example, some of the smaller West European navies specialised in mine-sweeping, which the US Navy comparatively neglected. The argument would be that after the Cold War, the changes under way in the American armed forces will fundamentally transform them, while there is no realistic prospect of West European states following suit. The problem here would not be a mere issue of technical compatibility but rather the more basic problem of entirely different conceptions of warfare that might make it impossible for forces from either side of the Atlantic to work together in a fully integrated way. The alternative of role specialisation would not necessarily take the narrow form of dividing up individual military capabilities. This approach involves disadvantages in terms of institutionalising dependence on other states, which could lead to a situation where a gap existed if a presumed partner with responsibility for a critical capability refused to participate in a particular operation. In any case, such a narrow view of burden sharing would not solve the problem of how to allow a post-RMA United States and its allies to co-operate. The role specialisation envisaged here would be more at the military strategic and grand strategic levels of policy; that is, the less well-equipped European states would specialise in certain types of operations, particularly those requiring troops on the ground when the US was unwilling to do this.[12] Such an approach has advantages and disadvantages. On the one hand, it would keep the two sides of the Atlantic alliance together politically, while European intervention in some regions might be more politically acceptable to local parties than having American troops used. On the other, it could lead to suspicion that the Europeans (or other allies elsewhere) were risking the casualties in support of American interests. Further, there would be no guarantee that disputes over political and military strategy would not reduce the effectiveness of co-operation that was possible at a purely practical level. In theory it might seem attractive to combine US strategic intelligence and combat air power with European troops on the ground. In practice, the experience might not be a wholly happy one, as is suggested by the 1992-95 UNPROFOR deployment in Bosnia, where significant differences emerged over political and military strategy.

It would be wrong to characterise this issue as a US-versus-European one, as some degree of role specialisation seems to be developing among the European states. Caused by a combination of hugely varying military capability and will to commit forces, an arrangement could be proposed by which some states commit combat forces while others concentrate on combat support, support and strategic lift. Movement in this direction would risk replicating US-European tensions within Europe, as the states that were ready and willing to commit combat forces might be reluctant to concede as much decision-making weight as the less capable states might seek. Arguments about burden sharing and concerns over some states suffering disproportionate casualties would be inevitable. If an increasing disparity emerges within Europe in terms of expeditionary capability and will to deploy troops, then disputes could also arise between European states similar to those that occasionally cause squalls between Europe and the US.[13]

This form of burden sharing will probably not be needed in such formal, general terms. For this to be the case there would have to be a very radical shift in the way the US forces function. It will remain in the interests of both the US and its allies to retain the capability to operate together, and given a certain degree of political will it should be technically feasible to do so. Where a form of burden sharing similar to that outlined above might be applicable would be on a more limited, ad hoc basis rather than as a broad strategy. This more restricted conception might see some solely European operations, such as a limited peace support operation or non-combatant evacuation operation either in Europe or close to it. Such operations could see the US providing combat support or participating with some strike systems, either of which could be made easier by RMA technology. It would be more likely to involve an extension of current practice, by which states participating in an operation undertake different sorts of roles depending on a host of factors particular to the state concerned and to the circumstances of the conflict at hand. Some allies, such as Britain, France or the Netherlands might supply combat forces, while others, that are constrained for technical or political reasons, might contribute forces for escorting sealift vessels or defending bases in the theatre and other rear-area tasks. An alternative model would be more sequential: the US and UK could undertake combat operations, the UK with the more capable Europeans the immediate post-war stabilisation and then less capable allies look after the peacekeeping phase.

Conclusion

An RMA, however limited or far-reaching its effect on capabilities, is bound to have considerable effects on alliances. This chapter has explored some of the consequences it could have for the trans-Atlantic relationship and for intra-European relations. The clearest conclusion is that technological issues of compatibility are not the most significant factor; here, as much as in any other aspect of the RMA, the primacy of political issues over narrowly military and technical ones is clear. The far end of the range of possibilities is a migration by US forces to an entirely new model of warfare that is quite incompatible with the old model. Even in this case, however, any practical problems of interoperability could be either solved or worked around if the broader political relationship were favourable. If there were to be a serious breach, in the overall relationship or over a specific policy issue, either between Europe and the US or within Europe, then even totally compatible forces would not be able to work together. At the broadest level, then, the technical impact of the RMA on alliances is subordinate to their underlying political health. The fact that each of the perspectives on the RMA that are used in this book could reach either optimistic or pessimistic conclusions about its impact on alliances demonstrates that it is not the RMA that is the decisive variable here but political factors.

That is not to say, of course, that the RMA cannot affect alliances. This chapter has suggested a number of ways in which emerging RMA concepts and capabilities could have positive or negative effects on alliances. (Many of these advantages, or disadvantages do not depend on there being a genuine RMA: even an 'evolutionary' model could lead to an incremental improvement or worsening of tendencies that have long existed.) At best, it could make co-operation far easier, allowing the more and less technologically gifted to interact far more easily than they do at present, or providing the US with far more effective and less intrusive ways to support allies around the world. The US would still be able to co-operate at the grand strategic and military-strategic levels, and its forces could step down to co-ordinate and co-operate with allies (if not integrate with all of them) at the operational and tactical levels. Even technical incompatibility need not cause insuperable difficulties, as long as the political circumstances were positive. At worst, an RMA could magnify existing disputes over burden sharing and decision making, exacerbate differences in world view and policy between allies, and introduce new strategic, legal and ethical disputes over the use of new means of intervention. Seduced by dazzling new technological opportunities, the US could embrace a truly unilateralist policy, with allies simply too much trouble to be worth the political restraint and military complications that co-operation would involve.

The RMA will affect even the most ambitious European state far less than it will the US. For this reason, the possible effects of the RMA on intra-European relations are likely to be far less dramatic, for good or ill, than on the trans-Atlantic relationship. The same issues could be significant, however, even if to a lesser degree. Positively, an RMA could make coalition operations easier even if they are conducted by technologically very different partners. Negatively, an RMA could widen the gap between those capable of sophisticated military operations and those who can only sit on the sidelines, with all the political implications that such a split could have. Any political, ethical or legal disagreements thrown up by RMA capabilities are likely to have a serious impact on Europe, as an entity that is still very far from unitary. A beneficial RMA could make co-operation far easier for the Europeans; a harmful one could exacerbate existing disparities in capability and will to deploy military forces. At best, the RMA could allow European forces to co-operate with the US and with each other; at worst, the more advanced European states might be incompatible with both the US and other European states

If the political backdrop is unfavourable, the RMA could lead to disputes that will worsen relations. On the whole, however, if the RMA does become a problem it is likely to be largely the result of a major breach, not its cause. That is, it would have detrimental effects only if serious disputes arise in some major area of policy, grave enough to cause a major breach in broad US-European or intra-European relations. Short of such a catastrophic parting of the ways, the potential problems that could be caused by the RMA should be solvable with a modicum of sensible discussion. If there were to be a split in US-European relations or within Europe, whether sudden or a more gradual drifting apart, then the RMA could exacerbate them. Any failure to work together would not be down to a technological shortcoming but a political one; any catastrophic breakdown will not be caused by the RMA but rather by political decisions or indecision.

Conclusions

There is a wide range of competing definitions of what a Revolution in Military Affairs is. There is an equally great variety of opinions about what the effects might be if, in fact, one is underway at all, which is also a matter of intense debate. The history of previous attempts to interpret change that some believe to be revolutionary suggests that this profusion of views is likely to include some wild overstatements. It is notoriously difficult to predict the future course of technological change; looking back to visions of the year 2000 from the 1950s or 1960s, it was expected that at the millennium we would be driving floating cars, eating nourishment pills instead of food and wearing one-piece shiny grey suits that would make a Dr Who costume designer wince. There is undoubtedly a need for wariness towards the occasional dubious and metaphorical use of language and concepts: 'dominance of the info-sphere' does not necessarily provide a degree of control comparable to troops occupying territory; 'information superiority' is not the same thing as air superiority; and 'control of cyberspace' is not the same as control of the sea. However, another conclusion that is suggested by history is that just because some exaggeration is involved does not mean that there is no substance in the debate.

The competing approaches to defining an RMA in general turn on different views about how military capabilities change, each of which is quite consistent and sustainable. First, the whole concept of RMA may be rejected as concealing more than it reveals, on the grounds that it places transitory change on an analytical pedestal, overlooking both continuity and broader processes of evolution. Second, it may be accepted that some truly momentous changes do very rarely occur and the term RMA should be used, most sparingly, for these. A third approach would be to acknowledge these enormously significant turning points but to coin a different, grander term for them, such as 'Military Revolution' or even 'Major RMA', allowing the term RMA (or 'Minor RMA') to be used less strictly to designate important shifts within the longer epochs. Finally, a large number of RMAs may be recognised across history, with no more than an informal hierarchy of greater or lesser examples. These models, each of which has its adherents, apply to understanding the concept of RMA in the abstract; the issue of whether one is currently underway is different.

There is, mercifully, rather more consensus regarding the sources of RMAs. Technology is recognised as an important factor but is usually seen as neither the only one nor even necessarily as the most significant. It is accompanied and sometimes relegated to a subordinate place by other political, economic and social factors, which are particularly emphasised by those who incline towards the stricter definitions of the term. There is also broad agreement that for a potential RMA to be realised in practice requires that its contributing elements must be recognised, fully understood and incorporated into new military doctrine and organisation.

A variety of opinions can be discerned over the significance of the changes in warfare that are a feature of the contemporary period. First, it may be denied that the present era represents anything more than the normal evolution, though perhaps at a faster rate than usual. This view could be held by those who reject the idea of RMAs at any time or by those who see them as possible but simply do not perceive the current period as amounting to one. Second, post-Cold War developments may be seen as a precursor stage to a genuine revolution according to the more rigorous definitions of RMA; some in this school would go further, assessing the current period as the tail-end of a previous RMA. For the adherents of the more permissive approach to identification, a third approach is to assert that the world is undergoing a true RMA that is fully comparable with many previous historical examples. Finally, at the most ambitious end of the scale, even those who are the most parsimonious in conferring the title may accept that the contemporary period amounts to one of very few (perhaps two or three) authentic RMAs in history. Once again, each of these perspectives is internally consistent and has its advocates.

As has been noted in this book, disputes over the exact label to be used might seem frustrating and pedantic. Surely, it might be argued, what counts is not what the current period is called but rather its effects on warfare? The thought of sweeping away the mass of terminological wrangling that confounds this subject is undoubtedly appealing; nonetheless, it does matter. Debates over how to designate the current period are not simply turgid scholastic rituals but involve competing views of precisely how great the effects of recent developments will be: are the current events more accurately assessed as routine evolution, as a noteworthy change of the sort that occurs every couple of decades or as a historical 'big bang' that is seen maybe once or twice a millennium? Casting aside the competing labels is, alas, no short-cut to resolving this question.

The argument of this book has been that the current period does not amount to an RMA in the most restrictive sense of the term. Significant changes are undoubtedly afoot but they are as yet far from the extent of those accompanying the transition from the Agricultural to the Industrial Age, as some would assert. The competing approach of acknowledging a greater number of RMAs has been found to be more useful, since otherwise even developments such as those surrounding the French Revolution or the advent of nuclear weapons would be excluded. Moreover, this latter approach provides a greater number and wider range of historical comparisons. By this more lenient definition, the current period could be seen as an RMA, perhaps comparable to the changes of the interwar period or, if it should advance as far as foreseen by what this book has characterised as the 'Radical' perspective, those of the Industrial Revolution.

The changes currently underway are hugely significant. Building on technological and conceptual advances of the 1970s and 1980s, the effects of information technology and digitisation are making possible the integrated 'system of systems' so cherished by RMA enthusiasts. It will result in forces that are very much better equipped, better informed and able to fight smarter. The ability to gather, process and exploit information that the emerging network makes possible will truly revolutionise conventional force-on-force warfare which, contrary to some opinion, will still be an unpleasantly frequent feature of international affairs. It will also offer many useful, if incremental benefits in the types of conflict that are likely to be more prevalent, namely lower intensity, intra-state warfare and other forms of asymmetric response.

The effects that should be anticipated from this RMA, however, are considerably less than some of its advocates predict. Its proponents tend to underestimate several factors that in practice will reduce the impact of the RMA far below their hopes. First, they overlook the ever present companions of all commanders throughout history, uncertainty (the fog of war), chance and the tendency of complex activities to fall victim to problems such as human error or mechanical failure (friction). Technology is not going to solve these problems, which have a particularly detrimental impact on many ideas about Information Warfare. Second, they overlook one of the defining characteristics of strategy, which is the existence of a thinking opponent who is seeking actively to frustrate your plans while advancing his own. Reactions to the RMA, as with all previous examples of momentous changes in military capability, will take the form of a combination of imitation and countering, with a mixture of high- and low-technology responses. Third, they overlook that fact that most conflict is not the conventional force-on-force warfare for which the RMA is best adapted but is lower intensity and more complicated. Wars between states will still occur and even in other cases, emerging capabilities offer considerable steps forward, yet this factor does restrict the overall impact of the RMA. The second and third factors are linked by the issue of asymmetric warfare, which gives the RMA an almost self-negating character: the more it improves the capabilities of the leading military powers in traditional military operations, the greater incentive it provides for any challenger to sidestep their advantages and to confront them with something more difficult (which might in turn be facilitated by some advances thrown up in the wake of the RMA). Finally, RMA aficionados tend to overlook the effect of political factors, which tower over all forms of warfare. Ethical and legal constraints, diplomatic and alliance considerations, the effect of domestic and international public opinion and even the difficulties involved in imposing one's will on an opponent all come into this category. It is surprising how often analysts of strategy and warfare fail to pay sufficient attention to politics; no doubt fish rarely contemplate the importance of water.

For some, all of these provisos and limitations might suggest that the current period does not, in fact, merit being designated an RMA. However, the magnitude of what remains even after all of these reservations are taken into account should not be dismissed. If both the potential and the limitations of the new technology are properly understood and married to appropriate doctrine, then in suitable cases, where the politics are right and the strategy is appropriate, it will bring about stunning results that do justify the label 'RMA'. As has been argued, however, this might not be quite as far-reaching a conclusion as might be thought. First of all, the definition used is on the more permissive end of the scale. Second, it does not require that an RMA be a total paradigm shift with no elements of continuity whatsoever. Third, and even more important, an RMA does not amount to some sort of strategic lottery win. It would be inappropriate to attach to the definition of an RMA the requirement that it must provide a military option that was equally applicable to all types and intensities of conflict, let alone insisting that it must offer a solution to every political-strategic dilemma that might be thrown at it. These criteria would rule out plausible candidate RMAs such as the developments during the Napoleonic Wars, the period of the two world wars, or nuclear weapons; even the transition from agricultural to industrial societies would fail such a stringent test. Establishing a definition as demanding as this one would not represent setting the bar too high as much as replacing analysis with a search for some kind of strategic Holy Grail.

What contemporary developments will not and cannot do, any more than previous RMAs, is to provide a guaranteed low-cost, high-success military solution to every complex political and strategic problem that might arise. This qualification does not indicate that the current period is not a Revolution in Military Affairs. It means simply that no RMA amounts to a magic bullet.

Notes

Chapter 1

1   Williamson Murray, 'Thinking about revolutions in military affairs', *Joint Forces Quarterly*, Summer 1997, p.69. Freedman also cites this as being the first usage of the term; Lawrence Freedman, *The Revolution in Strategic Affairs: Adelphi Paper 318* (Oxford, OUP for IISS, 1998), p.7.
2. Robert R. Tomes, 'Revolution in Military Affairs: A History', *Military Review*, September-October 2000.
3. This point is made in Colin Gray, *The American RMA: An Interim Assessment* (SCSI Occasional, No. 28, 1997), pp.12-13.
4. Alvin Toffler and Heidi Toffler, *War and Anti-War: Survival at the Dawn of the 21st Century* (London, Warner, 1994).
5. Martin Creveld, *Technology and War From 2000 BC to the Present* (London, Brasseys, 1991), p.14. He does accept some developments as truly revolutionary, such as the changes of the French Revolutionary and Napoleonic Wars; see p.21
6. Andrew F. Krepinevich, 'Cavalry to Computer: The Pattern of Military Revolutions', *National Interest*, Fall 1994.
7. James Adams, *The Next World War: The Weapons and Warriors of the New Battlefields in Cyberspace* (London, Arrow, 1998), p.54.
8. Gray, *The American RMA*, pp.13-14, 21-22
9. Steven Metz and James Kievit, *Strategy and the Revolution in Military Affairs: From Theory to Policy* (US Army Strategic Studies Institute, 1995), pp.v, 9-11. They believe that the world is currently undergoing a minor RMA and is on the verge of a major one.
10. Murray, pp.70-73. For example, he sees the Military Revolution of the First World War as being preceded by the Preshock RMA of the Fisher Revolution (1905-1914) and followed by aftershock RMAs including combined arms, blitzkrieg, strategic bombing, carrier warfare, unrestricted submarine warfare, amphibious warfare, intelligence, information warfare (1940-45) and stealth.
11. Krepinevich, p.30
12. John Keegan, *A History of Warfare* (New York, Knopf, 1993), chapters 2-3.
13. Creveld, *Technology and War*, especially pp.10-13, 37-49, 112.
14. Murray, pp.67-70.
15. For example, Beaumont suggests the alternative of 'On-going Military Technical Evolution', to stress the continuous nature of development, combinations and re-combinations; Roger Beaumont, 'OMTE: An Alternative Paradigm to "The Revolution in Military Affairs"', *Defense Analysis*, December 1995.
16. Creveld, *Technology and War*, pp.55-61, 132-33; he explains that galleys were eventually rendered obsolete with the introduction of gunpowder, since sailing ships proved capable of carrying more and heavier guns.
17. Freedman, *Revolution in Strategic Affairs*, pp.7-8. It is striking, however, that William Owens (the godfather of the RMA) derides the term 'transformation' as less ambitious than 'RMA', see his 'The Once and Future Revolution in Military Affairs', *Joint Forces Quarterly*, Summer 2002, pp.58-59.

Chapter 2

1. For example, Martin van Creveld, who is generally restrained in his use of the term 'revolutionary' sees the impact of these developments as 'revolutionary, indeed explosive'; see his *Technology and War* p.21
2. The literature on Napoleon is legion. A good starting point can be found in Peter Paret, 'Napoleon and the Revolution in War', and the bibliographical essay, in Peter Paret, (ed.) *Makers of Modern Strategy from Machiavelli to the Nuclear Age* (Oxford, Oxford University Press, 1986).
3. Metz and Kievit see the division and corps structures of Napoleon's armies, like the introduction of rifled guns in nineteenth century, as minor RMAs that formed 'constituent parts of a "major" revolution which included fundamental social, economic, and political change rather than simply a

radical increase in combat effectiveness.' Metz and Kievit, *Strategy and the Revolution in Military Affairs: From Theory to Policy*, pp.9-11.

4. It is tempting to compare Napoleon in this respect with Alexander the Great, who did not introduce major military reforms but rather demonstrated an unmatched ability to use the formidable combined-arms force that was his legacy from his father, Philip of Macedon.

5. David Gates, *The Napoleonic Wars, 1803-1815* (London, Arnold, 1997), p.272.

6. Carl von Clausewitz, (Michael Howard and Peter Paret, eds.) *On War* (Princeton, Princeton University Press, 1989), Book Eight, Chapter Six, pp.609-10.

7. Clausewitz suggested that war could be analysed using a trinity of violence, chance and politics, represented by a second trinity of the people, the army and the government; *On War*, Book One, Chapter One.

8. Initially, however, the range of gunfire was reduced; Archer Jones notes that the range of the Prussian breech loading rifle was actually half that of the Austrian muzzle loader, but this disadvantage was compensated by the higher rate of fire and by the ability of a soldier with a breech-loader to fire and, crucially, reload from a prone position rather than standing, as the Austrians had to; Archer Jones, *The Art of War in the Western World* (Oxford, Oxford University Press, 1987), pp.397-98. New weapons systems often have some initial disadvantages: for example it took many years for firearms to match the range and accuracy of the long bow.

9. Creveld writes that problems encountered in the 1852 war with Austria led to concerted efforts by France to improve the situation and hence produced a far better performance in 1859 against Italy; see *Technology and War*, pp.158-59.

10. Jones, *Art of War*, pp.396-98, 404-5.

11. Victor Hanson argues that the technological prowess of the West Europeans, as well as the way they conceived of war and battle were all crucial in their imperial successes – and that all were the product of their culture. Victor D. Hanson, *Carnage and Culture: Landmark Battles in the Rise of Western Power* (New York, Doubleday, 2001).

12. A helpful general account of the nineteenth century changes in navies and naval warfare can be found in Bernard Brodie, *Sea Power in the Machine Age* (Princeton, Princeton University Press, 1942).

13. Bernard Brodie, 'Technological Change, Strategic Doctrine and Political Outcomes' in K Knorr, (ed.) *Historical Dimensions of National Security Problems* (Lawrence, Kansas, University Press of Kansas, 1976), p.280-81.

14. Bryan Ranft, 'Sir Julian Corbett' in Geoffrey Till, (ed.) *Maritime Strategy and the Nuclear Age* (2nd edition, London, Macmillan, 1984), p.42.

15. Earl Tilford, *The Revolution in Military Affairs: Prospects and Cautions* (Strategic Studies Institute, US Army War College, 1995), p.2.

16. Jonathan Bailey, *The First World War and the Birth of the Modern Style of Warfare* (Strategic and Combat Studies Institute, Occasional Paper Number 22, 1996); also 'Deep Battle 1914-1941: The Birth of the Modern Style of Warfare', and 'The Century of Firepower', *British Army Review*, December 1998.

17. Murray, 'Thinking about revolutions in military affairs', p.72.

18. Giulio Douhet, *Command of the Air* (Trans. D. Ferrari: London, Faber and Faber, 1943 - original 1921); William Mitchell, (General, US Army) *Winged Defense: The Development and Possibilities of Modern Air Power - Economic and Military* (New York, Putnams, 1925); Alexander P. de Seversky, *Victory through Air Power* (New York, Simon & Schuster, 1942).

19. Douhet, p.146.

20. An interesting example of this sceptical school was written by the pseudonymous 'Neon', *The Great Delusion: A Study of Aircraft in Peace and War* (London, Ernst Benn, 1927); for example: 'The development of aircraft for war purposes is a sheer waste of men and money'; p.xxxvii. His writing is strikingly similar to that of Bernard Acworth, who published several books in the 1930s, so perhaps that is Neon's secret identity.

21. R H Fredette, *The First Battle of Britain, 1917-1918, and the Birth of the Royal Air Force* (London, Cassell, 1966).

22. Similarly, it is often overlooked that the German air campaign that led to the Battle of Britain was *not* a strategic bombing campaign, intended to knock Britain out of the war by itself; it was rather an attempt to gain air superiority that would allow Germany to neutralise British naval power and thus permit an invasion.
23. J F C Fuller, *The Reformation of War* (London, Hutchinson, 1923) and *On Future Warfare* (London, Sifton Praed, 1928); Basil H. Liddell Hart, *Paris: The Future of Warfare* (London, Kegan Paul, Trench, Trubner & Co, 1925); Brian Bond and Martin Alexander, 'Liddell Hart and de Gaulle: The Doctrines of Limited Liability and Mobile Defence' in Peter Paret, (ed.) *Makers of Modern Strategy from Machiavelli to the Nuclear Age* (Oxford, Oxford University Press, 1986).
24. Creveld, *Technology and War*, p.180.
25. Eliot Cohen, 'A Revolution in Warfare', *Foreign Affairs*, March-April 1996, p.46.
26. Beaumont, 'OMTE: An Alternative Paradigm to the "Revolution in Military Affairs"'.
27. For example, Beaumont, p.323.
28. For an overview of developments at sea in this period, again, see Brodie, *Sea Power in the Machine Age*.
29. A good place to start would be Lawrence Freedman's chapter, 'The First Two Generations of Nuclear Strategists', and the helpful bibliographical notes, in Paret, *Makers of Modern Strategy*; also Bernard Brodie, *Strategy in the Missile Age* (Princeton, Princeton University Press, 1959).
30. Andrew Lambert, 'The Royal Navy in the Last Long Peace', in Eric Grove, and Peter Hore, (eds.) *Dimensions of Sea Power* (Hull University Press, 1998).
31. Parliamentary Debates, Official Report ('Hansard'), 537 HC DEB, 1 March 1955, cc. 1898-99.
32. Robert Tomes explains how the Soviet reaction to the nuclear RMA thereby drove the US to take the first steps towards a new RMA, with new conventional technologies and, more significantly, new ideas and concepts for their use. Tomes, 'Revolution in Military Affairs: A History', p.99. In this piece, he provides an interesting account of theories regarding how conventional forces might respond and adapt to a nuclear battlefield; many of the concepts, such as the need for more dispersion and mobility, are similar to those currently embraced by RMA enthusiasts.
33. An interesting account of the rethinking of US Army doctrine between Vietnam and the Gulf can be found in H G Summers, (Colonel, US Army) *On Strategy II: A Critical Analysis of the Gulf War* (New York, Dell, 1992).
34. Freedman quotes a senior DOD official referring as early as 1974 to new military technologies promising 'a true revolution in conventional warfare'; Lawrence Freedman, *The Revolution in Strategic Affairs: Adelphi Paper 318* (Oxford, OUP for IISS, 1998), p.22.
35. Mary C. FitzGerald, 'Marshal Ogarkov and the New Revolution in Soviet Military Affairs', *Defense Analysis*, March 1987; D L Smith and A L Meier, 'Ogarkov's revolution: Soviet military doctrine for the 1990s', *International Defense Review*, July 1987; Cohen, 'A Revolution in Warfare', p.39.
36. Robert H. Scales, *Certain Victory: The US Army in the Gulf War* (Washington, Brasseys, 1994), pp. 12-27. It is significant that he refers to Air-Land Battle as 'the war-fighting doctrine applied by the American Army in Desert Storm', see pp.106-07. Note that he refers to it as being applied by the US Army, not necessarily the USAF.
37. See Toffler and Toffler discussed in Chapter 1.

Chapter 3

1. Toffler and Toffler, War and Anti-War, p.79.
2. CSIS Study Group on Lessons Learned from the Gulf War *Interim Report - The Gulf War: Military Lessons Learned* (Washington, CSIS, 1991), p.11.
3. Randall Bowdish, (Lt. Cmdr., USN), 'The Revolution in Military Affairs: The Sixth Generation', *Military Review*, November-December 1995, p.26.
4. Metz and Kievit, p.v.
5. Department of Defense (US) *Conduct of the Persian Gulf War: Final Report to Congress* (Washington, US Government Printing Office, April 1992), p.xx; W Perry, 'Desert Storm and Deterrence', *Foreign*

Affairs, Fall 1991; both quoted in T A Keaney and E A Cohen, *Revolution in Warfare? Air Power in the Persian Gulf* (Annapolis, Naval Institute Press, 1995); originally published as *Gulf War Air Power Survey Summary Report* (1993), pp.188-89.

6.   The title of A Bin, R Hill and A Jones, *Desert Storm: A Forgotten War* (Westport, Praeger, 1998) does not seem to be meant ironically.

7.   See for example Lawrence Freedman and Efraim Karsh, *The Gulf Conflict 1990-91: Diplomacy and War in the New World Order* (Princeton, Princeton University Press, 1993); R Atkinson, *Crusade: The Untold Story of the Gulf War* (London, Harper Collins, 1994); M R Gordon and B Trainor, (General, USMC, retired) *The Generals' War: The Inside Story of the Conflict in the Gulf* (Boston, Little Brown, 1995).

8.   The Gulf War Air Power Survey (GWAPS) remarked that the weather was apparently the worst for 14 years but also noted that it may not in fact have been atypical, since poor historical weather data for the region left some uncertainty; Keaney and Cohen, pp.144-46.

9.   Freedman and Karsh, *The Gulf Conflict* p.283.

10. See for example Mary Kaldor, *The Baroque Arsenal* (London, Abacus, 1983).

11. H. Norman Schwarzkopf, (General, US Army) *It Doesn't Take a Hero* (New York, Bantam, 1992), p.582.

12. For a fascinating, and often entertaining example, see United States General Accounting Office *Operation Desert Storm: Evaluation of the Air Campaign* (General Accounting Office, Washington DC, 1997).

13. IISS *Strategic Survey 1990-91* (Brasseys for IISS, 1991), p.95.

14. James Taylor and James Blackwell, 'The Ground War in the Gulf' in *Survival*, May-June 1991, p.242.

15. For the debate, see Theodore Postol, 'Lessons of the Gulf War Experience with Patriot', *International Security*, Winter 1991/92; and subsequent 'Correspondence', *International Security*, Summer 1992; also Bin, Hill and Jones, pp.100-01.

16. CSIS Study Group, *Interim Report*, p.12.

17. Donald B. Rice, 'Air Power in the New Security Environment', in Richard Shultz and Rohet Pfaltzgraff, *The Future of Air Power in the Aftermath of the Gulf War* (Maxwell AFB Alabama, Air University Press, 1992), pp.11-12.

18. Charles D. Link, (Major General, USAF) 'Role of USAF in Employment of Air Power', in Shultz and Pfaltzgraff, p.85.

19. J F Jones, (Lt. Col., USAF), 'Giulio Douhet Vindicated: Desert Storm 1991' in *Naval War College Review*, Autumn 1992, pp.97, 99, 101. See also P S Meilinger, (Colonel, USAF), 'Giulio Douhet and Modern War', *Comparative Strategy*, July-September 1993, pp.321, 326.

20. James Blackwell, (Major, US Army) *Thunder in the Desert: The Strategy and Tactics of the Persian Gulf War* (New York, Bantam, 1991). As will be argued below, this was not quite what the interwar air theorists advocated.

21. Meilinger, pp.321, 326.

22. John A. Warden, (Colonel, US Air Force) 'Employing Air Power in the Twenty-First Century' in Shultz and Pfaltzgraff, p.75. For his view of the theoretical basis of air power, see *The Air Campaign: Planning for Combat* (Washington DC, National Defense University Press, 1988).

23. Edward N. Luttwak, 'Victory through air power', *Commentary*, August 1991, pp.28, 30.

24. Edward N. Luttwak, 'Air power in US Military Strategy' in Shultz and Pfaltzgraff, p.30.

25. Charles Bowie, et al., *The New Calculus: Analysing Airpower's Changing Role in Joint Theater Campaigns* (Santa Monica, RAND, 1993). This report was the result of a project funded by the US Air Force which was called, with impressive if unusual candour, 'Project Air Force'.

26. See Keaney and Cohen, passim; Gordon and Trainor, pp. 75-101; Lawrence Freedman and Efraim Karsh, 'How Kuwait was won: Strategy in the Gulf War' in *International Security*, Fall 1991, pp.19-21.

27. Keaney and Cohen, pp.29-31; L Aspin and W Dickinson, *House Armed Services Committee – Defense for a New Era: Lessons of the Persian Gulf War* (Washington DC, US Government Printing Office, 1992) p. 8; Atkinson, pp.56-62.

28. Keaney and Cohen, p. 37

29. Colonel Warden, speaking at a conference in April 1991, acknowledged that air power had not toppled the regime but confidently predicted that it had set the stage for a widespread rebellion that might succeed because of the damage to Saddam's internal control mechanisms. Warden, p.70. Unfortunately for many of the inhabitants of Iraq, these control mechanisms proved to have been weakened far less than Warden believed.

30. *Final Report to Congress*, p.92.

31. Murray, a member of the GWAPS, states that after one night of such attacks they were stopped, because among the targets was the Al Firdos bunker in which several hundred civilians died. Williamson Murray, 'Air War in the Gulf: The Limits of Air Power', *Strategic Review*, Winter 2000, p.34.

32. Edward N. Luttwak, 'Towards Post-Heroic Warfare', *Foreign Affairs*, May-June 1995, pp.118-119. This argument brings to mind the wartime objections of Bomber Command to the 'diversion' of long-range aircraft to Coastal Command, where they would be used to prevent Britain being knocked out of the war at the expense of the single-minded pursuit of Harris' strategic bombing dogma.

33. Luttwak, 'Air Power in US Military Strategy', p.19.

34. The difference between targeting will and capability is explored in Robert A. Pape, *Bombing to Win: Air Power and Coercion in War* (Ithaca, Cornell University Press, 1996).

35. At the start of the air campaign, two known and two suspected nuclear facilities were targeted; this figure increased to eight by the end of the war. Postwar UN inspectors located more than 20, including 16 main facilities. They also found 16 Scud warheads loaded with 200 KG of nerve gas and barometric fuses, plus 13 empty warheads; over 25,000 bombs, artillery shells and rocket warheads filled with mustard and nerve gas; and a total of 500 tons of chemical agents (including 80 tons of nerve gas) and about 3000 tons of chemicals which could be used to produce weapons. Bin, Hill and Jones, p.228; Keaney and Cohen, pp.71-72, 107; Atkinson, pp.495-96.

36. After the war, the UN Special Commission reported that it had found no evidence of any mobile Scud launchers being destroyed by aircraft; and of 28 fixed launch sites, 12 were destroyed, 14 slightly damaged and two untouched. Jeffrey McCausland, *The Gulf Conflict: A Military Analysis - Adelphi Paper 282* (London, Brasseys for IISS, 1993), p.35.

37. The Pentagon Report to Congress notes that 31 per cent of 'strategic' strikes were conducted against the Republican Guard. *Final Report to Congress*, p.159.

38. Keaney and Cohen, pp.91-92; they also note that the level of losses varied widely between Iraqi units.

39. The GWAPS summary volume refers to the 'destruction or permanent disabling of some 50 percent of the Republican Guard (in roughly equal proportions by air and ground action)'. Keaney and Cohen, p.224.

40. See, for example, the detailed account of some of the battles in Stephen Biddle, 'Victory Misunderstood: What the Gulf War Tells us About the Future of Conflict', *International Security*, Fall 1996; he shows that most Republican Guard and many heavy army divisions had a great deal of their armour left and fought back hard.

41. Scales, *Certain Victory*, pp.209-10, 358-68.

42. Jones, 'Giulio Douhet Vindicated'. See also Luttwak, 'Air power in US Military Strategy', p.30.

43. Scales, *Certain Victory*, pp.192-94.

44. See Tim Benbow, 'Maritime Power in the 1990-91 Gulf War and the Conflict in the Former Yugoslavia' in A. Dorman, et al. (eds.) *The Changing Face of Maritime Power* (London, Macmillan, 1999).

45. *Final Report to Congress*, pp.xxi-xxii.

46. Krepinevich points out that during the 1972 Linebacker air campaigns in Vietnam, the US dropped around 9000 laser-guided bombs, about same number as in Desert Storm; Krepinevich, p.40

47. *Final Report to Congress*, pp.113, 343.

48. Keaney and Cohen, p.95; Scales, *Certain Victory*, pp.167-68. Another analyst reported that JSTARS proved able to spot enemy movements as far away as 155 miles in all weather; in 49 sorties it identified more than 1000 targets and controlled 750 aircraft. T S Swalm. 'Joint STARS in Desert

Storm', in A D Campen, (ed.) *The First Information War: The Story of Communications, Computers and Intelligence Systems in the Persian Gulf War* (Fairfax, VA: AFCEA International Press, 1992), pp.167-69.

49. Quotation *Final Report to Congress*, p.176; also Freedman, *The Revolution in Strategic Affairs*, p.30
50. Scales, *Certain Victory*, pp.200-04.
51. Gordon and Trainor, p.x.
52. Campen, p.vii; original emphasis.
53. See McCausland, pp.57-58; also Major General Rupert Smith in Royal United Services Institute *Whitehall Papers 14 – Command in War: Gulf Operations* (London, RUSI, 1992), p.51.
54. Campen, p.182.
55. Krepinevich, p.40, for example, views Desert Storm as a 'precursor war' that demonstrated the possibilities of new techniques, like the Battle of Cambrai in 1917.
56. Metz and Kievit, pp.v, 17.
57. Adams, *The Next World War*, p.28.
58. Richard J. Harknett, et al. 'The Risks of a Networked Military', *Orbis*, Winter 2000, p.138.
59. G I Rochlin and C C Demchak, *Lessons of the Gulf War: Ascendant Technology and Declining Capability - U.C.B. Institute of International Studies Policy Papers in International Affairs No. 39* (Berkeley, UCB Institute of International Studies, 1991).
60. See Schwarzkopf, pp.368-69, for his concerns about this possibility.
61. An 'Innovations' catalogue distributed with a daily newspaper in August 2000 offered, among various helpful gadgets for home and garden, a hand-held GPS set, accurate to 50m anywhere in the world, for £129.
62. McCausland noted in 1993 that missiles of much greater range than Iraq's Scuds were under development in more than 30 states. McCausland, p.65.
63. The Pentagon Report to Congress estimated that it might have been able to assemble one or two crude weapons six months to one year after the start of the invasion; *Final Report to Congress*, pp.15-16.

Chapter 4

1. Freedman, *The Revolution in Strategic Affairs*, pp.9-10.
2. Creveld even goes so far as to doubt on the continuing relevance of Clausewitz's state-centric analysis of war; Martin van Creveld, *On Future War*, (London, Brasseys, 1991).
3. For example: 'Theory becomes infinitely more difficult as soon as it touches the realm of moral values.' Clausewitz, (Howard and Paret ed.) *On War*, Book Two, Chapter Two, p.136; also Book One, Chapter One, p.78; Book One, Chapter Seven, p.119-21.
4. Arthur K. Cebrowski and John J. Gartska, 'Network-Centric Warfare: Its Origin and Future', *Proceedings of the US Naval Institute*, January 1998, p.29. Their article was written when Vice Admiral Cebrowski was the US Navy's Director for Space, Information Warfare, Command and Control, having previously been the Pentagon Director for C4 systems.
5. In November 2002, in Yemen, a Predator UAV fired a Hellfire missile that destroyed a car containing suspected al Qaeda activists, quite independently of any US deployment of forces on the ground in that country.
6. 'Stealthy' is often misunderstood as meaning 'invisible'; in fact, it simply means *less* visible, as comes across better in the more precise term 'low observable'. Just how difficult stealthy platforms are to detect is, of course, subject to change; there is no reason to believe that they are immune to the usual action-reaction dynamic of technological change that provides responses to every advance.
7. William Owens, 'The Once and Future Revolution in Military Affairs', *Joint Forces Quarterly*, Summer 2002, p.57; see also 'The Emerging System of Systems', *US Naval Institute Proceedings*, May 1995.
8. J Arquilla and D Ronfeldt, 'Cyberwar is coming', *Comparative Strategy*, April-June 1993, pp.143-44, 146.

9. William Owens, 'The American Revolution in Military Affairs', *Joint Forces Quarterly*, Winter 1995-96, p.38.

10. Cohen, 'A Revolution in Warfare', pp.48-50.

11. Steven Metz, 'Racing Toward the Future: The Revolution in Military Affairs', *Current History*, April 1997, p.185.

12. This parallel is explored in greater depth in Cebrowski and Gartska, p.29.

13. Cebrowski and Gartska explain how CEC unifies a sensor grid and an engagement grid; pp.33-34.

14. There is an earlier case of an author who was pondering the effect of a new technology taking an analogy from naval warfare and applying it to combat on land: in 1903, H G Wells wrote of powerful armoured vehicles and their impact on the battlefield, which he named 'land ironclads'. H G Wells, 'The Land Ironclads' (1903), reproduced in David G. Hartwell and Kathryn Cramer, *The Ascent of Wonder: The Evolution of Hard SF* (London, Orbit, 1994).

15. Cebrowski and Gartska, pp.32-33.

16. Metz and Kievit, p.7.

17. Arquilla and Ronfeldt, pp.147-48, 155.

18. Such concepts are by no means restricted to the US. In the UK, which is considerably more cautious than the Pentagon about the potential of the RMA, the heads of defence studies of the three armed services held a conference in May 2003 on effects-based warfare.

19. Owens, 'The American Revolution in Military Affairs', pp.37-38.

20. Owens, 'Once and Future RMA', p.58-59.

21. Owens, 'Once and Future RMA', p.59. For earlier evidence of bureaucratic weight in the side of the RMA, see William Owens, 'JROC: Harnessing the Revolution in Military Affairs', *Joint Forces Quarterly*, Summer 1994.

22. Richard J. Harknett, et al. 'The Risks of a Networked Military', *Orbis*, Winter 2000.

23. Any US advocacy of arms control measures to restrict anti-satellite weapons might well appear to other states like British attempts to prohibit submarines at the start of the twentieth century appeared to France or Germany in view of Britain's dominance in battleships.

24. Owens argues this, which is why he urges an acceleration of the RMA. Owens, 'Once and Future RMA', p.60.

25. An interesting parallel can be found in the decision of the Royal Navy to introduce in 1906 a new battleship class, the *Dreadnought*, which left all existing capital ships obsolete. It was objected that it was not in British interests thus to negate its existing naval supremacy, making it easier for rivals (particularly Germany) to catch up.

26. See for example Owens, 'The American Revolution in Military Affairs'; Colin Gray, *The American RMA: An Interim Assessment* (SCSI Occasional, No. 28, 1997).

27. *Economist*, 'The software revolution: a survey of defence technology', 10 June 1995, p.6.

28. Owens, 'Emerging system of systems', p.39.

29. Joseph Nye and William Owens, 'America's Information Edge', *Foreign Affairs*, March/April 1996, p.28.

30. S Cattermull, 'Digitization: Its Effects on the British Way of Warfighting', *British Army Review*, Summer 2001, p.19.

31. There is a useful summary of the British approach in the UK government's response to the attacks of 11 September 2001: Secretary of State for Defence, *The Strategic Defence Review: A New Chapter*, Cm 5566 (London, HMSO, July 2002), especially paras. 35-41.

32. David Shukman, *The Sorcerer's Challenge: Fears and Hopes for the Weapons of the Next Millennium* (London, Coronet, 1995), p.161.

33. Nye and Owens, 'America's Information Edge', pp.23-24.

34. Owens, 'The American Revolution in Military Affairs', p.38.

35. Alan Beyerchen, 'Clausewitz, Nonlinearity, and the Unpredictability of War', *International Security*, Winter 1992/93, pp.69-72.

36. Bill Toti, 'Stop the Revolution; I Want to Get Off', *Proceedings of the US Naval Institute*, July 2000, p.32; original emphasis.

37. Charles J. Dunlap, *Technology and the 21st Century Battlefield: Recomplicating Moral Life for the Statesman and the Soldier* (Strategic Studies Institute, January 1999), pp.9-22.
38. Stephen Blank, 'How we will lose the next war with Russia: A Critique of US Military Strategy', *Defense Analysis*, August 1999, p.132.
39. Metz and Kievit, pp.26, 28.
40. The analogy could be drawn with naval strategy: a state that does not need to use the sea can greatly complicate its exploitation by an intervening navy, and do so relatively cheaply, by looking to sea denial systems. This approach can be seen in German naval strategy in the Second World War and that of the USSR during the Cold War, as well as in the highly effective, and cost effective, use of naval mines by North Korea (1950-53) and Iraq (1991).
41. Martin Libicki, 'The emerging primacy of information', *Orbis*, Spring 1996, pp.265, 269-72.
42. See for example Dunlap, *Technology and the 21st Century Battlefield* pp.33-34; Shukman, pp.ix, 8.
43. Blank also notes that even if a weaker state could not escalate a conflict in this way, successful information attacks could lead to its implosion, threatening to demand deeper and more prolonged commitment. Blank, p.134.
44. For a useful general account of modern terrorism, see Bruce Hoffman, *Inside Terrorism* (London, Indigo, 1999).
45. Freedman, *Revolution in Strategic Affairs*, p.78.
46. It should be recalled that there have been plenty of premature obituaries written for heavy armoured vehicles, manned aircraft and surface warships. This is not, of course, to deny that they will ever be left obsolete but rather to introduce a note of caution with regard to claims that this change has arrived.
47. Colin Gray, rejoinder to Martin Libicki, *Orbis*, Spring 1996, pp.275-276.
48. James Adams, *The Next World War*, p.28.
49. Arquilla and Ronfeldt, p. 143
50. Steven Metz, 'The Next Twist of the RMA', *Parameters*, Autumn 2000, pp.41-43.
51. See, for example, Metz and Kievit, p.vi; Shukman, pp.7, 175-82, 193; Adams, *The Next World War*, especially p.150.
52. Many works on the RMA do use distinctly loaded terminology. A particularly clear example is Adams, who writes of 'traditionalists' versus 'revolutionaries', and 'conservatives' versus 'visionaries'; although these are not inherently loaded terms, he makes it abundantly clear which side he agrees with. He also tends to describe any scepticism in terms of bureaucratic obstructionism, without any concession that there might be reasonable grounds for some degree of scepticism. Adams, *The Next World War*, especially pp.5-6, 80-84, 106-07, 248-49. Another example can be found in the distinction between 'Platform-oriented traditionalists' and 'Information-oriented Modernists' drawn in IISS, 'Is there a Revolution in Military Affairs?', Strategic Survey, 1995-96, pp.32-34.

Chapter 5

1. This school of thought is most famously represented by Toffler and Toffler.
2. *Economist*, 'The software revolution: a survey of defence technology', 10 June 1995, p.18.
3. Colin Gray, noting the breadth of definitions of IW, remarks that 'information warfare' is frequently 'used to mean nothing more arcane than warfare in an information age which exploits high electronic prowess.' Colin Gray, *The American RMA: An Interim Assessment* (SCSI Occasional, No. 28, 1997), p.iii.
4. *Joint Warfare Publication 0-01: British Defence Doctrine* (second edition, October 2001), pp.1-2 to 1-4.
5. See Chapter Two for references to their works.
6. For example, James Adams refers to Washington lobbying by foreign governments as 'information warfare'; *The Next World War*, p. 315
7. *Economist*, 'The software revolution', p.18; emphasis added.
8. Joseph Nye and William Owens, 'America's Information Edge', *Foreign Affairs*, March/April 1996, p.22.

9.   Arquilla and Ronfeldt, p.144-45. They use a different term, 'cyberwar' to refer to a more distinctly military phenomenon; see below.
10.   This thesis is set out in Samuel Huntington, *The Clash of Civilizations and the Remaking of the World Order* (New York, Touchstone, 1997).
11.   Adams, *The Next World War*, pp.5-6.
12.   Arquilla and Ronfeldt, pp.141, 144-47, 155. It should be noted that, unlike many authors, they intend the term to mean something considerably wider than just computer warfare.
13.   Martin Libicki, pp.261-65. The term 'cyberspace' was first coined by the science fiction author William Gibson in *Neuromancer* (London, Victor Gollancz, 1984).
14.   Nye & Owens, p. 20.
15.   Freedman, *The Revolution in Strategic Affairs*, p.67.
16.   Gray, *Interim Assessment*, p.30.
17.   This operation is often cited as a success of strategic bombing; in fact, the strategic effect was achieved by the combination of air strikes and action by ground forces, as well as diplomatic moves and the longer-term effects of economic sanctions. See Benbow, 'Maritime Power in the 1990-91 Gulf War and the Conflict in the Former Yugoslavia'.
18.   Szafranski defines 'neocortical warfare' as attempts to 'control or shape the behaviour of enemy organisms, but without destroying the organisms', by manipulating the perceptions of the enemy leadership, ideally without fighting him at all. Richard Szafranski, 'Neocortical Warfare? The Acme of Skill', *Military Review*, November 1994.
19.   'Pentagon gets ready to wage a cyber-war', *The Times*, 9 November 1999.
20.   James Adams reports that the US government believes that more than 30 states have offensive computer warfare programmes; 'Virtual Defense', *Foreign Affairs*, May/June 2001, p.102.
21.   One useful exception to this rule is William J. Bayles, 'The Ethics of Computer Network Attack', *Parameters*, Spring 2001.
22.   'Pentagon gets ready to wage a cyber-war', *The Times*, 9 November 1999. Interestingly, the article refers to Russian suggestions that there should be a UN resolution governing the use of IT as a weapons, which invites comparison with the Russian Czar in the 1890s calling for a disarmament conference, prompted by his inability to fund artillery modernisation.
23.   US Air Force Basic Doctrine, AFDD-1, September 1997, quoted in Charles J. Dunlap, *Technology and the 21ˢᵗ Century Battlefield: Recomplicating Moral Life for the Statesman and the Soldier* (Strategic Studies Institute, January 1999), p.35.
24.   Indeed, one author has referred to the conflict as 'the first information war'. He argues that Desert Storm 'differed fundamentally from any previous conflict', because 'the outcome turned as much on superior management of knowledge as it did upon performances of people or weapons'. Campen, p.vii.
25.   See Campen for accounts of this and other aspects of the information conflict in the Gulf.
26.   The US General Accounting Office provides a devastating reminder of the limitations of intelligence: 'While known nuclear sites were severely or moderately damaged, overall program was *virtually* intact because only less than 15 percent of the facilities were known and, therefore, attacked'. *Operation Desert Storm: Evaluation of the Air Campaign* (General Accounting Office, Washington DC, 1997), p.151, emphasis added.
27.   After the war, the UN Special Commission reported that it had found no evidence of any mobile Scud launchers being destroyed by aircraft. McCausland, p.35.
28.   For a detailed account of the operation, in which numerous problems of information can be found, see Mark Bowden, *Black Hawk Down* (London, Bantam, 1999). It is interesting that Adams refers to the failure of this raid as representing a 'successful information attack' on the US by General Aideed, which is an example of how widely such terms are used. Adams, *The Next World War*, pp.74-75.
29.   Timothy L. Thomas, 'Kosovo and the current myth of information superiority', *Parameters*, Spring 2000.
30.   Richard J. Harknett, et al. 'The Risks of a Networked Military', *Orbis*, Winter 2000, p.131.
31.   Campen, p.182.

32. S. Cattermull, 'Digitization: Its Effects on the British Way of Warfighting', *British Army Review*, Summer 2001, pp.23-29.
33. According to *The Times*, 27 March 2002, problems emerged with the Predator unmanned aerial vehicle. According to 'senior US officers in Afghanistan', its 'constant streaming of images back to the US during fighting at Shah-i Kot earlier this month encouraged commanders thousands of miles away, who had only its limited view of the battlefield, to chip in with unhelpful advice.' They suggested that it 'would be better restricted to tasks such as pinpointing the position of the enemy'.
34. Charles J. Dunlap, 'How we lost the high-tech war of 2007', *Weekly Standard*, January 29, 1996, p.24.
35. Clausewitz stressed this problem: see the quotation in the conclusion, below.
36. Dunlap imagines a rogue state using freelance hackers to attack US computer systems – as well as those in neighbouring Mexico, to affect the US indirectly – as part of a broader campaign. 'How we lost the high-tech war of 2007'.
37. See for example, *Economist*, 'Asia's Lethal Computers – Nerd World War', October 30, 1999. Adams suggests that between October 2000 and January 2001, computer attacks between Israelis and Palestinians 'took down more than 250 Web sites'; *Virtual Defense*, p.98.
38. Bayles cites analysts who see CNA as more proportionate than traditional force, and hence more usable, but also others who argue that it approaches the destructive potential of WMD due to its broader effects.
39. Douhet, *Command of the Air*, pp.51-58.
40. H G Wells, *The War in the Air* (London, George Bell and Sons, 1908).
41. A related concept, which has begun to be taken up in the UK armed forces, is that of 'effects-based warfare', which seeks to focus on the results that might be achieved by military action rather than the means used. Even without an RMA, such an approach promises useful, albeit not 'revolutionary' results.
42. Sun Tzu, *The Art of War* (trans. Ralph Sawyer: New York, Barnes and Noble, 1994), p.179.
43. Clausewitz, *On War* (Howard and Paret) Book One, Chapter Six, p.117.
44. Clausewitz, *On War*, Book One, Chapter Seven, p.120.
45. Clausewitz, *On War*, Book One, Chapter Two, p.97.
46. Arthur Conan Doyle, *Penguin Complete Sherlock Holmes* (London, Penguin, 1981), 'The Adventure of the Blue Carbuncle', p.246. Among several other apposite comments, Sherlock Holmes also tells Watson, "You see, but you do not observe. The distinction is clear."; 'A Scandal in Bohemia', p.162.

Chapter 6

1. The extent of UK involvement in such conflicts is demonstrated by the startling fact that since the end of the Second World War (when the UK has been involved in traditional state-against-state war only in 1950-53, 1956, 1982, 1991 and 2003), there has only been one year in which no British service personnel have been killed in action.
2. See in particular, Creveld, *On Future War*.
3. This last has long been cited as a cause of major wars: 'What made war inevitable was the growth of Athenian power and the fear which this caused in Sparta.' Thucydides, *History of the Peloponnesian War* (trans. R Warner: London, Penguin, 1972), p.49.
4. In much of the world, internal conflict has long been far more prevalent than wars between states; indeed, it is quite possible that in some regions, inter-state conflict might be *more* common in the post-Cold War era than hitherto.
5. See for example, Jean de Bloch, *The Future of War in Its Technical, Economic and Political Relations* (trans. R C Long: New York, Garland, 1972: original 1899); Norman Angell, *The Great Illusion: A study of the relation of military power in nations to their economic and social advantage* (London, Heinemann, 1910).
6. Indeed, there has been a tendency to seek terms other than 'high intensity' and 'low intensity' (with the latter giving way to 'operations other than war' or 'other operations') precisely because they give a misleading impression that there is a strict dichotomy between the two.

7.   Secretary of State for Defence (UK) *The Strategic Defence Review*, Cm 3999 (London, HMSO, July 1998), especially paras. 45, 54-55, 59; and para. 78, which states 'Moreover, only forces equipped and trained for warfighting will have the range of specific capabilities – as well as the deterrent effect – to be effective across the full range of peace support and humanitarian operations.'

8.   The concept has emerged from the US Marine Corps (associated in particular with General Charles C. Krulak) of the 'three-block war': that is, in a single conflict, deployed forces might be delivering humanitarian aid on one city block, be performing peacekeeping tasks on an adjacent block and be conducting warfighting operations on a third.

9.   An interesting account of future conflict can be found in Charles Dick, 'Conflict spills into the 21st Century', *Jane's Intelligence Review*, 1 December 2000.

10. For example, Brower states that there are short-term fluctuations between platforms and anti-platform weapons, and also longer term trends which can lead to obsolescence. He believes that we are in one of the latter periods, with platforms in decline. Kenneth Brower, 'Technology and the Future Battlefield: The Impact on Force Structure, Procurement and Arms Control', *RUSI Journal*, Spring 1990.

11. Secretary of State for Defence (UK) *The Strategic Defence Review: Supporting Essays* (London, HMSO, July 1998), Essay Three, 'The Impact of Technology', para. 12.

12. The UK Ministry of Defence refers to 'Network Enabled Capability', which suggests a more modest view than the US 'Network Centric Warfare'.

13. William Safire, an American newspaper columnist, has referred to this inclination as the 'drive-by shooting' approach to foreign policy.

14. This last term is suggested by Gwyn Prins in *Strategy, Force Planning and Diplomatic/Military Operations* (London, RIIA, 1998). He explicitly rejects the divisions between 'war' and 'other operations' and between 'high' and 'low' intensity conflicts.

15. These terms are so fraught with potential to mislead that alternatives might well be preferable; they have been retained here because they are in common use and because other available terms seem little better.

16. During the Cold War, when the argument was made that a British force structure designed for World War III could also cover low intensity conflicts, it was occasionally expressed as 'the dog that can deal with the cat can also deal with the kittens'. This sentiment could mislead if it were taken to suggest that low-intensity conflicts were simply smaller versions of conventional wars.

17. Joseph Nye and William Owens, 'America's Information Edge', *Foreign Affairs*, March/April 1996, pp.29-33.

18. Arquilla and Ronfeldt, pp.158-60.

19. See for example Libicki, pp.261-65.

20. Tom Donnelly, 'Strategic Strife', *Jane's Defence Weekly*, 29 November 2000.

21. Chairman of the Joint Chiefs of Staff, *Joint Vision 2020* (US Government Printing Office, Washington DC, June 2000).

22. Metz and Kievit suggest that a force suitable for use against opponents in low intensity conflicts would be very different from the US Army's planned Force XXI: it would need to be composed of small units of great flexibility, 'able to deal with enemies with a tremendous range of capabilities, from high-tech niche opponents to low-tech warlord militias'. Metz and Kievit, p.25.

23. One journal referred to US forces in the Former Yugoslavia benefitting from a suitcase-sized device that prematurely detonated proximity fuses of incoming artillery and mortar rounds. 'Warfare in the Modern Age', in *Popular Science*, July 1996: quoted in Robert Gaskin, 'A Revolution for the Millennium', in W. Murray (ed.) *The Emerging Strategic Environment: Challenges of the Twenty-First Century* (Westport, Praeger, 1999).

24. This is a 1991 Pentagon definition, quoted in David Shukman, *The Sorcerer's Challenge: Fears and Hopes for the Weapons of the Next Millennium* (London, Coronet, 1995), p.213.

25. For non-lethal weapons, see International Institute for Strategic Studies, 'The role of non-lethal weapons', in *Strategic Survey 1995-96* (London, OUP, 1996); Shukman, *Sorceror's Challenge*, pp.203-27; Adams, *Next World War*, pp.157-178.

26. This concern seems to be borne out by the apparent inadequacy for follow-on stabilisation and peace

support operations of the relatively small US force that defeated the regular Iraqi forces in 2003.

Chapter 7

1. Sun Tzu, *The Art of War*, translated by Thomas Cleary (Boston, Shambala, 1988), p.95.
2. Indeed, given earlier al Qaeda attacks against Western embassies in East Africa and against the USS *Cole*, and many previous suicide attacks, it could be seen as different only in scale rather than in kind.
3. There was also a symmetric element to Napoleon's demise, as his initial successes compelled his opponents to learn, adapt and imitate, reforming their conventional forces and eventually matching and overwhelming their symmetrical French counterparts. The symmetric and asymmetric responses complemented and reinforced each other.
4. Much the same applies to other similar terms; 'unorthodox', 'unconventional', 'non-traditional' and even 'irregular' equally assume some standard model that is 'orthodox', 'conventional', 'traditional' or 'regular'.
5. Schwarzkopf, pp.368-69.
6. One of the most interesting and challenging is Charles Dunlap's masterpiece of the nasty thought-experiment genre, 'How we lost the high-tech war of 2007', *Weekly Standard*, January, 1996. It suggests some of the acts that could be committed by a truly ruthless opponent.
7. See Christopher Coker, *Waging War Without Warriors? The Changing Culture of Military Conflict* (Boulder, CO: Lynne Rienner, 2002); he highlights the difficulties encountered by Western powers when fighting peoples for whom war is a way of life rather than an instrument of politics.
8. Hoffman notes that terrorism could be perceived as 'the poor man's air power'; Bruce Hoffman, *Inside Terrorism* (London, Indigo, 1999), p.33.
9. Dunlap's piece, cited above, includes his fictional fanatical regime detonating a nuclear weapon in its own capital to blame on the US, discrediting it and justifying 'retaliatory' terrorist attacks and atrocities against captured US servicewomen.
10. It has been suggested that one unintended consequence of the September 2001 al Qaeda attacks has been to create some common interests among the US, Russia and China, in addition to important regional actors such as Iran and India.
11. 'Administration's Big Three get to grips with the counter attack', *The Times*, 13 September 2001.
12. An interesting analysis that could be read usefully well beyond the United States, and which is all the more striking for having been written before the 9/11 attacks, is the work of the US Hart-Rudman commission. 'New World Coming: American Security in the 21st Century', September 1999; 'Seeking a National Strategy: A Concept for Preserving Security and Promoting Freedom', April 2000; and 'Roadmap for National Security: Imperative for Change', February 2001, by the US Commission on National Security/21st Century (these documents, and supporting papers, are available online at www.nssg.gov). In response to the attacks of September 11, and acknowledging the arguments of this cross-party commission, the Bush administration announced on 22 September 2001 that it had established a new 'Office of Homeland Security' headed by a Cabinet-level official.
13. Terrorism can cause grievous casualties, severe disruption and serious economic losses for Western societies but despite what is sometimes suggested, short of the use of WMD, it does not amount to a military threat on the scale that could be presented by another state.
14. The response of the UK government was measured, arguing that the attacks did not undermine the analysis that underlay the 1998 Strategic Defence Review, nor did they require wholesale reform of the resulting force structures, which accurately recognised the increasingly joint and expeditionary nature of future UK military operations and emphasised more flexible and deployable forces. Rather, some additional thinking was necessary, which resulted in a 'New Chapter', devoted specifically to countering terrorism, that sought to complement the earlier review. Secretary of State for Defence, *The Strategic Defence Review: A New Chapter*, Cm 5566 (London, HMSO, July 2002).
15. See for example William Owens, 'The Once and Future Revolution in Military Affairs', *Joint Forces Quarterly*, Summer 2002, p.60.

16. Clausewitz, (Howard & Paret) *On War*, Book Eight, Chapter Six, p.605.

Chapter 8

1. One author believes that the respective world views of the US and Europe are increasingly diverging, with that of the US being based on military power while the Europeans emphasise international institutions and international law. Robert Kagan, *Paradise and Power: America and Europe in the New World Order* (London, Atlantic Books, 2003). There is a danger that such a stark two-fold division overlooks differences among European states, some of which (not least France, as well as the UK) still perceive an important role for military power in international politics.
2. This last epithet, aimed specifically at the French, was first coined by Willie the Scottish groundskeeper on the television series *The Simpsons*.
3. A report in *The Times*, 'Allies fail to share vision thing over rogue states', 14 June 2001, listed France and Germany as opposed to US plans for missile defence; the UK, Spain, Italy, Poland, Hungary and Turkey as supportive; and, significantly, Iceland, Belgium, Norway, Denmark, Ireland, the Netherlands, Portugal, Greece and the Czech Republic as undecided. See also *The Economist*, June 16, 2001, pp.53-54.
4. One striking statistic is that in June 2001, US expenditure on defence research was *four times* the combined European total. *The Economist*, June 2, 2001, p.29. The post-9/11 increases in US defence spending have widened this gap still further.
5. See in particular Nye and Owens, *passim* and Libicki, *passim*.
6. Suggested contributions of ground troops to the European Rapid Reaction Force were Germany 13,500; UK 12,500; France 12,000; Italy 6,000; Spain 6,000: Netherlands 5,000: Greece 3,500; Austria 2,000; Finland 2,000; Sweden 1,500; Portugal 1,000; Belgium 1,000; Ireland 1,000; Luxembourg 100; Denmark nil, due to its opt out. *The Times*, 21 November 2000.
7. Though Irish fears about this possibility were a significant factor in the rejection of the Nice Treaty in the first referendum held on the issue.
8. Christopher Coker, *Waging War Without Warriors? The Changing Culture of Military Conflict* (Boulder, CO: Lynne Rienner, 2002), p.62.
9. Chairman of the Joint Chiefs of Staff, *Joint Vision 2020* (US Government Printing Office, Washington DC, June 2000), p.13. The reference to multinational operations in this paper is more than merely paying lip service; it takes up one page out of a total of about 24 pages of text.
10. Freedman, *The Revolution in Strategic Affairs*, p.72.
11. A proposal along this lines is made in D Gombert, R Kugler and M Libicki, *Mind the Gap: Promoting a Transatlantic Revolution in Military Affairs* (Washington DC, National Defense University Press, 1999).
12. It would be unwise to draw too strong a distinction between US and European readiness to accept risks to personnel: the US has repeatedly deployed troops since the end of the Cold War, while not every European state is abundantly endowed with the will to fight.
13. Signs of such disagreements could be seen between 1992 and 1995, when many German and other European politicians were vocal in asserting the moral case for British and French troops to be deployed to Bosnia.

Bibliography

Adams, James *The Next World War: The Weapons and Warriors of the New Battlefields in Cyberspace* (London, Arrow, 1998)

Adams, James 'Virtual Defense', *Foreign Affairs*, May/June 2001

Angell, Norman *The Great Illusion: A study of the relation of military power in nations to their economic and social advantage* (London, Heinemann, 1910)

Arquilla, John & Ronfeldt, David, 'Cyberwar is coming!', *Comparative Strategy*, April-June 1993

Aspin, L. & Dickinson, W. *Defense for a New Era: Lessons of the Persian Gulf War* (Washington, US Government Printing Office, 1992)

Atkinson, R. *Crusade: The Untold Story of the Gulf War* (London, Harper Collins, 1994)

Bacevich, A.J. 'Preserving the Well-Bred Horse', *National Interest*, Fall 1994

Bailey, Jonathan *The First World War and the Birth of the Modern Style of Warfare* (Strategic and Combat Studies Institute, Occasional Paper Number 22, 1996)

Bailey, Jonathan 'Deep Battle 1914-1941: The Birth of the Modern Style of Warfare', and 'The Century of Firepower', *British Army Review*, December 1998

Barnaby, F. (ed.) *Future War: Armed Conflict in the Next Decade* (London, Michael Joseph, 1984)

Bayles, William J. 'The Ethics of Computer Network Attack', *Parameters*, Spring 2001

Beaumont, Roger, 'OMTE: An Alternative Paradigm to "The Revolution in Military Affairs"', *Defense Analysis*, December 1995

Beedham, Barry, 'Defence in the 21st Century', *Economist*, 5 September 1992

Benbow, Tim 'Maritime Power in the 1990-91 Gulf War and the Conflict in the Former Yugoslavia' in Dorman, A., Smith, M., & Utley, M. (eds.) *The Changing Face of Maritime Power* (London, Macmillan, 1999)

Benbow, Tim 'The "Revolution in Military Affairs": An Introductory Survey', *Journal of Defence Science*, May 2001

Benbow, Tim 'British Naval Aviation: Limited Global Power Projection', in Till, Geoffrey (ed.) *Seapower at the Millennium* (London, Sutton, 2001)

Bernstein, A., Libicki, M. & Kagan, F., 'High-Tech: The Future Face of War? A Debate', *Commentary*, January 1998

Beyerchen, Alan 'Clausewitz, Nonlinearity, and the Unpredictability of War', *International Security*, Winter 1992/93

Biddle, Stephen, 'Victory Misunderstood: What the Gulf War Tells Us About the Future of Conflict', *International Security*, Fall 1996

Billiere, Peter de la (General, British Army) *Storm Command: A Personal Account of the Gulf War* (London, Harper Collins, 1992)

Bin, A., Hill, R. & Jones, A. *Desert Storm: A Forgotten War* (Westport, Praeger, 1998)

Blackwell, J. (Major, US Army) *Thunder in the Desert: The Strategy and Tactics of the Persian Gulf War* (New York, Bantam, 1991)

Blaker, Jim 'The Owens Legacy', *Armed Forces Journal International*, July 1996

Blank, Stephen 'How We Will Lose the Next War with Russia: A Critique of US Military Strategy', *Defense Analysis*, August 1999

Bloch, Jean de *The Future of War in Its Technical, Economic and Political Relations* (trans. Long, R.C.: New York, Garland, 1972: original 1899)

Bond, B. & Alexander, M. 'Liddell Hart and De Gaulle: The Doctrines of Limited Liability and Mobile Defense', in Paret, Peter (ed.) *Makers of Modern Strategy from Machiavelli to the Nuclear Age* (Oxford, Oxford University Press, 1986)

Bowden, Mark *Black Hawk Down* (London, Bantam, 1999)

Bowdish, Randall (Lt. Cmdr., USN), 'The Revolution in Military Affairs: The Sixth Generation', *Military Review*, November-December 1995

Bowie, C. (et al) *The New Calculus: Analysing Airpower's Changing Role in Joint Theater Campaigns* (Santa Monica, RAND, 1993)

Brodie, Bernard *Sea Power in the Machine Age* (Princeton, Princeton University Press, 1942)

Brodie, Bernard *Strategy in the Missile Age* (Princeton, Princeton University Press, 1959)

Brodie, Bernard & Brodie, F.M. *From Cross-Bow to H-Bomb* (Bloomington, Indiana University Press, 1973)

Brodie, Bernard 'Technological Change, Strategic Doctrine and Political Outcomes' in Knorr, K. (ed.) *Historical Dimensions of National Security Problems* (Lawrence, Kansas, University Press of Kansas, 1976)

Brower, Kenneth 'Technology and the Future Battlefield: The Impact on Force Structure, Procurement and Arms Control', *RUSI Journal*, Spring 1990

Caddick, D.J. 'The Revolution in Military Affairs – Panacea or Myth?', *British Army Review*, Autumn 1999

Campen, Alan D. (ed.) *The First Information War: The Story of Communications, Computers and Intelligence Systems in the Persian Gulf War* (Fairfax, VA: AFCEA International Press, 1992)

Cattermull, S. 'Digitization: Its Effects on the British Way of Warfighting', *British Army Review*, Summer 2001

Cebrowski, Arthur K. & Gartska, John J. 'Network-Centric Warfare: Its Origin and Future', *Proceedings of the US Naval Institute*, January 1998

Chairman of the Joint Chiefs of Staff (US), *Joint Vision 2010* (US Government Printing Office, Washington DC, July 1996)

Chairman of the Joint Chiefs of Staff (US), *Joint Vision 2020* (US Government Printing Office, Washington DC, June 2000)

Clausewitz, Carl von (Howard, M. & Paret, P., eds. and trans.) *On War* (Princeton, Princeton University Press, 1989)

Cohen, Eliot 'The mystique of US air power', *Foreign Affairs*, January/February 1994

Cohen, Eliot 'A Revolution in Warfare', *Foreign Affairs*, March/April 1996

Coker, Christopher *Waging War Without Warriors? The Changing Culture of Military Conflict* (Boulder, CO: Lynne Rienner, 2002)

Collins, J.M. *Desert Shield and Desert Storm: Implications for Future US Force Requirements* (Washington, Congressional Research Service, April 1991)

Commission on National Security/21st Century (US), a.k.a. Hart-Rudman Commission, *New World Coming: American Security in the 21st Century* (September 1999); *Seeking a National Strategy: A Concept for Preserving Security and Promoting Freedom* (April 2000); and *Roadmap for National Security: Imperative for Change* (February 2001): available online at www.nssg.gov

Conan Doyle, Arthur *Penguin Complete Sherlock Holmes* (London, Penguin, 1981)

Cordesman, Anthony *The Lessons and Non-lessons of the Air and Missile War in Kosovo* (Washington DC, Centre for Strategic and International Studies, July 1999)

Creveld, M. van *On Future War* (London, Brasseys, 1991), published in the United States as *The Transformation of War* (New York, Free Press, 1991)

Creveld, M. van *Technology and War From 2000 BC to the Present* (London, Brasseys, 1991)

Creveld, M. van 'High Technology and the Transformation of War – Parts I and II', *RUSI Journal*, October 1992 & December 1992

CSIS Study Group on Lessons Learned from the Gulf War *Interim Report - The Gulf War: Military Lessons Learned* (Washington, CSIS, 1991)

Department of Defense (US) *Conduct of the Persian Gulf Conflict: An Interim Report to Congress* (Washington, US Government Printing Office, July 1991)

Department of Defense (US) *Conduct of the Persian Gulf War: Final Report to Congress* (Washington, US Government Printing Office, April 1992)

Dick, C. 'Conflict spills into the 21st Century', *Jane's Intelligence Review*, 1 December 2000

Donnelly, Tom 'Strategic Strife', *Jane's Defence Weekly*, 29 November 2000

Douhet, G. *Command of the Air* (Trans. Ferrari, D.: London, Faber and Faber, 1943 – original 1921)

Dunlap, Charles J. 'How we lost the high-tech war of 2007', *Weekly Standard*, January 29, 1996

Dunlap, Charles J. *Technology and the 21st Century Battlefield: Recomplicating Moral Life for the Statesman and the Soldier* (Strategic Studies Institute, January 1999)

Echevarria, Antulio (Major, US Army), 'War, Politics and RMA: The Legacy of Clausewitz', *Joint Forces Quarterly*, Winter 1995-96

Economist, 'The software revolution: a survey of defence technology', 10 June 1995

Economist, 'The future of warfare', editorial, 8 March 1997

Economist, 'Asia's lethal computers – Nerd world war', 30 October 1999

Economist, 25 January 2003, 'Digital dilemmas: A survey of the internet society'

Ellen, T.A. 'Is There Really a "Revolution in Military Affairs" Going On At The Moment, or Several?' *British Army Review*, Spring 2000

Emmett, Peter (Squadron Leader, RAF), 'Information Mania: A New Manifestation of Gulf War Syndrome?', *RUSI Journal*, February 1996

FitzGerald, Mary C. 'Marshal Ogarkov and the New Revolution in Soviet Military Affairs', *Defense Analysis*, March 1987

Fredette, R.H. *The First Battle of Britain, 1917-1918, and the Birth of the Royal Air Force* (London, Cassell, 1966)

Freedman, Lawrence 'The First Two Generations of Nuclear Strategists', in Paret, Peter (ed.) *Makers of Modern Strategy from Machiavelli to the Nuclear Age* (Oxford, Oxford University Press, 1986)

Freedman, Lawrence & Karsh, Efraim 'How Kuwait was won: Strategy in the Gulf War' in *International Security*, Fall 1991

Freedman, Lawrence & Karsh, Efraim *The Gulf Conflict 1990-91: Diplomacy and War in the New World Order* (Princeton, Princeton University Press, 1993)

Freedman, Lawrence, 'Britain and the Revolution in Military Affairs', *Defense Analysis*, April 1998

Freedman, Lawrence *The Revolution in Strategic Affairs: Adelphi Paper 318* (Oxford, OUP for IISS, 1998)

Friedman, George and Friedman, Meredith *The Future of War: Power, Technology and American World Dominance in the Twenty-First Century* (New York, St Martin's Griffin, 1998)

Friedman, Norman *Desert Victory: The War for Kuwait* (Annapolis, US Naval Institute, 1991)

Fuller, J.F.C. *The Reformation of War* (London, Hutchinson, 1923)

Fuller, J.F.C. *On Future Warfare* (London, Sifton Praed, 1928)

Gaskin, Robert 'A Revolution for the Millennium', in Murray, W. (ed.) *The Emerging Strategic Environment: Challenges of the Twenty-First Century* (Westport, Praeger, 1999)

Gates, D. *The Napoleonic Wars, 1803-1815* (London, Arnold, 1997)

General Accounting Office (United States) *Operation Desert Storm: Evaluation of the Air Campaign* (Washington DC, General Accounting Office, 1997)

Gibson, William *Neuromancer* (London, Victor Gollancz, 1984)

Gombert, D., Kugler, R. & Libicki, M. *Mind the Gap: Promoting a Transatlantic Revolution in Military Affairs* (Washington DC, National Defense University Press, 1999)

Gordon, M.R. & Trainor, B. *The Generals' War: The Inside Story of the Conflict in the Gulf* (Boston, Little Brown, 1995)

Gray, Chris H. *Post Modern War: The New Politics of Conflict* (London, Routledge, 1997)

Gray, Colin *The American RMA: An Interim Assessment* (SCSI Occasional, No. 28, 1997)

Gray, Colin *Modern Strategy* (Oxford, Oxford University Press, 1999)

Hanson, Victor D. *Carnage and Culture: Landmark Battles in the Rise of Western Power* (New York, Doubleday, 2001)

Harknett, Richard J. et al. 'The Risks of a Networked Military', *Orbis*, Winter 2000

Henry, Ryan & Peartree, C. Edward 'Military Theory and Information Warfare', *Parameters*, Autumn 1998

Hoffman, Bruce *Inside Terrorism* (London, Indigo, 1999)

Huntington, Samuel P. *The Clash of Civilizations and the Remaking of the World Order* (New York, Touchstone, 1997)

International Institute for Strategic Studies *Military Balance* - various years (London, Brasseys for IISS, various years)

International Institute for Strategic Studies *Strategic Survey* - various years (London, Brasseys for IISS, various years)

International Institute for Strategic Studies, 'Is there a revolution in military affairs?', in *Strategic Survey 1995-96* (London, OUP, 1996)

International Institute for Strategic Studies, 'The role of non-lethal weapons', in *Strategic Survey 1995-96* (London, OUP, 1996)

International Institute for Strategic Studies, 'Information Technology: Vulnerability and Threats', in *Strategic Survey 1998-99* (London, OUP, 1999)

Jones, Archer *The Art of War in the Western World* (Oxford, Oxford University Press, 1987)

Jones, J.F. (Lt. Col., USAF) 'Giulio Douhet Vindicated: Desert Storm 1991' in *Naval War College Review*, Autumn 1992

Kagan, Robert *Paradise and Power: America and Europe in the New World Order* (London, Atlantic Books, 2003)

Kaldor, M. *The Baroque Arsenal* (London, Abacus, 1983)

Katzenbach, E.L. 'The Horse Cavalry in the 20th Century' in Art, R.J. & Waltz, K.N. *The Use of Force: International Politics and Foreign Policy* (Boston, Little Brown, 1971)

Keaney, Thomas A. & Cohen, Eliot A. *Revolution in Warfare? Air Power in the Persian Gulf* (Annapolis, Naval Institute Press, 1995) – originally published as *Gulf War Air Power Survey Summary Report* (1993)

Keegan, J. *A History of Warfare* (New York, Knopf, 1993)

Krepinevich, Andrew F. 'Cavalry to Computer: The Pattern of Military Revolutions', *National Interest*, Fall 1994

Lambert, Andrew 'The Royal Navy in the Last Long Peace', in Grove, Eric and Hore, Peter (eds.) *Dimensions of Sea Power* (Hull, Hull University Press, 1998)

Libicki, Martin, 'The emerging primacy of information', *Orbis*, Spring 1996

Liddell Hart, B.H. *Paris: The Future of Warfare* (London, Kegan Paul, Trench, Trubner & Co, 1925)

Link, C.D. (Major General, USAF) 'Role of the USAF in the Employment of Air Power', in Shultz, R. & Pfaltzgraff, R. *The Future of Air Power in the Aftermath of the Gulf War* (Maxwell AFB Alabama, Air University Press, 1992)

Luttwak, E. *Strategy: The Logic of War and Peace* (Cambridge MA, Belknap, 1987)

Luttwak, E. 'Victory through air power', *Commentary*, August 1991

Luttwak, E. 'Air power in US Military Strategy' in Shultz, R. & Pfaltzgraff, R. *The Future of Air Power in the Aftermath of the Gulf War* (Maxwell AFB, Alabama, Air University Press, 1992)

Luttwak, E. 'Towards Post-Heroic Warfare', *Foreign Affairs*, May/June 1995

Mahnken, Thomas 'War and Culture in the Information Age', *Strategic Review*, Winter 2000

Mason, R.A. (Air-Vice Marshal, RAF) 'The air war in the Gulf' in *Survival*, May-June 1991

Matthews, Lloyd J. (Colonel, US Army, retired) *Challenging the United States Symmetrically and Asymmetrically: Can America be defeated?* (US Army War College Strategic Studies Institute, Carlisle Barracks, Pennsylvania, July 1998)

Mazarr, M., Snider, D. & Blackwell, J. *Desert Storm: The Gulf War and What we Learned* (Boulder, Westview, 1993)

McCausland, Jeffrey (Lieutenant-Colonel, US Army) *The Gulf Conflict: A Military Analysis - Adelphi Paper 282* (London, Brasseys for IISS, 1993)

McInnes, Colin *Spectator Sport War: The West and Contemporary Conflict* (Boulder, CO: Lynne Rienner, 2002)

Meilinger, P.S. (Colonel, USAF), 'Giulio Douhet and Modern War', *Comparative Strategy*, July-September 1993

Metz, Steven and Kievit, James *Strategy and the Revolution in Military Affairs: From Theory to Policy* (US Army Strategic Studies Institute, 1995)

Metz, Steven 'Racing Toward the Future: The Revolution in Military Affairs', *Current History*, April 1997

Metz, Steven 'The Next Twist of the RMA', *Parameters*, Autumn 2000

Mitchell, W. (General, US Army) *Winged Defense: The Development and Possibilities of Modern Air Power - Economic and Military* (New York, Putnams, 1925)

Morton, Oliver, 'A Survey of Defence Technology', *Economist*, 10 June 1995

Munro, N. *Electronic Combat and Modern Warfare: The Quick and the Dead* (London, Macmillan, 1991)

Murray, Williamson 'Thinking about revolutions in military affairs', *Joint Forces Quarterly*, Summer 1997

Murray, Williamson 'Air War in the Gulf: The Limits of Air Power', *Strategic Review*, Winter 1998

Myers, Grover & Wolfe, Thad (Lt. Gen., USAF, ret.) 'The Price of Greatness: Air Power in the Balkans', *Strategic Review*, Summer 1999

'Neon' *The Great Delusion: A Study of Aircraft in Peace and War* (London, Ernst Benn, 1927)

Nye, Joseph & Owens, William 'America's Information Edge', *Foreign Affairs*, March/April 1996

O'Connell, Robert *Of Arms and Men: A History of War, Weapons and Aggression* (New York, OUP, 1989)

Odom, William E. 'Transforming the Military', *Foreign Affairs*, July/August 1997

Owens, Mackubin T. 'Technology, The RMA and Future War', *Strategic Review*, Spring 1998

Owens, William 'JROC: Harnessing the Revolution in Military Affairs', *Joint Forces Quarterly*, Summer 1994

Owens, William 'The Emerging System of Systems', *Proceedings of the US Naval Institute*, May 1995

Owens, William 'The American Revolution in Military Affairs', *Joint Forces Quarterly*, Winter 1995-96

Owens, William 'The Once and Future Revolution in Military Affairs', *Joint Forces Quarterly*, Summer 2002

Pape, Robert A *Bombing to Win: Air Power and Coercion in War* (Ithaca, Cornell University Press, 1996)

Paret, Peter (ed.) *Makers of Modern Strategy from Machiavelli to the Nuclear Age* (Oxford, Oxford University Press, 1986)

Paret, Peter 'Napoleon and the Revolution in War', in Paret, Peter (ed.) *Makers of Modern Strategy from Machiavelli to the Nuclear Age* (Oxford, Oxford University Press, 1986)

Perry, W. 'Desert Storm and Deterrence', *Foreign Affairs*, Fall 1991

Petersen, C.C. 'Lessons of the Persian Gulf War: The View from Moscow' in *Journal of Strategic Studies*, September 1994

Pimlott, John and Badsey, Stephen *The Gulf War Assessed* (London, Arms and Armour, 1992)

Postol, Theodore 'Lessons of the Gulf War Experience with Patriot', *International Security*, Winter 1991/92; also 'Correspondence', *International Security*, Summer 1992

Prins, Gwyn *Strategy, Force Planning and Diplomatic/Military Operations* (London, RIIA, 1998)

Ranft, Bryan 'Sir Julian Corbett' in Till, Geoffrey (ed.) *Maritime Strategy and the Nuclear Age* (2nd edition, London, Macmillan, 1984)

Rathmell, Andrew, 'Cyberterrorism: The Shape of Future Conflict?', *RUSI Journal*, October 1997

Record, Jeffrey 'Defeating Desert Storm (and why Saddam didn't)', *Comparative Strategy*, April-June 1993

Rice, D.B. 'Air Power in the New Security Environment' in Shultz, R. & Pfaltzgraff, R. *The Future of Air*

Power in the Aftermath of the Gulf War (Maxwell AFB Alabama, Air University Press, 1992)

Rochlin, G.I. & Demchak, C.C. 'The Gulf War: Technological and Organizational Implications' in *Survival*, May-June 1991

Rochlin, G.I. & Demchak, C.C. *Lessons of the Gulf War: Ascendant Technology and Declining Capability* - U.C.B. *Institute of International Studies Policy Papers in International Affairs No. 39* (Berkeley, UCB Institute of International Studies, 1991)

Rohde, W.E. 'What is Info Warfare?', *Proceedings of the US Naval Institute*, February 1996

Rosen, S.P. *Winning the Next War: Innovation and the Modern Military* (Ithaca, Cornell, University Press, 1991)

Royal United Services Institute *Whitehall Papers 14 – Command in War: Gulf Operations* (London, RUSI, 1992)

Scales, Robert H. *Certain Victory: The US Army in the Gulf War* (Washington, Brasseys, 1994)

Scales, Robert (Major General, US Army) 'Adaptive Enemies: Dealing with the Strategic Threat After 2010', *Strategic Review*, Winter 1999

Schneider, Barry & Grinter, Lawrence *Battlefield of the Future: 21st Century Warfare Issues* – Air War College Studies in National Security No. 3 (Maxwell AFB, Air War College, 1995)

Schwartau, Winn 'Asymmetrical Adversaries', *Orbis*, Spring 2000

Schwarzkopf, H.N. (General, US Army) *It Doesn't Take a Hero* (New York, Bantam, 1992)

Secretary of State for Defence (UK) *The Strategic Defence Review*, Cm 3999 (London, HMSO, July 1998)

Secretary of State for Defence (UK) *The Strategic Defence Review: Supporting Essays* (London, HMSO, July 1998)

Secretary of State for Defence, *The Strategic Defence Review: A New Chapter*, Cm 5566 (London, HMSO, July 2002)

Seversky, A.P. de *Victory through Air Power* (New York, Simon & Schuster, 1942)

Shukman, David *The Sorcerer's Challenge: Fears and Hopes for the Weapons of the Next Millennium* (London, Coronet, 1995)

Shultz, R. & Pfaltzgraff, R. *The Future of Air Power in the Aftermath of the Gulf War* (Maxwell AFB Alabama, Air University Press, 1992)

Sloan, Elinor *The Revolution in Military Affairs: Implications for Canada and NATO* (Montreal, McGill-Queen's University Press, 2002)

Smith, D.L. & Meier, A.L. 'Ogarkov's revolution: Soviet military doctrine for the 1990s', *International Defense Review*, July 1987

Stanley, R.A. & Pokrant, M. 'Desert Storm at Sea' in *Proceedings of the US Naval Institute*, May 1991

Stone, John, 'The Future of Armoured Warfare: Prospects for the Tank', *RUSI Journal*, June 1996

Storr, Jim 'The Impact of Technology on War in the 21st Century', in RUSI, *International Security Review 2000* (London, RUSI, 1999)

Summers, H.G. (Colonel, US Army) *On Strategy II: A Critical Analysis of the Gulf War* (New York, Dell, 1992)

Sun Tzu, *The Art of War* (trans. Ralph Sawyer: New York, Barnes and Noble, 1994)

Swalm. T.S., 'Joint STARS in Desert Storm', in Campen, A.D. (ed.) *The First Information War: The Story of Communications, Computers and Intelligence Systems in the Persian Gulf War* (Fairfax, VA: AFCEA International Press, 1992),

Szafranski, Richard 'Neocortical Warfare? The Acme of Skill', *Military Review*, November 1994

Taylor, W.J. & Blackwell, J. 'The Ground War in the Gulf' in *Survival*, May-June 1991

Thomas, Timothy L. 'Kosovo and the current myth of information superiority', *Parameters*, Spring 2000

Thucydides *History of the Pelopponesian War* (trans. Warner, R.; London, Penguin, 1972)

Tilford, Earl *The Revolution in Military Affairs: Prospects and Cautions* (Strategic Studies Institute, US Army

War College, 1995)

Toffler, A. & Toffler, H. *War and Anti-War: Survival at the Dawn of the 21st Century* (London, Warner, 1994)

Tomes, Robert R. 'Revolution in Military Affairs: A History', *Military Review*, September-October 2000

Toti, Bill 'Stop the Revolution; I Want to Get Off', *Proceedings of the US Naval Institute*, July 2000

Van Riper, Paul & Scales, Robert H. 'Preparing for War in the 21st Century', *Strategic Review*, Summer 1997

Warden, John A. 'Employing Air Power in the Twenty-First Century' in Shultz, R. & Pfaltzgraff, R. *The Future of Air Power in the Aftermath of the Gulf War* (Maxwell AFB Alabama, Air University Press, 1992)

Warden, John A. *The Air Campaign: Planning for Combat* (Washington DC, National Defense University Press, 1988)

Watkins, Bryan, 'The Aftermath of the Storm', *RUSI Journal*, June 1993

Watson, B.W. (ed.) *Military Lessons of the Gulf War - Revised Edition* (London, Greenhill, 1993)

Wells, H.G., 'The Land Ironclads' (1903), in Hartwell, David G. & Cramer, Kathryn *The Ascent of Wonder: The Evolution of Hard SF* (London, Orbit, 1994)

Wells, H.G. *The War in the Air* (London, George Bell and Sons, 1908)

Zimm, Alan (Cmdr., USN, ret.) 'Desert Storm, Kosovo and "Doctrinal Schizophrenia"', *Strategic Review*, Winter 2000

Index

All abbreviations are listed in full on page 7.